**GOOD
HOUSEKEEPING**

ULTIMATE GRILLING
COOKBOOK

GOOD
HOUSEKEEPING

ULTIMATE GRILLING

COOKBOOK

250 SIZZLING RECIPES

HEARST
books

HEARSTBOOKS

An Imprint of Sterling Publishing Co., Inc.
1166 Avenue of the Americas
New York, NY 10036

ISBN 978-1-61837-267-3   33614080612897

The Good Housekeeping Cookbook Seal guarantees that the recipes in this publication meet the strict
standards of the Good Housekeeping Research Institute. The Institute has been a source of reliable
information and a consumer advocate since 1900, and established its seal of approval in 1909. Every
recipe in this publication has been triple-tested for ease, reliability, and great taste by the Institute.

Hearst Communications, Inc. has made every effort to ensure that all information in this publication is accurate.
However, due to differing conditions, tools, and individual skills, Hearst Communications, Inc. cannot be responsible
for any injuries, losses, and/or damages that may result from the use of any information in this publication.

Distributed in Canada by Sterling Publishing
c/o Canadian Manda Group, 664 Annette Street
Toronto, Ontario, M6S 2C8, Canada
Distributed in Australia by NewSouth Books
45 Beach Street, Coogee, NSW 2034, Australia

For information about custom editions, special sales, and premium and corporate purchases,
please contact Sterling Special Sales at 800-805-5489 or specialsales@sterlingpublishing.com.

Manufactured in China

2 4 6 8 10 9 7 5 3 1

sterlingpublishing.com
goodhousekeeping.com

Cover Design by Scott Russo
Interior Design by Susan Welt
For photography credits see page 314

Contents

Foreword

If America had a national cooking method it would be grilling. We celebrate the start and finish of summer with the enticing aromas and incomparable flavors of traditional backyard barbecues: grilled chicken, burgers, steaks, and ribs. More recently, we've embraced grilling as a go-to cooking method for healthy eating—and easy cleanup. Now we're grilling more than just meat, including pizzas and vegetables, too! And, with the help of a grill pan, even those of us in the North are enjoying luscious grilled food year-round.

Enter the *Good Housekeeping Ultimate Grilling Cookbook*: Making delicious grilled meals indoors and out is easy with this collection of favorite year-round grilling recipes and tips—all triple-tested in our test kitchens. Our recipes for starters and salads will have you turning out smoky dips, charred pizzas, and grilled salads with ease. To keep you in step with the burger craze, we include a total of thirty burgers, from beefy to veggie along with hot dogs with inventive toppings. And, of course, we haven't forgotten the classics: Try our succulent recipes for every cut of steak, chops, and ribs, including sometimes overlooked items like butterflied leg of lamb.

Fish and shellfish are luscious on the grill, too. Enjoy favorites like salmon and shrimp, plus tempting takes on sea bass, snapper, catfish, swordfish, scallops, and even squid. We even included an option for a New England Lobster Bake (page 225). And we offer an entire chapter starring vegetables, from meatless mains to flame-charred sides. Plus, we thought about the basics to accompany any backyard barbecue—the slaws, the pasta salads, baked beans, and pickles, too! Lastly, our rubs, marinades, and sauces will add mouthwatering flavor to even a simple chicken breast.

But before you start up your grill (or heat your grill pan), bone up on essential tools, techniques, and safety procedures reviewed in "The Joys of the Grill" on page 9 or at the beginning of each chapter. Happy grilling!

SUSAN WESTMORELAND
Food Director, *Good Housekeeping*

The Joys of the Grill

Grilling imparts an incomparable flavor that no other cooking method can. The intense heat, the savory smoke, and the pleasure of cooking outdoors all enhance the natural flavor of food. Before you fire up your grill, spend a few minutes with these pages to assess your grill and utensils, bone up on techniques and flavor-enhancing tricks, and review safety procedures.

TYPES OF GRILLS

Manufacturers now offer an enticing array of options for gas, charcoal, and electric grills (and some avid grillers own more than one type).

GAS GRILL. With its speed and ease of operation, the gas grill has become America's favorite type of grill. And what's not to like? Open the gas valve, turn on the controls, preheat for about ten minutes, and you're ready to go.

With gas grills—fueled by either liquid propane or natural gas—you've got a world of features to choose from, including a wide range of BTU capacities, stainless-steel, cast-iron, or porcelain-enameled cooking grates and flavor bars, V-shaped bars, and infrared burners for searing. Other features include side burners, rotisserie burners, warming racks, built-in thermometers, grill lights, and storage. In terms of size, you can find a gas grill to fit your needs, whether you're cooking for one or the entire neighborhood.

CHARCOAL GRILL. Fueled by charcoal briquettes or natural hardwood charcoal chunks, charcoal grills are, on the whole, less expensive than their gas-powered brethren. Look for a charcoal grill made of heavy-gauge steel; a porcelain-enamel coating will give you better protection from rust. Sturdy legs will keep the grill steady. Other features you might find in a charcoal grill include plated-steel, preseasoned–cast iron, or porcelain-enameled cooking grates, adjustable-height fire grates, side shelves and bottom storage, warming racks, temperature gauges, and a removable ashtray for easy cleanup.

As with gas grills, you can find a charcoal grill in whatever size fits your needs. If you're cooking for one or two, consider the hibachi, a small cast-iron grill that's just right for a pocket-size patio.

ELECTRIC GRILL. The electric grill offers an alternative to messing around with gas tanks and charcoal. Plug it in, and you're good to go. If you live where charcoal or gas is not allowed on the terrace, patio, or deck, there are tabletop versions as well as full-size electric grills that you can even use indoors; just be sure to position your grill within reach of a grounded outlet.

WHAT'S THE PURPOSE OF V-SHAPED FLAVOR BARS?

These hollow triangular bars catch dripping fat and juices, evaporate them, and create the tasty smoke that flavors the food.

GRILLING EQUIPMENT

Cooking over fire calls for some specialized tools, and there are also optional gadgets to consider for easier grilling of fish, kabobs, and so on. Here are the basics, plus some extras.

GRILL TOPPER. If you often grill delicate foods such as seafood and vegetables, you'll want a grill topper, a perforated metal sheet, tray, or basket that provides a nearly smooth surface for grilling. Food is less likely to break up or fall through, and you can virtually "stir-fry" cut-up foods over the flames.

TONGS. Better than a fork for turning foods because they don't pierce the surface and release juices. Barbecue tongs should have heatproof handles and rounded ends that won't cut into the food.

SPATULA. Use one with a long, heatproof handle for flipping burgers and moving food around on a grill topper.

SKEWERS. Long metal skewers are the best for kabobs. Choose skewers with flat shafts rather than round ones; food will be less likely to slip or spin around as you turn the skewers.

BASTING BRUSH. A heatproof handle and a long shaft are two definite brush requirements. As for bristles, silicone is the way to go—it's nearly indestructible and has the added benefit of being nonstick, making cleanup a snap. Your next best bet is a brush with natural bristles, which will stand up to heat better than synthetic bristles other than silicone.

GRILLING MITTS. A more serious version of oven mitts, these are longer and better insulated, to protect more of your arm from higher heat. Heavy suede mitts are excellent.

BRASS-BRISTLED SCRUB BRUSH. Use this to clean the grill rack. The best time for this? While the grill is still hot.

THERMOMETERS. Consider two different types of thermometers for grilling ease. The first measures the internal temperature of the food you're cooking (see "Is It Done?" on page 13). You can do this with an instant-read thermometer, which is inserted into the center of the food when you think it's getting close to done. There are also digital thermometers consisting of a probe that is inserted into the food as it goes onto the heat and attaches to a device that sits beside the grill and provides a continual temperature reading.

The other kind of thermometer is a grill surface thermometer, which measures the heat of the fire. When you're cooking with charcoal, it takes the guesswork out of determining whether you have a hot or medium fire (see "How Hot Is Your Fire?" on page 12). It is especially useful when you are cooking "low and slow," which requires that you maintain an even temperature over many hours.

GETTING STARTED ON YOUR CHARCOAL GRILL

Gas and electric grills are easy to light; just follow the manufacturer's directions. A charcoal fire requires a little more finesse. Be sure to leave enough time after starting the fire for the coals to develop a light layer of ash before you start cooking. Allow twenty minutes to be on the safe side.

You don't want to run out of heat before your food is cooked, so start with enough briquettes. Estimate the right amount by spreading an even layer over the bottom of the firebox. Before lighting, stack them into a pyramid to allow air to circulate among them. The following are options to help you get the fire going:

CHIMNEY STARTER. This is an open-ended metal cylinder with a handle. Crumple newspaper and stuff it in the bottom of the cylinder, fill the top portion with briquettes, then light the paper through an opening in the bottom. The briquettes will burn to ash-covered readiness.

ELECTRIC STARTER. A loop-shaped heating element with a handle—place this in a bed of briquettes, plug it in, and the briquettes will ignite.

LIQUID FIRE STARTER. Saturate briquettes with the liquid, then wait for a minute before lighting. By the time the coals are ready for proper cooking, the fluid will have burned off and will not affect the flavor of the food. Never add liquid starter to a fire that's already burning or to hot coals; a spark could ignite the whole can.

SOLID FIRE STARTER. Place these waxy-looking cubes in the firebox, pile briquettes on top, and light. They're safer to handle than liquid starter.

SELF-STARTING BRIQUETTES. These are impregnated with starter fluid. A match will ignite them immediately. Don't add them to a fire that's already lit.

CHOOSE YOUR COOKING METHOD

One of the keys to successful grilling is knowing the right kind and level of heat to use for the food you're preparing.

DIRECT COOKING. The gasgrill is preheated with all the burners on or, in a charcoal grill, the prepared coals are spread evenly. Food is placed on the grill rack directly over the heat source. This method works best with foods that take less than twenty-five minutes, such as steaks, chops, and vegetables. Direct heat is necessary for searing, which gives meats that nice crusty surface.

INDIRECT COOKING. For a gas grill, plan to place your food on the grill rack over the drip pan. Preheat the burners on the two outer sides for a three-burner grill (or on one side for a two-burner grill). Set the food over the unheated burner. For a charcoal grill, push the briquettes to the edges of the kettle and place a drip pan in the middle before placing your food on the rack. Indirect cooking is best for longer-cooking meats such as roasts and whole chickens or turkeys, or for delicate foods like fish fillets that might be scorched or dried out by direct heat. Consider placing the food in a pan rather than directly on the grill rack.

TO COVER OR NOT TO COVER? Most grill manufacturers—both gas and charcoal—recommend closing the cover for all grilling. It reduces flare-ups, helps prevent charring, and greatly shortens cooking time.

HIGH VERSUS MEDIUM HEAT. Use medium-high heat for thin cuts of meat that cook quickly: skirt steak, thin pork or lamb chops, frankfurters, or shrimp and other shellfish. It's a good idea to sear thick steaks over high heat first. Use medium heat for ¾- to 1-inch-thick rib-eye, tenderloin, or flank steaks, as well as hamburgers, chicken parts, vegetables, fruit, or whole fish.

MAINTAINING PROPER HEAT. For long, slow cooking, adjust the controls on your gas grill. It's a bit trickier with a charcoal model. If the fire is too hot, you should close or partially close the vents (top, bottom, or both); if it's not hot enough, open the vents fully or add more briquettes after each additional hour as the manufacturer recommends. Most gas and some charcoal grills have thermometers that permit you to monitor the interior temperature without lifting the lid (uncovering the grill causes the temperature to drop immediately).

IS IT DONE?

The best way to know if your food is done is to measure its internal temperature. Below are the temperatures, as determined by the USDA, that you want your food to register before you take it off the grill. Temperatures should be taken in the thickest part of the food; the thermometer should not touch bone, fat, or gristle. For internal temperatures and approximate grilling times organized by type and cut of meat, poultry, and seafood, see "Recommended Safe Minimum Internal Temperatures" on page 312.

Chicken breasts and whole poultry	165°F
Ground meat	160°F
Pork	145°F
Beef steaks and roasts	145°F
Lamb steaks, ribs, or leg	145°F
Fish	145°F

FLAVORING THE FIRE

It's the delicious taste of food cooked over flames that makes grilling such a popular cooking method. You can enhance the effect by adding flavor to the fire itself, or, more specifically, the smoke that rises from it. This works best in a covered grill, which holds the smoke in. Aromatic woods, such as mesquite or hickory, are well known for the tang they add to grilled meats. Herbs, spices, and other cooking ingredients like citrus peel or whole garlic cloves add their own flavors when placed in the smoker box or on the fire.

TYPE OF WOOD	FLAVOR	BEST FOR
Oak and Mesquite	Intense	Beef and pork
Hickory	Sweet	Turkey, chicken, and pork
Fruitwoods (like apple and cherry)	Mild	Chicken and seafood

Grilling woods are sold in chunks or chips to be tossed onto a charcoal fire or into foil packets or the smoker box of a gas grill. You want the wood to smoke slowly, not burn quickly, so soak chips in water for 30 minutes before adding them. Larger chunks should be soaked for up to two hours.

If you have a gas grill, use wood chips, not chunks. If your gas grill doesn't have a smoker box, wrap the chips up in heavy-duty foil, punch a few holes in it, and place it over the flavor bars.

If you're using a charcoal grill, add chunks of wood to the fire from the start; place chips on the coals later in the cooking process.

Whole spices or fresh or dried herbs can be placed in the smoker box or on the fire, or experiment with strips of lemon or orange peel or whole garlic cloves. Soak them for about thirty minutes before using. Fennel is traditional for grilling fish, while rosemary, thyme, bay leaves, and cilantro are other options. Dried grapevines give off a subtle wine flavor.

8 Safety Rules for the Backyard Chef

1 Make sure the grill is on a level surface and not too close to the house, trees, fences, or even deck railings—all can catch fire from flare-ups or flying sparks.

2 Don't line the bottom of a gas or charcoal grill with foil; it will obstruct airflow, and the fire will die out faster.

3 Use lighter fluid only to start a fire; don't squirt it onto hot coals to get a dying fire going again, because it can ignite in the can as you pour it.

4 We can't say it too often: Reduce the risk of cross-contamination and food poisoning by transferring cooked food from the grill to a clean plate, not the one that held the raw meat, fish, or poultry.

5 Boil used marinades and glazes for 2 minutes if you want to serve them with cooked meat. Or reserve some in a separate dish before it comes in contact with the meat, fish, or poultry.

6 Use long-handled barbecue utensils (not your regular kitchen set) for good reach and control. And watch out for dangling sleeves.

7 Be careful not to serve undercooked meat, poultry, or fish. (See "Is It Done?" on page 13, for guidelines.)

8 Don't throw water on flare-ups; it produces steam, which can cause severe burns. Instead, remove the food from the grill until the fire subsides or cover the grill for a few minutes. To prevent flare-ups, trim excess fat from meats.

HEALTHY GRILLING 101

Grilling is generally a healthy way to cook. But research shows that grilling meat, poultry, or fish at high temperatures produces chemicals called heterocyclic amines (HCAs), which may pose a cancer risk. When fat drips onto the heat source, it produces smoke that contains potentially harmful polycyclic aromatic hydrocarbons (PAHs), which stick to the foods. To minimize risk, follow these tips.

BURN ANY RESIDUE OFF YOUR GRATES before or after grilling, then scrub it away with a stiff-bristled grill brush. If the inside of your hood is covered with grease, or black char is flaking off onto your food, clean the lid with a nonabrasive cleaning pad and a mild dish detergent.

CHOOSE LEAN CUTS OF MEAT AND TRIM EXCESS FAT. Cook larger cuts more slowly (at low temperatures) to produce fewer HCAs. (Indirect grilling over a drip pan is a good choice.)

MARINATE YOUR MEAT. This can decrease HCA formation by more than 90 percent. (Scientists believe that some of the ingredients in marinades may act as protective antioxidants.) See "The Best Way to Marinate" on page 285 for tips.

USE A MEAT THERMOMETER to make sure meat is cooked to safe temperatures (see "Is It Done?" on page 13). And remove any charred areas from the food before eating.

DON'T GRILL MEAT IF IT'S STILL FROZEN. If you do, its surface is likely to be overexposed to high heat while the inside is cooking. Make sure to thaw it thoroughly before grilling.

PARTIALLY COOK MEAT in the microwave or conventional oven and pour off any juices before grilling; this can cut HCA production by 90 percent. Try giving these items a zap:

Chicken quarters (3 pounds): Microwave on High for 12 to 15 minutes or until tender, rotating pieces halfway through cooking.

Italian sausage links (1 pound): Cut slashes into tops of sausages before microwaving on High for 5 to 6 minutes, until sausages are no longer pink.

GRILL MORE FRUITS AND VEGETABLES, which don't contain the substances—amino acids and creatine—that are linked to the production of HCAs. For great vegetarian dishes on the grill, see "Vegetables and Sides," page 231.

GRILLING INDOORS

Even if you're an intrepid, all-weather sort of grillmeister, sometimes grilling outdoors just isn't an option—or you'd simply prefer to get your grill on indoors. Happily, you can still enjoy the great taste of grilled food. When you think indoors, think grill pan.

A grill pan is essentially a skillet with ridges in the bottom. Grill pans come in a wide range of sizes, including griddle-style pans without sides built for cooking over two stovetop burners at once. You've also got your choice of materials, from the classic cast iron and enameled cast iron to stainless steel and hard-anodized aluminum. We do not recommend buying a grill pan with a nonstick coating; these should not be preheated empty, and if they are heated over more than medium heat, the coating can begin to degrade, releasing harmful chemicals. Seasoned cast-iron pans are naturally nonstick. Whether you've seasoned your pan or you've bought it preseasoned from the factory, all you need to clean it after each use is a rinse in hot water and a good scrubbing with a stiff brush—no detergent, as that can remove the seasoning. Immediately dry your pan to keep it from rusting. And if it does develop rust, just tackle it with a scouring pad, rinse well, towel dry, and reseason it.

So, can you prepare anything you cook on an outdoor grill in a grill pan? No, but there's an awful lot you can do—all manner of steaks, burgers, lamb, veal, and pork chops, fish steaks and fillets, scallops and shrimp, boneless chicken breasts, and turkey cutlets, along with vegetables and greens.

We've sprinkled an assortment of grill pan recipes throughout the book—including lots of great burgers you can grill up on your stovetop. From Our Best Burger (page 51) to Flank Steak Fajitas (page 152), these easy-to-execute recipes all boast great grilled flavor.

Starters and Side Salads

Tease your taste buds with these party-worthy appetizers and salads. They're so yummy, you just may want to make them the main course.

A Guide to Entertaining Outdoors

When you're planning a patio party or barbecue bash, there's nothing worse than running out of food or (gasp!) drinks. So make a menu, shopping list, and timetable for grilling and serving. Then cook, sit down, relax, and enjoy the delicious fruits of your labors. Here's how to plan a fun, safe cookout:

FOOD AND DRINKS For each person have 8 to 10 hors d'oeuvres, 8 ounces meat (about 2 burgers or chicken breasts), and ¼ pound to ½ pound of each side dish. Figure on 1½ drinks per hour.

TIMING Meats, salads, and cut-up fruits and veggies are fine out of the fridge for two hours. If it's superhot (80°F to 90°F), that drops to one hour. GH Lab Tip: Instead of prepping large platters or bowls, make a few small ones and swap them out as needed.

SEATING Set up comfortable chairs and benches for at least 80 percent of the guests. And don't forget a few side tables for drinks.

DÉCOR New disposable innovations are surprisingly sturdy—and stylish! Pick up chic paper plates, faux-fabric napkins, and no-mess tablecloths and runners for trendy tableware. Best part: minimal post-party cleanup required!

BACKYARD BASH ESSENTIALS

Playing hostess is a lot of work—not to mention you should be able to have fun with your guests, too! Check off these easy to-do's before your next party.

PUT OUT WELCOME MATS Doormats trap dirt so floors stay clean.

HANG A SIGN ON THE FRONT DOOR Guests will know to head straight for the backyard.

STOCK YOUR POWDER ROOM Stash towels and toilet paper in the bathroom closest to your yard.

CLEAR OUT THE KITCHEN Empty the fridge and dishwasher pre-party to make room for the leftovers and dirty dishes.

CREATE A PARTY SUPPLY STATION Set up a spot inside the back door to keep essentials like extra utensils, dishes, napkins, and stain wipes handy.

ADD MORE TRASH BINS Place receptacles lined with bags around the yard. Use clear ones for recyclables and colored ones for paper and trash.

BARBECUE ON A BUDGET

A summer barbecue can be hard on your budget. If you're trying to feed a crowd on a song, skip the ready-made burger patties and baby back ribs. Buying in bulk, shaping your own burgers, and choosing cheaper cuts will feed a crowd for less.

MENU	CHOOSE	WHY
Chicken	Bone-in pieces	They're flavorful and moist. Buy with skin; remove skin at home.
Burgers	Family-pack ground beef	You can shape the patties; freeze some to use for future meals.
Ribs	Pork spareribs	They're delicious and less pricey than baby back ribs.
Steaks	A club-store-size package	You can grill it all and use leftovers for tacos or salads the next day.

TEST KITCHEN HACK

Skewer Know-How

Chunks of chicken, steak, shrimp, or veggies—whatever you're skewering, follow these tips for kebab success!

If you use metal skewers, look for the kind that are twisted or square—not round. Food twirls around when you try to turn it on a round skewer. (Wooden and skinny bamboo skewers aren't slippery, so their round shape is no problem.) If you're grilling shrimp or other slippery items, use two parallel skewers, about ¾ inch apart.

Before using wooden or bamboo skewers, soak them in hot water for at least thirty minutes so they won't burn when exposed to the grill's heat and flames.

For even cooking, don't jam up foods against each other when you assemble the kebab—leave a little space between them on the skewer.

Use two parallel skewers for unwieldy items, like thick, large slices of onion.

Combine foods with similar cooking times on the same skewer.

Smoky Guacamole

PREP 10 MINUTES
TOTAL 15 MINUTES

2 ripe avocados, halved and pitted

2 teaspoons vegetable oil

3 tablespoons fresh lime juice

1 clove garlic, crushed with press

½ teaspoon chipotle chile powder

½ teaspoon salt

¼ cup finely chopped red onion

¼ cup finely chopped fresh cilantro

Tortilla chips, for serving

||||||||||||||||||||||||||||||||||||

To ripen a hard avocado, place it in a paper bag at room temperature for two days, until it yields to gentle pressure when squeezed lightly. Avocados can be stored in the refrigerator for a few days.

1 Prepare outdoor grill for direct grilling over medium-high heat. Brush cut sides of avocados with oil. Grill 2 to 4 minutes, or until grill marks appear.

2 Transfer avocados to cutting board; cool slightly. Scoop avocados from peel. Mash with lime juice, garlic, chipotle powder, and salt until almost smooth. Stir in red onion and cilantro. Transfer to serving bowl. Refrigerate, covered, until cold, about 1 hour. Serve with tortilla chips.

SERVES 4 (without chips) ABOUT 190 CALORIES, 2G PROTEIN, 11G CARBOHYDRATE, 17G FAT (2G SATURATED), 7G FIBER, 265MG SODIUM

Feta-Dill Greek Salad

 **PREP** 10 MINUTES
TOTAL 15 MINUTES

- 4 ounces feta cheese
- ⅔ cup extra-virgin olive oil
- ⅓ cup plain nonfat Greek yogurt
- 3 tablespoons lemon juice
- 1 clove garlic
- ¼ teaspoon salt
- ¼ teaspoon freshly ground black pepper
- ¼ cup packed fresh dill, chopped
- 3 romaine lettuce hearts
- ¼ cup roasted sunflower seeds

1 In blender or food processor, puree feta, olive oil, yogurt, lemon juice, garlic, salt, and pepper. Transfer to medium bowl; stir in dill.

2 Prepare outdoor grill for direct grilling over medium heat. Halve lettuce hearts lengthwise; grill about 2 minutes per side or until charred in spots.

3 Serve immediately, drizzled with yogurt dressing and sprinkled with roasted sunflower seeds.

SERVES 6 ABOUT 325 CALORIES, 6G PROTEIN, 5G CARBOHYDRATE, 32G FAT (7G SATURATED), 1G FIBER, 265MG SODIUM

Prosciutto-Wrapped Fig Salad

PREP 15 MINUTES
TOTAL 20 MINUTES

½ teaspoon fresh thyme leaves

½ teaspoon fennel seeds

4 ounces goat cheese

Salt

½ teaspoon ground black pepper

10 fresh figs, halved lengthwise

4 ounces very thinly sliced prosciutto, halved lengthwise

2 tablespoons sherry vinegar

1 tablespoon honey

1 tablespoon extra-virgin olive oil

5 ounces mixed baby greens

1 Prepare outdoor grill for direct grilling over medium heat.

2 Chop thyme and fennel together and transfer to bowl. Mix with goat cheese, pinch of salt, and ¼ teaspoon pepper.

3 Scoop 1 level teaspoon goat cheese mixture onto cut side of 1 fig half. Repeat with remaining cheese and figs. Wrap 1 strip prosciutto around each fig, enclosing cheese. If prosciutto doesn't stick to itself, secure with toothpicks.

4 Grill figs 2 to 3 minutes, turning over once, until prosciutto is lightly charred and cheese is soft.

5 Meanwhile, in bowl, whisk vinegar, honey, oil, and ¼ teaspoon each salt and pepper. Add greens; toss to coat.

6 Remove toothpicks, if any. Divide greens and figs among serving plates.

SERVES 4 ABOUT 285 CALORIES, 15G PROTEIN, 31G CARBOHYDRATE, 13G FAT (6G SATURATED), 4G FIBER, 1,050MG SODIUM

Smoked Mozzarella Salad

PREP 15 MINUTES
TOTAL 20 MINUTES

1½ pounds smoked mozzarella, cut into ½-inch-thick slices

3 tablespoons olive oil

½ cup panko bread crumbs

6 cups packed baby arugula

1 pint grape tomatoes, halved

2 tablespoons balsamic vinegar

⅓ cup packed fresh basil leaves, torn

Salt

Freshly ground black pepper

1 In large bowl, toss mozzarella slices with 2 tablespoons oil. Pour panko into large shallow dish. Press mozzarella slices into panko to coat both sides; place on small baking sheet. Freeze for 20 minutes.

2 Coat large ridged grill pan with nonstick cooking spray; heat on medium-high until hot but not smoking. Place cheese slices on pan. Cook for 2 minutes or until crumbs are golden and grill marks appear. With a thin spatula, turn cheese slices over. Cook for another 2 minutes. Transfer to large platter or cutting board.

3 In a large bowl, toss arugula with tomatoes, balsamic vinegar, basil, remaining 1 tablespoon oil, and ¼ teaspoon each salt and pepper. Serve cheese slices over salad.

SERVES 4 ABOUT 640 CALORIES, 39G PROTEIN, 19G CARBOHYDRATE, 47G FAT (23G SATURATED), 2G FIBER, 1,335MG SODIUM

Watermelon, Tomato and Feta Salad

 PREP 5 MINUTES
TOTAL 10 MINUTES

- 4 slices watermelon (½ inch thick)
- 5 ounces mixed greens
- 2 large yellow or red tomatoes, cut into 6 wedges each
- 1 bunch small radishes, halved
- 4 ounces feta cheese, crumbled
- 2 tablespoons balsamic vinegar
- 2 tablespoons extra-virgin olive oil
- ¼ teaspoon salt

1 Prepare outdoor grill for direct grilling over medium heat.

2 Pat watermelon slices dry and grill 3 to 4 minutes, turning over halfway through, until grill marks appear.

3 Using medium star cookie cutter, cut 8 to 9 stars from watermelon slices.

4 Arrange mixed greens on a serving platter and top with watermelon stars, tomato wedges, radishes, and feta. Drizzle with balsamic vinegar and olive oil; sprinkle with salt.

SERVES 4 ABOUT 230 CALORIES, 6G PROTEIN, 27G CARBOHYDRATE, 13G FAT (5G SATURATED), 3G FIBER, 447MG SODIUM

Shrimp and Pineapple Salad with Basil

 **PREP** 10 MINUTES
TOTAL 30 MINUTES

3 limes

3 tablespoons olive oil

1½ cups loosely packed fresh basil leaves

½ teaspoon salt

¼ teaspoon coarsely ground black pepper

1½ pounds large shrimp, shelled and deveined

1 pineapple (3 pounds)

12 corn tortillas

1 bag (5 to 6 ounces) baby greens

2 medium heads Belgian endive, sliced

1 Prepare outdoor grill for direct grilling over medium heat.

2 From limes, grate ½ teaspoon zest and squeeze ¼ cup juice. In blender, place lime zest and juice, oil, ½ cup basil leaves, salt, and pepper. Blend until pureed.

3 Spoon 2 tablespoons dressing from blender into medium bowl. Add shrimp to bowl and toss to coat with dressing.

4 Cut off crown and stem end from pineapple. Stand pineapple upright and slice off rind and eyes. Cut pineapple lengthwise into 8 wedges, then cut off core from each wedge.

5 Grill pineapple wedges about 10 minutes, turning over once, until lightly charred and tender. Place shrimp on skewers and cook 5 to 8 minutes, turning over once, until opaque throughout. Transfer shrimp to large bowl. Transfer pineapple to cutting board and cut into ½-inch chunks.

6 Lightly spray both sides of tortillas with cooking spray and place on grill. Cook tortillas 4 to 5 minutes, or until toasted, turning over once.

7 To bowl with shrimp, add greens, endive, pineapple, and remaining basil and dressing; toss to coat. Place 2 tortillas on each plate; top with salad.

SERVES 6 ABOUT 350 CALORIES, 23G PROTEIN, 43G CARBOHYDRATE, 11G FAT (2G SATURATED), 6G FIBER, 420MG SODIUM

Shrimp with Apple-Tomato Salad

PREP 25 MINUTES
TOTAL 30 MINUTES

- ½ cup packed fresh cilantro leaves
- ½ cup reduced-fat sour cream
- ¼ cup light mayonnaise
- 4 tablespoons lemon juice
- 1 tablespoon red wine vinegar
- ⅜ teaspoon salt
- ¾ teaspoon freshly ground black pepper
- 1 pound (26/30 count) shelled and deveined shrimp
- 1 tablespoon olive oil
- 1 teaspoon ground coriander
- 2 romaine lettuce hearts, chopped
- 1 pint cherry tomatoes, halved
- 1 Granny Smith apple, cut into ¼-inch sticks

1 If using bamboo skewers, soak in hot water at least 30 minutes. Prepare outdoor grill for direct grilling over medium-high heat.

2 In blender, puree cilantro, sour cream, mayonnaise, 2 tablespoons lemon juice, vinegar, ¼ teaspoon salt, and ½ teaspoon pepper; set dressing aside.

3 In large bowl, combine shrimp, oil, coriander, remaining 2 tablespoons lemon juice, ⅛ teaspoon salt, and ¼ teaspoon pepper, tossing to coat.

4 Thread shrimp, ½ inch apart, on skewers. Grill 3 to 4 minutes, turning over once, until shrimp just turn opaque. Transfer to plate.

5 In another large bowl, toss lettuce with half of dressing until well coated. Divide among serving plates. In same bowl, toss tomatoes and apple with half of remaining dressing until well coated; place on lettuce with shrimp. Drizzle with remaining dressing.

SERVES 4 ABOUT 270 CALORIES, 19G PROTEIN, 18G CARBOHYDRATE, 14G FAT (4G SATURATED), 3G FIBER, 1,010MG SODIUM

Cayenne Eggplant with Fresh Tomatoes

PREP 15 MINUTES
TOTAL 30 MINUTES

- 2 pounds medium eggplants, cut lengthwise into ½-inch-thick slices
- ¼ cup plus 3 tablespoons extra-virgin olive oil
- 1 teaspoon ground coriander
- 1 teaspoon cayenne pepper
- Salt
- ¼ cup packed fresh mint leaves, finely chopped, plus more for garnish
- 3 small fresh red Fresno chiles or other hot chiles, finely chopped
- 2 tablespoons lemon juice
- 2 tablespoons red wine vinegar
- ½ pint (about 1½ cups) multicolored cherry or grape tomatoes, halved
- ¼ cup plain Greek yogurt
- 2 tablespoons milk

1 Prepare outdoor grill for direct grilling over medium heat. Brush eggplant all over with ¼ cup oil. Sprinkle with coriander, cayenne, and ¼ teaspoon salt. Grill 10 to 12 minutes, or until tender.

2 Meanwhile, in medium bowl, whisk mint, chiles, lemon juice, vinegar, remaining 3 tablespoons oil, and ½ teaspoon salt until well combined. Add tomatoes to vinaigrette; toss to combine. In a small bowl, stir yogurt and milk.

3 Arrange eggplant on large serving platter. Top with tomato mixture. Drizzle with yogurt mixture. Garnish with additional mint leaves, if desired.

SERVES 6 ABOUT 205 CALORIES, 3G PROTEIN, 12G CARBOHYDRATE, 17G FAT (3G SATURATED), 5G FIBER, 260MG SODIUM

Artichokes with Harissa-Honey Dip

PREP 20 MINUTES
TOTAL 1 HOUR

4 medium artichokes

1 lemon, halved

½ cup mayonnaise

1 tablespoon harissa

1 tablespoon honey

1¼ teaspoons freshly ground black pepper

1 tablespoon salt

1 With serrated knife, cut ½ inch off top of each artichoke. Halve each vertically and, using scissors, trim pointy ends off leaves. Carefully cut out fuzzy choke in center and discard. Rub artichokes all over with lemon. Fill large pot with water and fit with steaming rack. Place artichokes on rack, cover, and steam until tender and easily pierced with a fork, about 30 minutes. Set aside to cool for 15 minutes.

2 Meanwhile, prepare outdoor grill for direct grilling over high heat. In small bowl, stir together mayonnaise, harissa, honey, and ¼ teaspoon pepper. Set dipping sauce aside.

3 Coat cut sides of artichokes with nonstick cooking spray. Sprinkle with salt and remaining pepper. Grill artichokes, cut side down, 4 to 5 minutes, or until nicely charred. Serve hot with dipping sauce.

SERVES 8 ABOUT 140 CALORIES, 2G PROTEIN, 10G CARBOHYDRATE, 11G FAT (2G SATURATED), 4G FIBER, 1,006MG SODIUM

Onion Dip with Naan Chips

PREP 20 MINUTES
TOTAL 45 MINUTES

2 tablespoons olive oil

1 teaspoon fresh thyme leaves, chopped

Freshly ground black pepper

1 medium sweet onion, cut into ½-inch-thick slices

1 clove garlic

4 ounces cream cheese, softened

½ cup low-fat sour cream

¼ cup mayonnaise

2 tablespoons lemon juice

2 tablespoons Worcestershire sauce

Salt

Naan chips or pita chips, for serving

1 Prepare outdoor grill for direct grilling over medium-low heat. Combine oil, thyme, and ¼ teaspoon pepper; brush over onion. Grill onion and garlic for 15 minutes, turning once, until tender and slightly charred. Transfer to cutting board and let cool.

2 Peel garlic and place in bowl of food processor along with onion. Pulse just until chopped. Add cream cheese, sour cream, mayonnaise, lemon juice, Worcestershire sauce, and ½ teaspoon salt; pulse until combined but not smooth. Transfer to serving bowl. Refrigerate, covered, until cold. Serve with naan or pita chips.

SERVES 6 ABOUT 205 CALORIES, 2G PROTEIN, 8G CARBOHYDRATE, 19G FAT (6G SATURATED), 1G FIBER, 380MG SODIUM

Naan Chips

Cut **3 large naan** into 2-inch squares. Arrange squares in a single layer on a large baking sheet. Spray with **nonstick cooking spray** and sprinkle with **¼ teaspoon kosher salt**. Bake at 350°F for 25 minutes or until deep golden brown. Cool completely. Store in airtight container up to 1 week and serve with Grilled Onion Dip.

Thai Chicken Saté

PREP 45 MINUTES
TOTAL 55 MINUTES

1 seedless (English) cucumber, thinly sliced crosswise

1½ teaspoons salt

1 tablespoon Thai green curry paste

¼ cup well-stirred unsweetened coconut milk

4 medium skinless, boneless chicken-breast halves (1¼ pounds total), each cut diagonally into 6 strips

¼ cup rice vinegar

3 tablespoons sugar

2 medium shallots, thinly sliced

1 jalapeño, seeded and minced

12 skewers (12-inch), preferably metal

Peanut Sauce (recipe follows)

1 In medium bowl, toss cucumber with salt; let stand 30 minutes at room temperature.

2 In another bowl, stir together curry paste and coconut milk until blended. Add chicken and turn to coat. Let stand 15 minutes at room temperature, stirring occasionally.

3 Prepare outdoor grill for direct grilling over medium heat.

4 Drain cucumber, discarding liquid in bowl. Pat cucumber dry with paper towels. Return cucumber to bowl; stir in vinegar, sugar, shallots, and jalapeño; cover and refrigerate until ready to serve.

5 Thread 2 chicken strips, accordion-style, on each skewer. See tip (page 21). Discard marinade. Place skewers on hot grill grate. Grill covered for 5 to 8 minutes, turning skewers once, until cooked through (165°F).

6 Arrange skewers on platter. Serve with peanut sauce and cucumbers.

SERVES 6 (one tablespoon of sauce per serving) ABOUT 225 CALORIES, 25G PROTEIN, 12G CARBOHYDRATE, 9G FAT (4G SATURATED), 1G FIBER, 440MG SODIUM

Peanut Sauce

In small bowl, whisk ¼ cup creamy peanut butter, 2 teaspoons soy sauce, 1 teaspoon packed dark brown sugar, ⅛ teaspoon cayenne pepper, ⅓ cup well-stirred unsweetened coconut milk, and 1 tablespoon hot water until blended and smooth. Transfer sauce to serving bowl.

Skewered Shrimp

PREP 25 MINUTES
TOTAL 30 MINUTES PLUS
SOAKING SKEWERS

16 metal or bamboo skewers
   (10-inch)

2 lemons, plus lemon wedges
  for garnish

2 tablespoons olive oil

1 large clove garlic, crushed
  with press

4 tablespoons chopped fresh
  dill, plus sprigs for garnish

½ teaspoon salt

¼ teaspoon freshly ground
  black pepper

2¼ pounds shelled and deveined
    large shrimp

1 pint grape tomatoes

1 If using bamboo skewers, soak in hot water at least 30 minutes. Prepare outdoor grill for direct grilling over medium heat.

2 From lemons, grate 4 teaspoons zest and squeeze 2 tablespoons juice. In bowl, with wire whisk or fork, whisk lemon zest and juice, olive oil, garlic, 3 tablespoons chopped dill, salt, and pepper until blended. Add shrimp; toss to coat.

3 Thread shrimp and tomatoes alternately on skewers. Grill 4 to 5 minutes, turning skewers occasionally, until shrimp are opaque and tomatoes are slightly charred.

4 To serve, transfer skewers to platter; sprinkle with remaining 1 tablespoon chopped dill. Garnish platter with lemon wedges and dill sprigs.

SERVES 16 ABOUT 85 CALORIES, 13G PROTEIN, 2G CARBOHYDRATE, 3G FAT (1G SATURATED), 0G FIBER, 170MG SODIUM

Tomato-Eggplant Tartines

PREP 5 MINUTES
TOTAL 20 MINUTES

8 thick slices rustic Italian bread

1 large clove garlic, peeled and halved

4 tablespoons extra-virgin olive oil

3 small eggplants, thinly sliced

Kosher salt

1 cup shredded mozzarella cheese

4 small tomatoes, thinly sliced

¼ cup grated Parmesan cheese

Basil, for garnish

1 Prepare outdoor grill for direct grilling over medium heat. Grill bread 5 minutes, or until well toasted, turning once. Transfer to large platter. Rub toast lightly with garlic; drizzle with 2 tablespoons olive oil.

2 Toss eggplant with remaining olive oil; sprinkle with salt. Grill 5 minutes; turn slices over and top with mozzarella. Grill 5 minutes or until cheese melts. Top bread with tomatoes and salt. Layer with eggplant. Sprinkle with Parmesan. Garnish with basil.

SERVES 4 ABOUT 425 CALORIES, 32G PROTEIN, 45G CARBOHYDRATE, 22G FAT (7G SATURATED), 6G FIBER, 480MG SODIUM

Green and White Pizza

PREP 15 MINUTES
TOTAL 40 MINUTES

2 cups packed fresh basil leaves

¼ cup pine nuts

1 tablespoon lemon juice

1 clove garlic, peeled

¾ cup grated Parmesan cheese

⅓ cup plus 2 teaspoons extra-virgin olive oil

Salt

1 pound summer squash, thinly sliced

1¼ pounds pizza dough, divided into 4 balls

½ cup part-skim ricotta cheese

1 Fresno chile or red jalapeño, seeded and finely chopped

1 Prepare outdoor grill for direct grilling over medium-high heat.

2 In food processor, combine basil, pine nuts, lemon juice, garlic, ½ cup Parmesan, ⅓ cup oil, 1 tablespoon water, and ½ teaspoon salt; pulse until smooth. Transfer to medium bowl; set pesto aside.

3 In large bowl, toss squash with remaining 2 teaspoons oil and ¼ teaspoon salt until well coated. Grill 6 to 8 minutes, turning over once, until tender and grill marks appear. Transfer to bowl. Reduce grill heat to medium.

4 Stretch and roll dough balls as thinly as possible (to about 8-inch diameter). Place pieces of dough on grill grate. Grill 2 to 4 minutes, or until puffy and grill marks appear. Turn over. Working quickly, divide pesto, squash, ricotta, and chile among pieces of dough. Cover and grill another 2 to 4 minutes, or until cheese melts and bottoms of crusts are browned. With spatula and tongs, transfer pizzas to large platter or cutting board. Sprinkle pizzas with remaining ¼ cup Parmesan.

SERVES 4 ABOUT 700 CALORIES, 20G PROTEIN, 68G CARBOHYDRATE, 38G FAT (8G SATURATED), 5G FIBER, 1,800MG SODIUM

Pizza with Zucchini and Gruyère

🕑 **PREP** 10 MINUTES
TOTAL 20 MINUTES

- 2 **large zucchini, cut into ⅓-inch slices**
- 1 **clove garlic, crushed with press**
- 1 **tablespoon extra-virgin olive oil**
- ⅛ **teaspoon dried oregano**
- ⅛ **teaspoon crushed red pepper flakes**
- ⅛ **teaspoon salt**
- 1 **pound pizza dough (see Tip)**
- ½ **cup ricotta cheese**
- ½ **cup shredded Gruyère cheese**
- ¼ **cup grated Parmesan cheese**
- ¼ **cup packed fresh basil leaves, thinly sliced, plus whole leaves for garnish**

Look for fresh pizza dough in the dairy section of your supermarket, usually sold near the tortillas. (Frozen pizza dough is also available, but it takes several hours to thaw before it can be used.) Or you can purchase dough from a local pizzeria; they'll usually sell it to you in 1-pound balls if you ask.

1 Prepare outdoor grill for direct grilling over medium-high heat.

2 In large bowl, toss zucchini, garlic, oil, oregano, pepper flakes, and salt. Grill zucchini 4 minutes or until just tender, turning over once. Transfer to plate to cool.

3 Reduce grill heat to medium-low.

4 Divide dough into 4 balls; cover loosely with plastic wrap. Working with one ball at a time, transfer to large baking sheet and gently pat and stretch to form ¼-inch-thick free-form shape, as desired. Repeat.

5 Carefully lift shaped dough and lay flat on grill grate. Grill 2 to 3 minutes, or until puffed and dough releases easily from grate. Carefully turn crusts over.

6 Divide ricotta and Gruyère among crusts, spreading evenly. Top with zucchini, then Parmesan and sliced basil. Grill 3 to 5 minutes, or until cheese melts and dough is cooked through. Garnish with basil leaves.

SERVES 8 ABOUT 230 CALORIES, 11G PROTEIN, 29G CARBOHYDRATE, 8G FAT (4G SATURATED), 1G FIBER, 405MG SODIUM

Italian Sausage and Pepper Pie

PREP 15 MINUTES
TOTAL 25 MINUTES

Flour, for dusting

1 pound pizza dough, left out at room temperature for 30 minutes (see Tip on page 43)

2 teaspoons olive oil

2 small bell peppers (1 red and 1 orange), quartered

2 sweet Italian sausage links (about 8 ounces)

4 ounces part-skim mozzarella cheese, shredded

½ small red onion, thinly sliced

3 pepperoncini peppers, thinly sliced

1 Prepare outdoor grill for direct grilling over medium-high heat. Lightly dust baking sheet with flour. On floured surface, shape dough into 14-inch round; place on prepared sheet. Brush dough with 1 teaspoon oil.

2 Place bell peppers and sausages on grill grate, cut sides down, cover, and cook 3 minutes. Turn and grill, covered, 2 to 3 minutes more, or until sausages are cooked through and peppers are tender. Transfer to cutting board; slice in half lengthwise.

3 Transfer pizza dough to hot grill grate, oiled side down. Cover and grill about 2 minutes, until top begins to bubble and bottom is crisp. Brush top of dough with remaining 1 teaspoon oil.

4 Turn dough over and sprinkle with half of mozzarella, then all of onion. Top with grilled peppers, sausage, and pepperoncini; sprinkle with remaining mozzarella. Cover and grill about 3 minutes, until bottom is golden brown and crisp and mozzarella has melted. Transfer to cutting board; cut into pieces to serve.

SERVES 4 ABOUT 485 CALORIES, 19G PROTEIN, 55G CARBOHYDRATE, 19G FAT (6G SATURATED), 3G FIBER, 1,495MG SODIUM

Burgers and Dogs

Whether "naked" (aka: unadorned) or piled high with "the works," nothing beats a hot, juicy burger or dog.

A Guide to Burgers and Dogs

These tricks will make you the burger master of any backyard barbecue.

THE PERFECT DOGS

When cooked perfectly, hot dogs should be snappy and smoky on the outside and hot and juicy inside. Avoid burned, shriveled, split dogs with these tips.

USE MEDIUM HEAT. If the fire is too hot, the outsides of the hot dogs will burn before the insides heat to a safe temperature. Low temperatures take too long and won't allow you to develop a nice crust or snap. Medium heat is just right—get half the grill medium hot and keep the other half unheated. On a charcoal grill, bank the coals to one side. On gas, turn on half the burners.

STAY NEAR THE GRILL. Don't walk away! The dogs need to be turned constantly in order to get grill marks all around. Watch them carefully. When they start to expand, they are done. Roll them onto the unheated part of the grill and begin to toast your buns.

GROUND RULES FOR BURGERS

Ground chuck is a favorite for burgers. Its rich flavor is a perfect partner to just about any condiment; the fat content ensures that the meat is juicy—chuck is 81 to 85 percent lean. Be sure to get 1¼ pounds for 4 burgers, because 5 ounces raw meat cooks down to 4 ounces.

IF YOU WON'T BE USING THE MEAT RIGHT AWAY, refrigerate it in its supermarket wrap for up to two days. (And don't let the meat or its juice touch other foods; the spread of E. coli and other bacteria is a real risk.) For longer storage, repackage it in freezer wrap or foil and freeze it; use frozen meat within three months.

HANDLE BEEF GENTLY WHEN SHAPING IT, so you don't end up with a dense, dry burger. Start with a mound, flatten it slightly, and smooth around the edges.

MAKE SURE THE GRILL OR GRILL PAN IS HOT BEFORE PUTTING THE BURGERS ON. A hot surface sears the meat, so it won't stick.

DON'T FLATTEN THE PATTIES WITH A SPATULA WHILE THEY'RE GRILLING. Pressing squeezes out the flavorful juices, and it won't speed up the cooking process.

FOR SAFETY'S SAKE, COOK THE MEAT THOROUGHLY, until there's just a trace of pink in the center. Burgers don't have to be well done to be safe to eat, just not rare (an instant-read thermometer should register at least 160°F, for medium doneness). It's risky to eat undercooked burgers because bacteria on the surface of the meat before it's ground can be transferred to its interior during the grinding process. Cooking times vary, depending on the thickness of the burgers and the heat of the grill, so the only way to be sure they're done is to make them all the same size, then fork into one of them to check for doneness or use an instant-read thermometer (insert it horizontally into the patty).

DON'T GET MORE CHEESE ON THE GRILL GRATE THAN ON THE BURGERS. Once the patties are cooked to medium, blanket the tops with Cheddar, Swiss, or another favorite, and cook them with the grill cover down for about a minute.

TEST KITCHEN HACK

Burgers Shape Up

The difference between a tough and tender burger isn't just the meat, but how you shape it into patties. Here's how:

Chill your hands under cold running water. Cold, wet hands help prevent the fat in the meat from melting, which can make burgers tough.

Handle the meat as little as possible. Working quickly, divide the meat into equal mounds and loosely shape into balls.

Gently flatten the balls into patties and smooth the edges all around. Don't overwork, squeeze, or compress the meat as you shape it or you'll end up with a dense burger.

Press into the centers of the patties with your thumbs to make deep indentations. Ground meat expands as it cooks, so these dents will prevent the burgers from puffing up during cooking. The result: a flat, beautifully shaped, cooked burger—perfect for piling on lots of toppings. Stash the patties in the fridge until ready to cook (at least 30 minutes). Well-chilled patties will hold together better and cook more evenly.

Our Best Burger

PREP 10 MINUTES
TOTAL 20 MINUTES

1¼ pounds ground beef chuck

¾ teaspoon salt

½ teaspoon coarsely ground black pepper

4 hamburger buns, split

Lettuce leaves and sliced tomato, for serving

South of the Border Topping (recipe follows), optional

1 Divide ground beef into 4 mounds (about 5 ounces each) and loosely shape into balls. Gently flatten balls into patties ¾ inch thick, handling meat as little as possible. Smooth patty edges with your fingers. Place patties on flat surface. Using your thumbs, press into the centers of patties to make deep indentations. Refrigerate until ready to grill.

2 Prepare outdoor grill for direct grilling over medium-high heat, or heat ridged grill pan over medium-high heat until very hot. Sprinkle salt and pepper on both sides of patties.

3 Grill patties on grill 8 to 12 minutes for medium, or until desired doneness is reached, turning over once. About 1 minute before burgers are done, add buns, cut sides down, to grill grate. Grill just until toasted.

4 Serve burgers on buns with lettuce and tomato.

SERVES 4 ABOUT 380 CALORIES, 29G PROTEIN, 21G CARBOHYDRATE, 19G TOTAL FAT (7G SATURATED), 1G FIBER, 718MG SODIUM

South of the Border Burger

Prepare **Our Best Burger**. Serve burgers as in step 4, but omit lettuce and tomato. Dividing evenly, top burgers with **1 ripe avocado** (lightly mashed), **2 cups crumbled Cotija or feta cheese**, and **16 slices pickled jalapeño**.

SERVES 4 ABOUT 485 CALORIES, 32G PROTEIN, 26G CARBOHYDRATE, 28G TOTAL FAT (9G SATURATED), 5G FIBER, 874MG SODIUM

Extra, Extra Burgers

Start with our Best Burger (page 51) and then choose from these lip-smacking spin-offs.

Spicy Elvis Burger

Prepare **Our Best Burger**. Serve burgers as in step 4, but omit lettuce and tomato. Divide **¾ cup crunchy peanut butter** and **½ cup hot pepper jelly** among burgers. Top burgers evenly with **8 slices cooked bacon** (2 slices per burger).

SERVES 4 ABOUT 820 CALORIES, 46G PROTEIN, 50G CARBOHYDRATE, 49G FAT (13G SATURATED), 5G FIBER, 1,236MG SODIUM

Sriracha-Mayo Burger

Prepare **Our Best Burger**. Serve burgers as in step 4, but omit lettuce and tomato. Mix together **1 cup mayonnaise, ½ cup sour cream, 4 grilled green onions** (chopped), **1½ tablespoons Sriracha sauce, 1 teaspoon honey, 1 teaspoon lemon juice, ⅛ teaspoon salt,** and **⅛ teaspoon pepper.** Divide among burgers.

SERVES 4 ABOUT 840 CALORIES, 30G PROTEIN, 26G CARBOHYDRATE, 68G FAT (16G SATURATED), 1G FIBER, 1,277MG SODIUM

Chips 'n' Guac Burger

Prepare **Our Best Burger**. Serve burgers as in step 4, but omit lettuce and tomato. Top burgers evenly with ¼ **cup guacamole**, ¼ **cup sliced pickled jalapeños**, and **14 tortilla chips**.

SERVES 4 ABOUT 435 CALORIES, 30G PROTEIN, 27G CARBOHYDRATE, 22G TOTAL FAT (7G SATURATED), 3G FIBER, 871MG SODIUM

Crunchy Onion Burger

Prepare **Our Best Burger**. Serve burgers as in step 4, but omit lettuce and tomato. Top burgers evenly with ¼ **cup onion dip** and **1 cup canned fried onions** (we love French's®).

SERVES 4 ABOUT 495 CALORIES, 31G PROTEIN, 28G CARBOHYDRATE, 28G TOTAL FAT (10G SATURATED), 1G FIBER, 912MG SODIUM

Island Burger

Prepare **Our Best Burger**. Serve burgers as in step 4, but omit lettuce and tomato. Top burgers evenly with ½ **cup shredded pepper Jack cheese**, **1 green onion** (thinly sliced), and **4 fresh pineapple rings**.

SERVES 4 ABOUT 465 CALORIES, 32G PROTEIN, 29G CARBOHYDRATE, 23G TOTAL FAT (9G SATURATED), 2G FIBER, 806MG SODIUM

Vietnamese Bánh Mì Burger

In medium bowl, mix **1 medium Kirby cucumber** (sliced), **¼ cup shredded carrots**, **2½ tablespoons seasoned rice vinegar**, **2 tablespoons fresh mint leaves** (chopped), and **¼ teaspoon salt**. Cover and refrigerate 1 hour. Prepare **Our Best Burger**. Serve burgers as in step 4, but omit lettuce and tomato. Top burgers evenly with cucumber mixture.

SERVES 4 ABOUT 400 CALORIES, 29G PROTEIN, 26G CARBOHYDRATE, 19G TOTAL FAT (7G SATURATED), 1G FIBER, 1,132MG SODIUM

Pimiento Cheeseburger

Prepare **Our Best Burger**. Serve burgers as in step 4 but omit lettuce and tomato. In small bowl, mix **2 ounces Cheddar**, **pimientos**, **mayonnaise**, **green onion**, **hot pepper sauce**, and **Worcestershire sauce** until blended; set aside. Place burgers on buns and top with pimiento mixture.

SERVES 4 ABOUT 470 CALORIES, 32G PROTEIN, 23G CARBOHYDRATE, 26G FAT (10G SATURATED), 1G FIBER, 882MG SODIUM

Tapas Burger

Prepare **Our Best Burger**. Serve burgers as in step 4 but omit lettuce and tomato. Puree **1 cup jarred roasted red peppers**, drained and patted dry, and **¼ cup mayonnaise** in blender until smooth. Serve burgers on buns topped with **one ounce Manchego cheese** each and red pepper sauce.

SERVES 4 ABOUT 560 CALORIES, 35G PROTEIN, 27G CARBOHYDRATE, 33G FAT (14G SATURATED), 3G FIBER, 1,097MG SODIUM

Pepper and Onion Cheeseburger

Prepare **Our Best Burger**. Serve burgers as in step 4 but omit lettuce and tomato. Top each burger with **1 slice Monterey Jack cheese**. Cover and cook until cheese has melted, about 1 minute longer. Meanwhile, in 12-inch skillet, heat **2 tablespoons oil** over medium-high heat until hot. Add **1 red or yellow bell pepper**, sliced, and **1 red onion**, sliced; cook, stirring occasionally, until vegetables are tender. Place burgers on buns and top with pepper and onion mixture.

SERVES 4 ABOUT 540 CALORIES, 35G PROTEIN, 26G CARBOHYDRATE, 32G FAT (12G SATURATED), 2G FIBER, 857MG SODIUM

New England–Style Cheeseburger

Prepare **Our Best Burger**. Serve burgers as in step 4 but omit lettuce and tomato. Top each burger with **1 slice sharp Cheddar cheese**. Cover and cook until cheese has melted, about 1 minute longer. Place burgers on buns and top with **4 thin slices Granny Smith apples** each and **3 thin slices red onion** each.

SERVES 4 ABOUT 495 CALORIES, 37G PROTEIN, 31G CARBOHYDRATE, 24G FAT (10G SATURATED), 3G FIBER, 968MG SODIUM

Creamy Pesto Burger

Prepare **Our Best Burger**. Serve burgers as in step 4, but omit toppings. Beat together **3 ounces softened reduced-fat cream cheese, 1 ½ tablespoons pesto, 1 teaspoons lemon juice**. Divide pesto topping among the burgers and top with **shredded romaine lettuce**.

SERVES 4 ABOUT 510 CALORIES, 33G PROTEIN, 27G CARBOHYDRATE, 29G FAT (13G SATURATED), 1G FIBER, 1,200MG SODIUM

Deviled Burger

PREP 10 MINUTES
TOTAL 20 MINUTES

- 2 pounds ground beef chuck
- ⅓ cup prepared chili sauce
- 2 teaspoons finely chopped onion
- 2 teaspoons prepared horseradish
- 2 teaspoons spicy brown mustard
- 2 teaspoons Worcestershire sauce
- ½ teaspoon kosher salt
- ¼ teaspoon freshly ground black pepper
- 6 pretzel buns

  Pickles, lettuce, sliced tomato, sliced Cheddar cheese, for serving

1 In large bowl, mix together ground beef, chili sauce, onion, horseradish, mustard, Worcestershire sauce, salt, and pepper until combined.

2 Divide beef mixture into 6 portions and loosely shape into balls. Gently flatten into patties 1 inch thick. Using your thumbs, make deep indentation in center of each patty. Refrigerate until ready to grill.

3 Prepare outdoor grill for direct grilling over medium heat.

4 Grill over medium heat to desired doneness. Serve on pretzel buns with pickles, lettuce, tomato, and Cheddar.

SERVES 6 ABOUT 600 CALORIES, 41G PROTEIN, 43G CARBOHYDRATE, 28G FAT (13G SATURATED), 1G FIBER, 1,030MG SODIUM

Classic Sliders

PREP 10 MINUTES
TOTAL 15 MINUTES

- 1¼ pounds ground beef chuck, pork, lamb, chicken, or turkey
- ¾ teaspoon salt
- ½ teaspoon freshly ground black pepper
- 12 slider mini buns, split and toasted
  Plum tomato slices, small lettuce leaves, dill pickle slices, and/or onion slices (optional)

1 Prepare outdoor grill for direct grilling over medium heat.

2 Shape ground beef into 12 equal patties each ½ inch thick. Sprinkle salt and pepper on both sides of patties.

3 Grill patties 5 to 6 minutes for medium, or until desired doneness is reached, turning over once.

4 Serve burgers on buns with tomato, lettuce, pickles, and onion, if using.

SERVES 12 ABOUT 145 CALORIES, 10G PROTEIN, 9G CARBOHYDRATE, 8G FAT (3G SATURATED), 1G FIBER, 240MG SODIUM

If preparing these sliders with **ground chicken** or **turkey**, make sure to spray both sides of the patties with nonstick cooking spray and increase the cooking time to 6 to 7 minutes.

Pesto Sliders

Prepare **Classic Sliders** with **ground chicken**, **turkey**, **pork**, or **beef**, but in step 2, before shaping patties, mix ¼ **cup refrigerated or jarred pesto** with meat until blended, but do not overmix. Sprinkle patties with **salt** and **pepper**. Serve burgers as in step 4, but spoon additional pesto over burgers, if desired.

SERVES 12 ABOUT 140 CALORIES, 10G PROTEIN, 9G CARBOHYDRATE, 8G TOTAL FAT (3G SATURATED), 1G FIBER, 270MG SODIUM

Corn and Salsa Sliders

Prepare **Classic Sliders** with **ground chicken** or **turkey**, but in step 2, before shaping patties, mix **½ cup fresh or frozen (thawed) corn kernels** and **¼ cup medium salsa** with meat mixture until blended, but do not overmix. Do not sprinkle patties with salt and pepper. At the end of step 3, place slices of **pepper Jack cheese** (about 4 ounces total) on top of burgers; cover and grill about 1 minute for cheese to melt. Serve burgers as in step 4, but spoon additional medium salsa over burgers, if desired.

SERVES 12 ABOUT 160 CALORIES, 12G PROTEIN, 11G CARBOHYDRATE, 8G TOTAL FAT (3G SATURATED), 1G FIBER, 170MG SODIUM

Ranch Sliders

Prepare **Classic Sliders** with **ground chicken** or **turkey**, but in step 2, before shaping patties, mix **1 medium carrot**, shredded (about ½ cup); **1 green onion**, chopped; and **¼ cup ranch salad dressing** with ground meat until blended, but do not overmix. Sprinkle patties with **pepper** but not salt. Serve burgers as in step 4, but spoon additional ranch dressing over burgers, if desired.

SERVES 12 ABOUT 140 CALORIES, 10G PROTEIN, 10G CARBOHYDRATE, 8G TOTAL FAT (0G SATURATED), 1G FIBER, 150MG SODIUM

Rosemary-Cabernet Sliders

Prepare **Classic Sliders** with **ground beef** or **lamb**, but in step 2, before shaping patties, mix **⅓ cup Cabernet Sauvignon** or other dry red wine and **2 teaspoons finely chopped fresh rosemary** with meat until blended, but do not overmix. Sprinkle patties with **salt** and **pepper**. Serve burgers as in step 4.

SERVES 12 ABOUT 145 CALORIES, 11G PROTEIN, 9G CARBOHYDRATE, 8G TOTAL FAT (3G SATURATED), 1G FIBER, 240MG SODIUM

Mediterranean Spiced Burger

PREP 15 MINUTES
TOTAL 25 MINUTES

1 pound ground lamb, beef, or turkey

½ cup packed fresh cilantro leaves, finely chopped

2 cloves garlic, crushed with press

1 teaspoon ground coriander

¼ teaspoon salt

1 medium red onion, cut into 1-inch rounds

4 hamburger buns, split

⅓ cup ketchup

1 teaspoon curry powder

2 tablespoons crumbled feta cheese

Fresh cilantro sprigs, for topping

1 Prepare outdoor grill for direct grilling over medium-high heat.

2 In medium bowl, combine ground meat, cilantro, garlic, and coriander until blended, but do not overmix.

3 Divide meat mixture into 4 portions and loosely shape into balls. Gently flatten into patties ¼ inch thick. Using your thumbs, make deep indentation in center of each patty. Sprinkle salt on both sides of patties. (For ground turkey, spray both sides of patties with nonstick cooking spray.)

4 Grill patties and onion slices 8 to 10 minutes for medium, or until desired doneness is reached, turning over once (onions should be browned and tender). About 1 minute before burgers are done, add buns, cut sides down, to grill. Grill just until toasted.

5 Meanwhile, in small bowl, stir together ketchup and curry powder until blended.

6 Serve burgers on buns with curry ketchup, feta, onion, and cilantro sprigs.

SERVES 4 ABOUT 390 CALORIES, 25G PROTEIN, 31G CARBOHYDRATE, 18G FAT (7G SATURATED), 2G FIBER, 667MG SODIUM

Green Chile Cheeseburger

PREP 10 MINUTES
TOTAL 25 MINUTES

½ teaspoon garlic powder

½ teaspoon onion powder

½ teaspoon salt

¼ teaspoon freshly ground black pepper

1 pound ground beef sirloin (90% lean)

¾ pound ground beef chuck (80% lean)

6 slices American or Cheddar cheese

¾ cup jarred or canned roasted diced green chiles (preferably Hatch), drained

6 brioche hamburger buns, split and toasted

1 Prepare outdoor grill for direct grilling over medium-high heat.

2 In small bowl, combine garlic powder, onion powder, salt, and pepper. In large bowl, gently combine sirloin and chuck. Divide beef into 6 portions and loosely shape into balls. Gently flatten into patties 4 inches wide. Using your thumbs, make deep indentation in center of each patty. Sprinkle both sides with garlic powder mixture.

3 Grill burgers 3 minutes; turn over. Top each with slice of cheese. Cover and cook 3 minutes or until desired doneness and cheese has melted. Top each with 2 tablespoons green chiles. Serve on buns.

SERVES 6 ABOUT 585 CALORIES, 35G PROTEIN, 47G CARBOHYDRATE, 26G FAT (13G SATURATED), 4G FIBER, 1,005MG SODIUM

Basic Chicken Burger

PREP 20 MINUTES
TOTAL 35 MINUTES

1 pound ground chicken breast

1 medium carrot, grated (1 cup)

2 green onions, minced

1 clove garlic, crushed with press

4 hamburger buns, split and warmed

Kosher salt

Freshly ground black pepper

Sliced cucumber, lettuce leaves, and green onion (optional)

||||||||||||||||||||||||||||||||||

Chicken patties
are delicate, so if you have a grill with widely spaced grates, we recommend placing the burgers on a **perforated grill topper** to keep them intact.

1 Prepare outdoor grill for direct grilling over medium heat.

2 In medium bowl, combine ground chicken, carrot, green onions, and garlic until blended, but do not overmix.

3 On waxed paper, divide chicken mixture into 4 portions and shape into patties 3½ inches wide, handling mixture as little as possible (mixture will be very soft and moist). Spray both sides of patties with nonstick cooking spray. Season with kosher salt and ground black pepper.

4 Grill patties about 12 minutes or just until chicken loses its pink color throughout, turning once.

5 Serve burgers on warmed buns with cucumber slices, lettuce leaves, and green onion, if using.

SERVES 4 ABOUT 275 CALORIES, 30G PROTEIN, 24G CARBOHYDRATE, 5G TOTAL FAT (1G SATURATED), 2G FIBER, 310MG SODIUM

Teriyaki Chicken Burger

Prepare **Basic Chicken Burger** as directed, but in step 2, add **2 tablespoons soy sauce, 1 tablespoon seasoned rice vinegar, 2 teaspoons grated peeled fresh ginger, and 2 teaspoons toasted sesame oil** to ground chicken mixture. (Prepare burger mixture just before cooking to prevent ginger from changing texture of meat.)

SERVES 4 ABOUT 305 CALORIES, 31G PROTEIN, 26G CARBOHYDRATE, 8G FAT (2G SATURATED), 2G FIBER, 940MG SODIUM

BBQ Chicken Burger

Prepare **Basic Chicken Burger** as directed, but in step 2, add **2 tablespoons chili sauce, 1 tablespoon light (mild) molasses, 2 teaspoons cayenne pepper sauce, 2 teaspoons Worcestershire sauce, and ¼ teaspoon salt** to ground chicken mixture.

SERVES 4 ABOUT 295 CALORIES, 31G PROTEIN, 30G CARBOHYDRATE, 5G FAT (1G SATURATED), 2G FIBER, 715MG SODIUM

Herb Chicken Burger

Prepare **Basic Chicken Burger** as directed, but in step 2, add **2 tablespoons finely chopped fresh dill, 1 tablespoon dried mint, 1 tablespoon lemon juice, 1 teaspoon ground cumin, ½ teaspoon salt, and ⅛ teaspoon cayenne pepper** to ground chicken mixture.

SERVES 4 ABOUT 280 CALORIES, 31G PROTEIN, 25G CARBOHYDRATE, 5G FAT (1G SATURATED), 2G FIBER, 605MG SODIUM

Buffalo Chicken Burger

 **PREP** 15 MINUTES
TOTAL 30 MINUTES

1¼ pounds ground chicken or turkey

1 stalk celery, finely chopped

3 tablespoons cayenne pepper sauce, plus more for serving

4 hamburger buns, split and toasted

Lettuce leaves

Blue Cheese Sauce (recipe follows)

Carrot and celery sticks

||||||||||||||||||||||||||||||||||||

If grill has widely spaced grates, place **burgers** on perforated grill topper to keep them intact.

1 Prepare outdoor grill for direct grilling over medium heat, or lightly spray ridged grill pan with nonstick cooking spray and heat over medium heat until hot.

2 In medium bowl, combine chicken, celery, and cayenne pepper sauce just until blended. Divide chicken mixture into 4 portions and loosely shape into balls. Gently flatten into patties ¾ inch thick. Using your thumbs, make deep indentation in center of each patty. Spray both sides of burgers with cooking spray.

3 Grill burgers on hot grill grate or grill pan. Grill 12 to 14 minutes, turning over once, until juices run clear when center of burger is pierced with tip of knife. (An instant-read meat thermometer inserted horizontally into center should register 165°F.)

4 Serve burgers on buns with lettuce and 1 tablespoon Blue Cheese Sauce. Serve remaining Blue Cheese Sauce with carrot and celery sticks for dipping. Pass additional cayenne pepper sauce with burgers if you like.

SERVES 4 ABOUT 385 CALORIES, 28G PROTEIN, 23G CARBOHYDRATE, 20G FAT (3G SATURATED), 2G FIBER, 895MG SODIUM

Blue Cheese Sauce

In small bowl, stir ¼ cup light mayonnaise, ¼ cup reduced-fat sour cream, ½ cup crumbled blue cheese (2 ounces), **2 teaspoons apple cider vinegar**, and ½ teaspoon Worcestershire sauce until blended. Refrigerate until serving. **Makes about ¾ cup.**

BBQ Chicken and Cheddar Burger

 **PREP** 10 MINUTES
TOTAL 20 MINUTES

1¼ pounds ground chicken

⅓ cup barbecue sauce

3 green onions, chopped

¼ teaspoon salt

¼ teaspoon freshly ground black pepper

2 teaspoons canola oil

4 slices sharp Cheddar cheese

4 whole wheat buns, split

Thinly sliced green apple

Microgreens

||||||||||||||||||||||||||||||||||||||

Consider using
Chunky Barbecue Sauce (page 303) on this burger.

1 In medium bowl, combine ground chicken, barbecue sauce, green onions, salt, and pepper. Divide into 4 portions and loosely shape into balls. Gently flatten into patties 1 inch thick. Using your thumbs, make deep indentation in center of each patty.

2 In a stovetop grill pan, heat canola oil over medium heat. Add patties and cook 7 minutes per side or until cooked through (165°F).

3 Top each patty with 1 slice sharp Cheddar cheese; remove from heat and cover skillet to melt cheese. Serve on whole wheat buns topped with green apple and microgreens.

SERVES 4 ABOUT 475 CALORIES, 36G PROTEIN, 35G CARBOHYDRATE, 23G FAT (8G SATURATED), 5G FIBER, 795MG SODIUM

Loaded Chicken Burger

PREP 5 MINUTES
TOTAL 20 MINUTES

1 pound ground dark-meat chicken

3 tablespoons Italian-style bread crumbs

¼ cup grated Parmesan cheese

1 large egg

¼ teaspoon salt

½ teaspoon freshly ground black pepper

2 teaspoons vegetable oil

4 buns, split and toasted

Tomato, sliced

Lettuce, shredded

2 cups barbecue-flavored potato chips

Mustard

Ketchup

1 In medium bowl, combine ground chicken, bread crumbs, Parmesan, egg, salt, and pepper. Divide into 4 portions and loosely shape into balls. Gently flatten into patties 4 inches wide. Using your thumbs, make deep indentation in center of each patty.

2 In a stovetop grill pan, heat oil on medium. Add patties and cook 8 to 10 minutes, or until cooked through (165°F), turning once.

3 Serve on toasted buns topped with tomato, lettuce, potato chips, mustard, and ketchup.

SERVES 4 ABOUT 470 CALORIES, 33G PROTEIN, 42G CARBOHYDRATE, 19G FAT (5G SATURATED), 2G FIBER, 960MG SODIUM

Turkey Burger with Sweet Potato Fries

PREP 20 MINUTES
TOTAL 40 MINUTES

- 2 small sweet potatoes (1 pound)
- 2 tablespoons olive oil
- 2 teaspoons chili powder
- ½ teaspoon salt
- 1 pound ground turkey breast
- 2 cloves garlic, crushed with press
- ½ cup chopped fresh cilantro
- ½ ripe avocado
- 2 teaspoons fresh lime juice
- 4 whole-grain sandwich thins, split and toasted
- Sliced tomato, sliced cucumber, lettuce leaves, and sprouts (optional)

1 Preheat oven to 450°F. Cut unpeeled potatoes lengthwise into ¼-inch-wide sticks. On large rimmed baking sheet, toss potatoes with oil, 1 teaspoon chili powder, and ¼ teaspoon salt. Roast potatoes 20 to 25 minutes, or until crisp, shaking pan once halfway through cooking.

2 Meanwhile, prepare outdoor grill for direct grilling over medium heat.

3 In medium bowl, combine ground turkey, garlic, cilantro, 1 teaspoon chili powder, and ¼ teaspoon salt. Divide into 4 portions and loosely shape into balls. Gently flatten into patties. Using your thumbs, make deep indentation in center of each patty. Spray both sides of patties with nonstick cooking spray.

4 Grill patties 12 to 15 minutes, or just until turkey loses its pink color throughout, turning once.

5 While burgers are cooking, in small bowl, mash avocado with lime juice.

6 Place burgers on sandwich thins and top with avocado mixture, tomato and cucumber slices, lettuce leaves, and sprouts, if using. Serve with fries.

SERVES 4 ABOUT 470 CALORIES, 30G PROTEIN, 46G CARBOHYDRATE, 21G FAT (4G SATURATED), 11G FIBER, 640MG SODIUM

Lamb Burger with Minted Yogurt Sauce

PREP 20 MINUTES
TOTAL 30 MINUTES

1 plum tomato, chopped

½ cup plain low-fat yogurt

2 tablespoons light mayonnaise

¾ cup loosely packed fresh mint leaves, coarsely chopped

1 teaspoon salt

¼ teaspoon ground black pepper

1¼ pounds ground lamb

¼ cup walnuts (optional), chopped

1 clove garlic, crushed with press

2 teaspoons ground cumin

4 pitas (6-inch)

1 medium Kirby cucumber, sliced

||||||||||||||||||||||||||||||||||||

Instant-read meat thermometer inserted horizontally into **patties** should register 160°F.

1 Prepare outdoor grill for direct grilling over medium heat, or lightly spray ridged grill pan with nonstick cooking spray, then place over medium heat until hot.

2 In small bowl, stir tomato, yogurt, mayonnaise, 2 tablespoons mint, ¼ teaspoon salt, and pepper until blended; set aside.

3 In medium bowl, combine lamb, walnuts (if using), garlic, cumin, ¾ teaspoon salt, and remaining mint until just blended.

4 Divide lamb mixture into 4 portions and loosely shape into balls. Gently flatten into patties ¾ inch thick. Using your thumbs, make deep indentation in center of each patty.

5 Grill patties, covered, 10 to 12 minutes for medium, or until desired doneness, turning over once.

6 To serve, cut off one-third from side of each pita; save for making crumbs another day. Place burgers in pitas with yogurt sauce and cucumber slices.

SERVES 4 ABOUT 485 CALORIES, 32G PROTEIN, 31G CARBOHYDRATE, 25G FAT (10G SATURATED), 3G FIBER, 985MG SODIUM

Asian Tuna Burger

PREP 15 MINUTES
TOTAL 20 MINUTES

1 tuna steak (about 1 pound)

1 green onion, thinly sliced

2 tablespoons lower-sodium
   soy sauce

1 teaspoon grated peeled
   fresh ginger

¼ teaspoon coarsely ground
   black pepper

¼ cup plain dried bread crumbs

2 tablespoons sesame seeds

4 buns

   Pickled ginger (optional)

||||||||||||||||||||||||||||||||||||||||

Finely chop tuna
by hand for a light
texture. Don't use a
food processor—it will
make the patties dense
and dry.

1 Prepare outdoor grill for direct grilling over medium heat.

2 Finely chop tuna and place in medium bowl. Add green onion, soy sauce, ginger, and pepper; mix until combined (mixture will be very soft and moist). Divide tuna mixture into 4 portions and gently flatten into patties 3 inches wide.

3 On waxed paper, combine bread crumbs and sesame seeds. Carefully press patties into mixture, turning to coat both sides. Spray both sides of tuna patties with nonstick cooking spray.

4 Grill patties 6 to 7 minutes, until browned on the outside and still slightly pink in the center, or to desired doneness, turning over once. Serve with pickled ginger and with, or without, the bun.

SERVES 4 ABOUT 210 CALORIES, 26G PROTEIN, 7G CARBOHYDRATE, 8G FAT (2G SATURATED), 1G FIBER, 400MG SODIUM

Salmon Burger with Cabbage-Apple Slaw

 **PREP** 10 MINUTES
TOTAL 30 MINUTES

3 **green onions**

1¼ **pounds salmon fillets, cut into chunks**

2 **teaspoons curry powder**

Salt

½ **medium head red cabbage**

½ **green apple, cut into matchsticks**

2 **tablespoons apple cider vinegar**

4 **brioche buns, split**

Mayonnaise

If using wild salmon, check for doneness sooner. It cooks faster, as it's leaner.

1   Prepare outdoor grill for direct grilling over medium-high heat.

2   Slice green onions. In food processor, pulse salmon fillets, half of green onions, curry powder, and ½ teaspoon salt until finely chopped. Divide mixture into 4 portions and gently flatten into patties ½ inch thick. Freeze 10 minutes.

3   Cut red cabbage into 1-inch-thick slices; spray with cooking spray. Grill, covered, 3 minutes per side or until lightly charred.

4   Spray patties with cooking spray. Grill 2 to 4 minutes per side to desired doneness.

5   Slice cabbage and toss with green apple, cider vinegar, remaining green onions, and ¼ teaspoon salt. Serve burgers on brioche buns with slaw and mayonnaise.

SERVES 4 ABOUT 565 CALORIES, 36G PROTEIN, 56G CARBOHYDRATE, 22G FAT (7G SATURATED), 7G FIBER, 970MG SODIUM

Southwestern Black Bean Burger

 PREP 10 MINUTES
TOTAL 15 MINUTES

1 can (15 to 19 ounces) black beans, rinsed and drained

6 tablespoons light mayonnaise

2 cups packed fresh cilantro leaves, chopped

1 tablespoon plain dried bread crumbs

1 teaspoon ground cumin

1 teaspoon hot pepper sauce

4 sesame hamburger buns, split and toasted

1 cup thinly sliced romaine lettuce

4 slices beefsteak tomato

1 cucumber, thinly sliced (optional)

1 In large bowl, with potato masher or fork, mash beans with 2 tablespoons mayonnaise until almost smooth (some lumps of beans should remain). Stir in cilantro, bread crumbs, cumin, and pepper sauce until combined.

2 With lightly floured hands, shape bean mixture into 4 equal patties. Spray both sides of patties with nonstick cooking spray.

3 Heat grill pan over medium heat until hot. Add patties and cook about 6 minutes or until heated through, turning over once.

4 Serve burgers on buns with remaining 4 tablespoons mayonnaise, lettuce, tomato, and cucumber (if using).

SERVES 4 ABOUT 395 CALORIES, 15G PROTEIN, 50G CARBOHYDRATE, 12G FAT (2G SATURATED), 10G FIBER, 770MG SODIUM

PLT Burger

 **PREP** 20 MINUTES

TOTAL 30 MINUTES

1 teaspoon fresh rosemary leaves, finely chopped

1 clove garlic, crushed with press

3 tablespoons olive oil

3 tablespoons light mayonnaise

2 tablespoons packed, finely chopped fresh basil leaves

4 large portobello mushroom caps, gills removed

2 teaspoons salt

2 teaspoons freshly ground black pepper

4 ciabatta or other crusty rolls, split

4 iceberg lettuce leaves

1 cup arugula (optional)

1 ounce Parmesan cheese, shaved

4 large tomato slices

1 Prepare outdoor grill for direct grilling over medium-high heat.

2 In small bowl, combine rosemary, garlic, and oil. In another small bowl, combine mayonnaise and basil.

3 Brush oil mixture all over mushrooms, then sprinkle with salt and pepper.

4 Place ciabatta halves, cut sides down, and mushrooms on hot grill grate. Cook ciabatta 3 minutes or until toasted, turning over once. Cook mushrooms 6 to 8 minutes, or until browned and tender, turning over once. Transfer to cutting board. Cut mushrooms at an angle into ½-inch slices, keeping mushroom shape intact.

5 Spread basil mayonnaise on cut sides of ciabatta. Divide lettuce and arugula (if using) among bottom halves. Place 1 mushroom on top, slightly fanning slices apart. Top with Parmesan, tomato, and ciabatta tops.

SERVES 4 ABOUT 435 CALORIES, 17G PROTEIN, 55G CARBOHYDRATE, 18G FAT (3G SATURATED), 4G FIBER, 880MG SODIUM

Mushroom-Quinoa Burger

PREP 15 MINUTES
TOTAL 45 MINUTES PLUS
        CHILLING

½ cup mayonnaise

1 teaspoon finely chopped
  fresh rosemary

1 teaspoon lemon juice

  Kosher salt

4 medium portobello
  mushroom caps (about
  1 pound), gills removed,
  chopped

½ cup walnuts

1 clove garlic, peeled

2 tablespoons canola oil

¾ teaspoon salt

¼ teaspoon freshly ground
  black pepper

¼ cup chopped red onion

3 green onions, chopped

2 teaspoons rice vinegar

1 cup cooked quinoa

½ cup cornstarch

  Whole-grain burger buns,
  split

  Sprouts, lettuce, and sliced
  tomatoes

1. Combine mayonnaise, rosemary, lemon juice, and pinch of salt. Set aside.

2. Preheat oven to 375°F.

3. In 3-quart, shallow baking dish, toss mushrooms with walnuts, garlic, 1 tablespoon oil, salt, and pepper; spread in even layer. Bake 20 minutes or until mushrooms are tender. Set aside to cool. Turn oven off.

4. In food processor, pulse mushroom mixture, red onion, green onions, and vinegar until mostly smooth, scraping side of bowl if necessary. Transfer mixture to large bowl and stir in quinoa and cornstarch until well blended. Cover bowl with plastic wrap and refrigerate 2 hours.

5. Preheat oven to 375°F. Line baking sheet with foil.

6. Divide quinoa mixture into 5 portions and gently form into patties about ½ inch thick and 3 inches wide.

7. In 12-inch nonstick skillet, heat remaining 1 tablespoon oil over medium heat. In 2 batches, cook patties 5 minutes or until well browned, turning over once. Transfer seared patties to prepared baking sheet. Bake 10 minutes or until hot in centers.

8. Serve burgers on buns with Rosemary Mayo, garnished with sprouts, lettuce, and tomato. Keep excess mayo in fridge for up to 5 days.

SERVES 5 ABOUT 495 CALORIES, 9G PROTEIN, 49G CARBOHYDRATE, 31G FAT (4G SATURATED), 7G FIBER, 700MG SODIUM

Sriracha Meatball Hoagies

 **PREP** 20 MINUTES
TOTAL 30 MINUTES

½ cup seasoned rice vinegar

½ medium jicama, peeled and cut into small strips

½ cup shredded carrots

¼ cup packed fresh mint leaves

3 cloves garlic, peeled

1 medium shallot, chopped

1 stalk lemongrass, tough outer layer discarded, sliced

1½ tablespoons fish sauce

1 pound ground pork

1 tablespoon Sriracha sauce, plus more for serving

⅓ cup mayonnaise

2 tablespoons Sriracha

4 soft hoagie or sub rolls (4 inches long), split and lightly toasted

Cilantro sprigs, for garnish

Thinly sliced jalapeños, for garnish

1 In 2-quart saucepot, heat vinegar and ¼ cup water to simmering on medium. Remove from heat; add jicama and carrots. Let vegetable mixture cool completely.

2 Meanwhile, prepare outdoor grill for direct grilling over medium heat.

3 In food processor, pulse mint, garlic, shallot, lemongrass, and fish sauce until finely chopped, stopping and scraping occasionally. Transfer to medium bowl

4 Add pork and 1 tablespoon Sriracha to bowl; mix just until well combined. Divide and shape into 16 meatballs. Grill, covered, 10 to 12 minutes, or until cooked through, turning occasionally.

5 Meanwhile, stir mayonnaise with Sriracha until well blended and spread Sriracha Mayo on insides of rolls. Drain jicama and carrots; add to rolls along with meatballs, cilantro, and jalapeños.

SERVES 4 ABOUT 575 CALORIES, 29G PROTEIN, 38G CARBOHYDRATE, 34G FAT (10G SATURATED), 5G FIBER, 1,160MG SODIUM

Taco Dogs

PREP 10 MINUTES
TOTAL 20 MINUTES

2 teaspoons olive oil

8 ounces ground beef sirloin

1 tablespoon chili powder

½ cup prepared salsa verde

6 all-beef hot dogs

6 hot dog buns, toasted

1 cup plus 2 tablespoons shredded Cheddar cheese, for serving

1 cup plus 2 tablespoons crushed tortilla chips, for serving

Shredded lettuce, for serving

1 Set ridged grill pan over medium heat until hot.

2 Place hot dogs on hot grill pan; cook for 7 to 9 minutes or until heated through, turning occasionally.

3 Meanwhile, in 10-inch skillet, heat oil on medium-high. Add ground beef and chili powder; cook 2 minutes or until cooked through, breaking up meat with thin, stiff spatula. Stir in salsa verde; cook for 1 minute.

4 Place hot dogs in buns; top evenly with beef mixture. Top each hot dog with 3 tablespoons Cheddar, 3 tablespoons tortilla chips and lettuce.

SERVES 6 ABOUT 435 CALORIES, 20G PROTEIN, 29G CARBOHYDRATE, 26G FAT (10G SATURATED), 2G FIBER, 1,000MG SODIUM

Top Dogs

Grill up your favorite wieners and buns, then top with one of these think-outside-the-bun combos.

 PREP 10 MINUTES
TOTAL 20 MINUTES

4 **hot dogs, grilled**

4 **hot dog buns, toasted**

Choice of toppings (see below)

Italian Dog

Prepare steps 1 and 2 for Taco Dogs. Top each dog with **1 ounce sautéed peppers and onions,** and **1 ounce roasted potato chunks.**

SERVES 4 ABOUT 490 CALORIES, 12G PROTEIN, 34G CARBOHYDRATE, 18G FAT (7G SATURATED), 2G FIBER, 942MG SODIUM

Sonoran Dog

Prepare steps 1 and 2 for Taco Dogs. Top each dog with **2 tablespoons fresh pico de gallo, 1 tablespoon pickled or fresh jalapeños, 1 tablespoon sour cream,** and **1 teaspoon cilantro.**

SERVES 4 ABOUT 345 CALORIES, 12G PROTEIN, 29G CARBOHYDRATE, 20G FAT (9G SATURATED), 1G FIBER, 941MG SODIUM

Cuban Frita Dog

Prepare steps 1 and 2 for Taco Dogs. Top each dog with **2 tablespoons potato sticks**, **1½ tablespoons raw chopped white onion**, and **1 tablespoon ketchup**.

SERVES 4 ABOUT 360 CALORIES, 12G PROTEIN, 34G CARBOHYDRATE, 19G FAT (8G SATURATED), 1G FIBER, 986MG SODIUM

Hawaiian Dog

Prepare steps 1 and 2 for Taco Dogs. Top each dog with **2 teaspoons yellow mustard**, **1 tablespoon garlic mayo**, **2 tablespoons finely chopped fresh pineapple**, and **1 tablespoon sliced green onions**.

SERVES 4 ABOUT 375 CALORIES, 11G PROTEIN, 32G CARBOHYDRATE, 23G FAT (8KG SATURATED), 1G FIBER, 998MG SODIUM

BLT Dogs

Prepare steps 1 and 2 for Taco Dogs. Divide **¼ cup mayonnaise**, **½ cup sliced romaine**, **1 chopped tomato**, and **6 slices crumbled cooked bacon** among **4 hot dogs** in **buns**.

SERVES 4 ABOUT 480 CALORIES, 16G PROTEIN, 28G CARBOHYDRATE, 33G FAT (11G SATURATED), 1G FIBER, 1,063MG SODIUM

Spicy Blue Cheese Dogs

Prepare steps 1 and 2 for Taco Dogs. In bowl, combine **1 cup celery**, **¼ cup mayonnaise**, **½ teaspoon apple cider vinegar**, **½ teaspoon hot sauce**, and **3 ounces crumbled blue cheese**; divide among **4 hot dogs** in **buns**.

SERVES 4 ABOUT 485 CALORIES, 16G PROTEIN, 27G CARBOHYDRATE, 34G FAT (13G SATURATED), 1G FIBER, 1,134MG SODIUM

Poultry

Inexpensive, versatile, and delicious, chicken and turkey are the triple threats of the grilling world. Your family is sure to vote "Yes!" on these easy dinners again and again.

A Guide to Grilling Chicken

Whether you're preparing breasts, thighs, or the whole bird, follow these tips for grilling succulent, mouthwatering chicken every time.

GREASE YOUR GRILL. Chances are you won't have a sticking problem if your chicken has skin, or if it's marinated or rubbed with some oil. But play it safe. Before you light the grill, spray the rack with nonstick cooking spray or brush it with oil.

KEEP IT HOT. Sear the chicken on a hot grill—this makes it easier to turn the chicken over, because it won't stick.

WATCH SEASONINGS CAREFULLY. Marinades and basting sauces, many of which have a high sugar content, will burn if the grill temperature is too high or if they're exposed to heat for too long. This is normally not a problem with quick-cooking chicken cuts (such as skinless, boneless breasts), but longer-cooking ones (such as bone-in chicken parts) should be placed over a lower temperature. It also helps not to start basting until the chicken is almost fully cooked.

CLOSE THE TOP. If your grill has a cover, cook bone-in chicken with the cover down. It will make your grill more oven-like, so that the heat comes into contact with the food more evenly. Also, because the cover cuts off some of the oxygen, you'll have fewer flare-ups.

BE PATIENT. Resist the urge to move the poultry around while it cooks. The chicken will cook more evenly (and more quickly!) if you follow the recipe cooking instructions or turn it over only once midway through grilling.

USE THE RIGHT UTENSIL. Use long-handled tongs or a wide metal spatula to move the chicken. Poking it with a fork will allow precious juices to escape.

TEST FOR DONENESS. Don't risk serving undercooked chicken. First, make a small cut into the thickest part so you can be positive that it's no longer pink inside. Then use an instant-read meat thermometer to see if your meat has reached a safe internal temperature—165°F for whole chicken and breasts.

BE SURE TO CLEAN UP. Scrape your grill grate after each use; otherwise the chicken will pick up charred bits from your last barbecue. Chicken has a tendency to stick to a dirty grill.

POULTRY SAFETY

Chicken and turkey are deliciously simple choices for dinner, but because of the possibility of salmonella contamination, they need to be treated with respect. Here are some sensible tips for keeping things safe in the kitchen and on the grill:

PROMOTE GOOD HYGIENE. Proper hand washing—20 seconds with hot, soapy water—is absolutely essential before and after handling raw poultry. Try this tactic: Wash as long as it takes to sing two rousing choruses of "Happy Birthday." You may even encourage good hygiene in your child with this tactic!

TACKLE CROSS-CONTAMINATION. Place the package of raw poultry in a plastic bag to separate it from other groceries. Take it straight home from the store and refrigerate it immediately (35° to 40°F). Set wrapped raw poultry on a plate on the bottom shelf of the refrigerator so juices don't drip onto other foods. Always thoroughly wash cutting boards, knives, utensils, and countertops after they come in contact with raw poultry. Immediately take away any plates that have held raw poultry, so you don't accidentally put cooked food back onto them.

MAKE SEASONING SAFE. Always place chicken that must marinate for longer than thirty minutes in the refrigerator. If you want to use the marinade as a basting or dipping sauce, set aside a portion of it before adding the raw food. It is important to wash basting brushes with hot, soapy water after use. Discard leftover marinade that has come in contact with raw poultry, or bring it to a boil for a minute before serving.

REFRIGERATE OR COOK. Thaw poultry in the refrigerator or in the microwave, never at room temperature. When you thaw it in the microwave, cook it immediately and completely to destroy harmful bacteria. Never partially grill poultry and finish cooking it later.

TEST KITCHEN HACK

The Gentle Art of Pounding

Here's how to pound a chicken breast to a uniform thickness.

1 On a cutting board or work surface, place a skinless, boneless chicken breast half between two sheets of plastic wrap. The plastic wrap will protect the surface of the chicken and prevent the meat from sticking to the mallet or work surface. Plus the plastic won't rip as easily as waxed paper. Bonus! The same two sheets of plastic wrap can be reused for the remaining chicken breasts.

2 Use the smooth side of a metal or wood meat mallet. (The textured side is good for tough cuts of meat that need to be tenderized.) If you don't have a meat mallet, you can use a sturdy rolling pin or the flat side of a heavy skillet. Gently strike the chicken breast until it has an even thickness, ½ to ¼ inch thick, depending on the recipe. It's not necessary to strike the meat with a great deal of force; let the mallet do the work!

Chicken with Herbed Corn Salsa

PREP 10 MINUTES
TOTAL 20 MINUTES

- 2¼ pounds skin-on, bone-in chicken thighs
- ¾ teaspoon salt
- ½ teaspoon freshly ground black pepper
- 1 cup packed fresh basil leaves
- ½ cup packed fresh mint leaves
- ¼ cup grated Parmesan cheese
- 1 clove garlic
- ¼ cup lemon juice
- 2 tablespoons extra-virgin olive oil
- 2 large ears corn, shucked

1 Prepare outdoor grill for direct grilling over medium heat.

2 Season chicken thighs with ½ teaspoon salt and pepper. Grill chicken, covered, 15 to 20 minutes, turning over once, until chicken is cooked through (165°F).

3 In food processor, pulse basil, mint, Parmesan, garlic, and ¼ teaspoon salt until finely chopped. Add lemon juice and olive oil; pulse until just combined. Transfer herb sauce to bowl.

4 Grill corn over medium heat for 10 minutes, turning occasionally. Cut kernels off cobs; stir into herb sauce. Serve chicken with corn salsa.

SERVES 4 ABOUT 495 CALORIES, 39G PROTEIN, 17G CARBOHYDRATE, 31G FAT (8G SATURATED), 3G FIBER, 690MG SODIUM

Chicken Fajitas for a Crowd

PREP 15 MINUTES
TOTAL 30 MINUTES, PLUS MARINATING

¼ cup tequila

½ cup fresh lime juice

2 teaspoons ground cumin

6 garlic cloves, minced

2¼ teaspoons salt

8 medium skinless, boneless chicken breast halves (3 pounds total)

12 (12-inch) bamboo skewers

3 medium red onions, cut into ½-inch-thick slices

2 tablespoons olive oil

4 large red and/or green peppers, stems and seeds removed, each cut lengthwise in half

24 (6-inch) flour tortillas, warmed

Salsa, sour cream, and cilantro leaves

1 In a large zip-tight plastic bag, combine tequila, lime juice, cumin, garlic, and 1 teaspoon salt. Add chicken to bag, turning to coat with marinade. Seal bag, pressing out excess air; refrigerate at least 2 hours or overnight, turning over several times.

2 Soak skewers in water to cover at least 30 minutes. Meanwhile, prepare outdoor grill for direct grilling over medium heat.

3 Thread skewers horizontally through onion slices. Brush onions with some oil; sprinkle with ¼ teaspoon salt. In medium bowl, toss ½ teaspoon salt and remaining oil with peppers.

4 Place onions and peppers on hot grill rack. Cover grill and cook vegetables until tender, 10 to 12 minutes, turning over once. Remove vegetables to large platter as they are done. Remove skewers from onions. Transfer peppers to cutting board; cut into ½-inch-wide slices. Return to platter with onions.

5 Remove chicken from bag; discard marinade. Place chicken on grill; sprinkle with remaining salt. Cover grill and cook chicken 7 to 9 minutes, or until internal temperature reaches 165°F.

6 Transfer chicken to cutting board; thinly slice. Transfer to platter with vegetables. Serve with warm tortillas, salsa, sour cream, and cilantro.

SERVES 24 ABOUT 485 CALORIES, 33G PROTEIN, 42G CARBOHYDRATE, 20G FAT (6G SATURATED), 2G FIBER, 660MG SODIUM

BBQ Herbed Chicken

PREP 5 MINUTES
TOTAL 1 HOUR 20 MINUTES

2 pounds chicken drumsticks

¾ cup Spicy Cilantro Pesto (page 295)

¼ teaspoon salt

Consider using

other pestos like **Smoky Almond** and **Hazelnut Arugula** for a tasty twist. See page 295 for your options.

1 Pat drumsticks dry and place in gallon-size resealable plastic bag with ½ cup pesto. Shake to coat, then refrigerate at least 1 hour or overnight.

2 Prepare outdoor grill for direct grilling over medium heat.

3 Remove chicken and wipe off excess pesto. Season all over with salt. Grill 15 minutes, turning occasionally, until golden and crisped. Brush with additional pesto and serve.

SERVES 4 ABOUT 355 CALORIES, 28G PROTEIN, 1G CARBOHYDRATE, 26G FAT (5G SATURATED), 0G FIBER, 326MG SODIUM

Serve this CHICKEN with a CRISP GREEN VEGETABLE or a MEDITERRANEAN STARTER like **CAYENNE EGGPLANT WITH FRESH TOMATOES** (page 33).

Roasted Baby Vine Tomato Chicken

PREP 20 MINUTES
TOTAL 45 MINUTES

2 pounds mixed-size cherry tomatoes, on the vine if desired (about 4 pints)

4 large cloves garlic, crushed with press

¼ cup plus 1 tablespoon olive oil

¼ teaspoon crushed red pepper flakes

1 teaspoon kosher salt

¼ teaspoon ground black pepper

1½ pounds chicken breast cutlets (about ⅓ inch thick)

1 tablespoon chopped fresh tarragon

1. Arrange oven rack in top third. Preheat oven to 500°F. Prepare outdoor grill for direct grilling over medium-high heat.

2. Cut about 1 cup of largest tomatoes in half. On rimmed baking sheet, toss all tomatoes with garlic, ¼ cup olive oil, pepper flakes, and ¾ teaspoon salt.

3. Roast tomatoes for 20 minutes, stirring halfway through, until they burst and soften and some are beginning to char. (If most juices have evaporated, stir in 1 to 2 tablespoons water to create more sauce.)

4. Meanwhile, coat chicken cutlets with remaining 1 tablespoon olive oil and season with ¼ teaspoon each salt and black pepper. Grill 2 to 3 minutes per side or until lightly charred and just cooked through.

5. Gently toss tomatoes with chopped tarragon. Spoon tomatoes and juices on top of chicken.

SERVES 4 ABOUT 390 CALORIES, 37G PROTEIN, 10G CARBOHYDRATE, 22G FAT (4G SATURATED), 2G FIBER, 595MG SODIUM

Chicken Quarters with Grape Tomato Salad

 **PREP** 25 MINUTES
TOTAL 55 MINUTES

4 to 5 lemons

3 cloves garlic, crushed with press

1 teaspoon olive oil

1¼ teaspoons kosher salt

¾ teaspoon coarsely ground black pepper

1 chicken (4 pounds), quartered

¼ cup finely chopped red onion

¼ cup loosely packed fresh basil leaves, chopped

2 pints grape or cherry tomatoes (4 cups), each halved

||||||||||||||||||||||||||||||||||||||||

If you want to deliver this dish to the dinner table even faster, replace the **chicken quarters** with 1½ pounds turkey cutlets or thinly sliced chicken cutlets. Proceed as above, but reduce grilling time to 5 to 7 minutes, turning cutlets once.

1 Prepare outdoor grill for direct grilling over medium heat.

2 From 3 to 4 lemons, grate 3 tablespoons plus 1 teaspoon zest and squeeze 1 tablespoon juice. Cut remaining lemon into 4 wedges and reserve for serving with chicken.

3 In small bowl, combine 3 tablespoons lemon zest with garlic, olive oil, 1 teaspoon salt, and ½ teaspoon pepper. With fingertips, gently separate chicken skin from meat on chicken breasts and thighs. Rub half of lemon-zest mixture on meat under skin; rub remaining mixture all over skin.

4 Grill chicken, covered, 30 to 40 minutes, turning over once, until cooked through (165°F), juices run clear, and skin is browned and crisp. Transfer chicken pieces to platter as they are done.

5 Meanwhile, place chopped onion in 1 cup ice water and soak 10 minutes; drain well. In medium bowl, combine onion, basil, tomato halves, lemon juice, and remaining ¼ teaspoon each salt and pepper and 1 teaspoon lemon zest.

6 Arrange each grilled chicken quarter on a dinner plate. Top each portion with 1 cup grape tomato salad. Garnish each plate with reserved lemon wedge.

SERVES 4 ABOUT 400 CALORIES, 47G PROTEIN, 11G CARBOHYDRATE, 24G FAT (7G SATURATED), 3G FIBER, 755MG SODIUM

Chicken Breasts with Tomato-Olive Relish

PREP 15 MINUTES
TOTAL 25 MINUTES

2 medium tomatoes (6 to 8 ounces each), cut into ¼-inch pieces

¼ cup Kalamata olives, pitted and coarsely chopped, plus whole olives for garnish

2 tablespoons minced red onion

2 tablespoons capers, drained

1 teaspoon red wine vinegar

3 teaspoons olive oil

4 small skinless, boneless chicken breast halves (1 pound total)

¼ teaspoon salt

¼ teaspoon coarsely ground black pepper

1 In small bowl, mix tomatoes, olives, onion, capers, vinegar, and 1 teaspoon oil; set aside.

2 Prepare outdoor grill for direct grilling over medium heat, or lightly spray ridged grill pan with nonstick cooking spray, then place over medium heat until hot.

3 In medium bowl, toss chicken with salt, pepper, and remaining 2 teaspoons oil until evenly coated.

4 Grill chicken 10 to 12 minutes, turning over once, until cooked through (165°F) and juices run clear.

5 To serve, top chicken with tomato-olive relish and garnish with olives.

If you'd like, you can double the **Tomato-Olive Mixture** and toss half with 8 ounces cooked **corkscrew pasta**. Serve the pasta at room temperature alongside the chicken.

SERVES 4 ABOUT 200 CALORIES, 27G PROTEIN, 5G CARBOHYDRATE, 7G TOTAL FAT (1G SATURATED), 0G FIBER, 565MG SODIUM

Herbed Chicken Cutlets with Mustard Sauce

 PREP 25 MINUTES
TOTAL 35 MINUTES

2 tablespoons light mayonnaise

3 tablespoons chopped fresh dill

2 tablespoons chopped fresh mint

1 tablespoon Dijon mustard

3 tablespoons white wine vinegar

1 teaspoon plus 2 tablespoons sugar

4 medium skinless, boneless chicken breast halves (1¼ pounds total)

1 teaspoon vegetable oil

1 teaspoon salt

¼ teaspoon coarsely ground black pepper

4 slices pumpernickel bread, warmed

1 Prepare outdoor grill for direct grilling over medium-high heat.

2 In small bowl, mix mayonnaise with 1 tablespoon each dill, mint, mustard, and vinegar, and 1 teaspoon sugar until blended; set sauce aside.

3 If necessary, pound chicken breasts to uniform ¼-inch thickness. In medium bowl, combine remaining 1 tablespoon mint and 2 tablespoons each dill, vinegar, and sugar. Add oil, salt, and pepper and stir until mixed. Add chicken; toss until evenly coated.

4 Grill chicken 8 to 10 minutes, turning over once, until cooked through (165°F) and juices run clear.

5 Serve chicken with mustard sauce and pumpernickel bread.

SERVES 4 ABOUT 330 CALORIES, 36G PROTEIN, 23G CARBOHYDRATE, 9G FAT (2G SATURATED), 0G FIBER, 955MG SODIUM

Beer-Can Chicken

PREP 15 MINUTES
TOTAL 1 HOUR 25 MINUTES

3 tablespoons paprika

1 tablespoon sugar

1 tablespoon salt

2 teaspoons coarsely ground black pepper

1 teaspoon onion powder

1 teaspoon garlic powder

1 teaspoon cayenne pepper

2 whole chickens (3½ pounds each)

2 cans beer (12 ounces each)

||||||||||||||||||||||||||||||||||||||||||

If you're using a charcoal grill and the chickens require more than an hour of cooking, you will need to add ten fresh **charcoal briquettes** per side.

1 Prepare charcoal fire for indirect grilling with drip pan as manufacturer directs, or preheat gas grill for indirect grilling over medium heat.

2 In small bowl, combine paprika, sugar, salt, black pepper, onion powder, garlic powder, and cayenne.

3 Remove giblets and necks from chickens and reserve for another use. Sprinkle 1 tablespoon spice mixture inside cavity of each chicken. Rub remaining spice mixture all over chickens.

4 Wipe beer cans clean. Open beer cans; pour off ½ cup beer from each can and reserve for another use. With church-key-style can opener, make four more holes in top of each can. Place partially filled beer can on flat surface; hold 1 chicken upright, with opening of body cavity down, and slide chicken over top of can so can fits inside cavity. Repeat with remaining chicken and can.

5 Carefully set chickens over drip pan on charcoal grill or away from heat source on gas grill. Spread out legs to balance chickens on grill grate. Cover grill and cook chickens 1 hour to 1 hour 15 minutes, or until cooked through (165°F) and juices run clear.

6 With tongs and barbecue mitts, carefully remove chickens and cans from grill, being careful not to spill beer. Let chickens stand 10 minutes before lifting from cans. Transfer chickens to large platter or carving board; discard beer. Cut each chicken into 8 serving pieces.

SERVES 8 ABOUT 350 CALORIES, 39G PROTEIN, 4G CARBOHYDRATE, 19G FAT (5G SATURATED), 0G FIBER, 985MG SODIUM

Black Beer Chicken

PREP 10 MINUTES
TOTAL 35 MINUTES PLUS
MARINATING

6 green onions, sliced

6 cloves garlic, peeled

⅓ cup soy sauce

¼ cup packed brown sugar

2 tablespoons olive oil

4 teaspoons coriander seeds

1 can or bottle (12 ounces) black beer, such as Guinness Black Lager

3 pounds chicken thighs

Beer marinade makes grilling meat safer to eat: When fat and juices burn up over charcoal or open flames, they create carcinogens that latch on to your meat. But marinating the meat in beer actually cuts the level of cancer-promoting compounds.

1 In food processor or blender, pulse green onions, garlic, soy sauce, brown sugar, oil, and coriander seeds until smooth. Stir in beer. Transfer to gallon-size plastic bag and add chicken. Seal and marinate in refrigerator for at least 3 hours. Turn the bag occasionally.

2 Prepare outdoor grill for direct grilling over medium heat.

3 Reserving marinade, remove chicken from bag. Grill, covered, for 20 to 25 minutes, turning once, until cooked through (165°F) and juices run clear.

4 Meanwhile, boil reserved marinade for 3 minutes to serve as a sauce along with chicken.

SERVES 6 ABOUT 410 CALORIES, 32G PROTEIN, 15G CARBOHYDRATE, 24G FAT (6G SATURATED), 1G FIBER, 913MG SODIUM

Sweet and Spiced Chicken Tacos

PREP 15 MINUTES

TOTAL 25 MINUTES

1¼ pounds skinless, boneless chicken breasts

1 tablespoon olive oil

3 tablespoons The Ultimate Rub (page 309)

10 corn tortillas, warmed

Cilantro, chopped

Radishes, sliced

Cotija cheese, crumbled

Salsa

Lime wedges

1 Prepare outdoor grill for direct grilling over medium heat.

2 Toss chicken with olive oil and The Ultimate Rub. Grill 15 to 18 minutes, turning once, until cooked through (165°F) and juices run clear.

3 Thinly slice chicken and divide among corn tortillas. Top with cilantro, radishes, Cotija, and salsa. Serve with lime wedges for squeezing.

SERVES 5 ABOUT 355 CALORIES, 29G PROTEIN, 34G CARBOHYDRATE, 12G FAT (4G SATURATED), 6G FIBER, 1,195MG SODIUM

Chicken Watermelon Tacos

Prepare Sweet and Spiced Chicken Tacos through step 2. Thinly slice chicken and divide among corn tortillas. In a bowl, toss **2 cups chopped seedless watermelon, 1 jalapeño, minced, 1 small red onion, minced, ¼ cup lime juice, ¼ cup chopped fresh cilantro** and **¼ teaspoon kosher salt.** Evenly top chicken with **salsa** and **¼ cup grated Cotija cheese.**

SERVES 4 ABOUT 330 CALORIES, 27G PROTEIN, 33G CARBOHYDRATE, 9G FAT (3G SATURATED), 3G FIBER, 1,041MG SODIUM

Mojito-Rubbed Chicken with Pineapple

 PREP 20 MINUTES
TOTAL 30 MINUTES

- 4 medium skinless, boneless chicken breast halves (6 ounces each)
- 2 limes
- 1 tablespoon olive oil
- 1 medium pineapple (3½ pounds), peeled and cut into ½-inch-thick slices
- ¼ cup loosely packed fresh mint leaves, chopped
- ½ teaspoon salt
- ¼ teaspoon freshly ground black pepper

To round out your meal, serve with steamed broccolini spears. Or you could serve this island-inspired dish with **TROPICAL RADICCHIO SLAW** (page 257).

1 Prepare outdoor grill for direct grilling over medium heat, or heat large ridged grill pan over medium heat until very hot.

2 Meanwhile, place chicken between two sheets plastic wrap; with meat mallet, pound to an even ½-inch thickness.

3 From 1 lime, grate 1 teaspoon zest and squeeze 2 tablespoons juice. Cut remaining lime into 4 wedges; set aside. In small bowl, combine oil, lime zest, and lime juice. Lightly brush pineapple on both sides with lime mixture; set aside remaining lime mixture in bowl.

4 Grill pineapple slices for 10 minutes, turning over once, until browned on both sides.

5 Stir mint into remaining lime mixture and pat onto both sides of chicken. Sprinkle chicken with salt and pepper to season both sides. Grill chicken for 5 minutes, turning over once, until chicken is browned on both sides and no longer pink throughout.

6 Serve chicken with pineapple and lime wedges.

SERVES 4 ABOUT 320 CALORIES, 40G PROTEIN, 27G CARBOHYDRATE, 6G FAT (1G SATURATED), 3G FIBER, 385MG SODIUM

Chicken with White BBQ Sauce

 **PREP** 5 MINUTES
TOTAL 30 MINUTES

4 pounds chicken parts: thighs, drumsticks, wings

Salt

Freshly ground black pepper

1 recipe White BBQ Sauce (below)

Parsley leaves, for garnish

1 Prepare outdoor grill for direct grilling over medium-low heat.

2 Season chicken all over with 1½ teaspoons salt and ½ teaspoon black pepper. Grill chicken, covered, 20 minutes, turning occasionally.

3 Place ¾ cup White BBQ Sauce in bowl. Uncover chicken; generously brush with sauce. Turn chicken pieces over. Cook 5 minutes, brushing and turning chicken 2 more times, until chicken is cooked through (165°F).

4 Garnish with parsley; serve with remaining sauce.

SERVES 8 ABOUT 375 CALORIES, 29G PROTEIN, 1G CARBOHYDRATE, 28G FAT (6G SATURATED), 0G FIBER, 660MG SODIUM

White BBQ Sauce

Whisk together **1½ cups mayonnaise, ¼ cup cider vinegar, 2 tablespoons prepared horseradish, drained; 1 tablespoon lemon juice, ¾ teaspoon sugar, ¾ teaspoon salt, ½ teaspoon freshly ground black pepper, and ¼ teaspoon cayenne pepper**, until smooth. **Makes about 13/4 cups.**

EACH ¼ CUP ABOUT 315 CALORIES, 1G CARBOHYDREATE, 35G FAT (5G SATURATED), 0G FIBER, 540MG SODIUM

You can serve this dish with **COOKED GREEN BEANS** and **WILD RICE PILAF**.

Chicken Romesco

4 small skinless, boneless chicken breast halves

3 tablespoons extra-virgin olive oil

¼ teaspoon plus ⅛ teaspoon kosher salt

¼ teaspoon freshly ground black pepper

½ cup roasted red peppers

⅓ cup slivered almonds

2 small cloves garlic

2 teaspoons sherry vinegar

Chopped parsley, for garnish

1 Prepare outdoor grill for direct grilling over medium heat.

2 Brush chicken breasts with 1 tablespoon olive oil; season with ¼ teaspoon each salt and pepper. Grill, covered, 20 minutes, turning over once, until just cooked (160°F).

3 In food processor, pulse roasted red peppers, almonds, garlic, sherry vinegar, and ⅛ teaspoon salt until finely chopped. With machine running, drizzle in remaining 2 tablespoons olive oil. Serve chicken with sauce. Garnish with parsley.

SERVES 4 ABOUT 470 CALORIES, 30G PROTEIN, 46G CARBOHYDRATE, 19G FAT (3G SATURATED), 7G FIBER, 680MG SODIUM

Chipotle-Orange Chicken

PREP 5 MINUTES
TOTAL 35 MINUTES

- 1 tablespoon brown sugar
- 2 teaspoons chipotle chile powder
- 1 teaspoon ground cumin
- 1 teaspoon garlic powder
- ½ teaspoon onion powder
- 1 teaspoon salt
- 1 teaspoon freshly ground black pepper
- 4 pounds small chicken thighs, trimmed of excess skin
- 2 tablespoons olive oil
- 2 small oranges, cut into quarters
- 2 green onions, thinly sliced

1 Prepare outdoor grill for direct grilling over medium heat.

2 In small bowl, combine brown sugar, chipotle powder, cumin, garlic powder, onion powder, salt, and pepper. In large bowl, toss chicken with oil; sprinkle with spice mixture, then rub spices into chicken to coat evenly.

3 Grill chicken, covered, 20 to 25 minutes, turning over once, until cooked through (165°F) and juices run clear. Grill oranges 5 to 10 minutes or until grill marks appear. Transfer chicken to serving platter. Squeeze juice from oranges all over chicken. Garnish with green onions.

SERVES 6 ABOUT 480 CALORIES, 42G PROTEIN, 6G CARBOHYDRATE, 31G FAT (8G SATURATED), 1G FIBER, 535MG SODIUM

Coffee-Spiced Chicken with Fruit-Basil Salsa

PREP 20 MINUTES

TOTAL 30 MINUTES

- 1 piece (4 pounds) seedless watermelon, cut into ½-inch chunks (3 cups)
- 1 large nectarine, pitted and cut into ½-inch chunks
- 3 tablespoons finely chopped red onion
- 1 tablespoon lemon juice
- 2 tablespoons instant coffee
- 1 tablespoon grated peeled fresh ginger
- 1 tablespoon olive oil
- 1¼ teaspoons ground allspice
- ¾ teaspoon salt
- 8 skinless, boneless chicken breast halves (6 ounces each)
- ½ cup packed fresh basil leaves, coarsely chopped

1. In medium bowl, combine watermelon, nectarine, red onion, and lemon juice. Cover and refrigerate salsa while preparing chicken.

2. Prepare outdoor grill for direct grilling over medium heat.

3. In large bowl, with spoon or fingers, press coffee to pulverize. Add ginger, oil, allspice, and ½ teaspoon salt; stir to combine. Add chicken and toss to evenly coat with spice mixture (you may need to pat spice mixture onto chicken with fingers).

4. Grill chicken covered for 8 to 10 minutes, turning over once, until chicken is cooked through (165°F) and juices run clear. Transfer chicken to cutting board and let rest 5 minutes.

5. Meanwhile, stir basil and remaining ¼ teaspoon salt into salsa. Slice chicken crosswise and serve with salsa.

SERVES 8 ABOUT 235 CALORIES, 40G PROTEIN, 8G CARBOHYDRATE, 4G FAT (1G SATURATED), 1G FIBER, 310MG SODIUM

Lemon-Oregano Chicken with Mint Zucchini

PREP 15 MINUTES

TOTAL 25 MINUTES

3 medium zucchini (8 ounces each)

2 tablespoons olive oil

½ teaspoon salt

½ cup loosely packed fresh mint leaves, chopped

4 medium skinless, boneless chicken breast halves (6 ounces each)

3 lemons

1 tablespoon chopped fresh oregano

½ teaspoon coarsely ground black pepper

Pounding all the **chicken breasts** to the same uniform thickness means they will cook at the same rate.

1 Prepare outdoor grill for direct grilling over medium heat.

2 With mandoline or sharp knife, slice zucchini very thinly lengthwise. In large bowl, toss zucchini with 1 tablespoon oil, ¼ teaspoon salt, and half of mint.

3 Pound chicken breasts to uniform ¼-inch thickness. From 2 lemons, grate 1 tablespoon zest and squeeze 2 tablespoons juice. Cut remaining lemon into 4 wedges; set aside. In medium bowl, combine lemon zest and juice with oregano, pepper, and remaining 1 tablespoon oil and ¼ teaspoon salt. Add chicken to bowl and toss until evenly coated.

4 In batches, grill zucchini slices 2 to 4 minutes, turning over once, until grill marks appear and zucchini is tender. Place zucchini on large platter and sprinkle with remaining mint.

5 Grill chicken, covered, for 6 to 8 minutes, turning over once, until cooked through (165°F). Transfer chicken to platter with zucchini; serve with lemon wedges.

SERVES 4 ABOUT 280 CALORIES, 42G PROTEIN, 8G CARBOHYDRATE, 9G FAT (2G SATURATED), 0G FIBER, 390MG SODIUM

Caribbean Chicken and Cauliflower Rice

PREP 10 MINUTES
TOTAL 30 MINUTES

- 4 cups riced cauliflower
- ¼ cup water
- 4 chicken breast cutlets
- 2 teaspoons olive oil
- ¾ teaspoon salt
- ½ teaspoon freshly ground black pepper
- ¼ cup sweetened cream of coconut
- 2 tablespoons hot sauce
- 2 limes, halved
- 1 can (15 ounces) black beans, rinsed and drained
- Chopped fresh cilantro, for garnish

1 Prepare outdoor grill for direct grilling over medium heat.

2 Combine riced cauliflower and water in a microwave-safe container; cover with vented plastic wrap and microwave on High 6 minutes.

3 Brush chicken with olive oil; season all over with ½ teaspoon salt and pepper. Grill for 5 minutes, turning over once. Whisk together cream of coconut and hot sauce; brush onto chicken. Grill about 5 minutes longer, brushing and turning 2 more times, until cooked through (165°F). Grill halved limes 2 to 3 minutes, until lightly charred.

4 Toss cooked cauliflower with black beans and remaining ¼ teaspoon salt. Serve chicken over cauliflower with grilled limes, garnished with chopped cilantro.

SERVES 4 ABOUT 370 CALORIES, 37G PROTEIN, 37G CARBOHYDRATE, 9G FAT (4G SATURATED), 10G FIBER, 990MG SODIUM

Chicken with Citrus Slaw

 **PREP** 15 MINUTES
TOTAL 25 MINUTES

1 large navel orange

4 medium skinless, boneless chicken breast halves (6 ounces each)

¾ cup bottled barbecue sauce

1 teaspoon Dijon mustard

8 ounces shredded cabbage mix for coleslaw

½ medium fennel bulb (8 ounces), thinly sliced, plus fennel fronds for garnish

1 tablespoon white wine vinegar

¼ teaspoon salt

¼ teaspoon freshly ground black pepper

1 From orange, grate 1½ teaspoons zest. With knife, cut remaining peel and white pith from orange and discard. Holding orange over small bowl to catch juice, cut out segments from between membranes; drop segments into bowl. With slotted spoon, transfer segments to cutting board; coarsely chop. Reserve 2 tablespoons orange juice.

2 With meat mallet, pound chicken (placed between two sheets plastic wrap) to an even ½-inch thickness.

3 Coat large ridged grill pan with olive oil cooking spray and place over medium-high heat until hot.

4 Meanwhile, combine barbecue sauce, mustard, and 1 teaspoon orange zest. Measure out ¼ cup sauce and set aside for serving.

5 Place chicken on grill pan; cook 4 minutes, turning once. Generously brush chicken with barbecue-sauce mixture; cook 3 to 4 minutes longer, turning over often and brushing with sauce frequently, until cooked through (165°F).

6 While chicken is cooking, make citrus slaw: In large bowl, place orange pieces, reserved juice, cabbage mix, fennel, vinegar, salt, pepper, and remaining ½ teaspoon orange zest; toss to combine.

7 Serve slaw with chicken; garnish with fennel fronds.

SERVES 4 ABOUT 265 CALORIES, 42G PROTEIN, 17G CARBOHYDRATE, 3G FAT (1G SATURATED), 4G FIBER, 600MG SODIUM

Basil-Orange Chicken

PREP 20 MINUTES
TOTAL 30 MINUTES

2 large navel oranges

3 lemons

½ cup packed fresh basil leaves, chopped

2 tablespoons olive oil

⅜ teaspoon salt

⅜ teaspoon ground black pepper

4 skinless, boneless chicken breast halves (6 ounces each)

½ teaspoon sugar

1 cup whole wheat couscous

8 ounces sugar snap peas

|||||||||||||||||||||||||||||||||||||||||

Citrus sauce in step 4 can be made up to 8 hours ahead, if refrigerated.

1 From 1 orange, grate 1½ teaspoons zest and squeeze ¼ cup juice. From 2 lemons, grate 1½ teaspoons zest and squeeze ⅓ cup juice. Cut remaining fruits into slices and set aside.

2 In medium bowl, combine 1 teaspoon of each zest, 1 tablespoon orange juice, half of basil, 1 tablespoon olive oil, and ¼ teaspoon each salt and pepper.

3 Pound chicken breasts (placed between two sheets plastic wrap) to an even ½-inch thickness. Add chicken to citrus marinade.

4 In small pitcher or bowl, combine sugar, remaining ⅛ teaspoon each salt and pepper, and remaining citrus zests and juices, basil, and oil; set aside.

5 Prepare outdoor grill for direct grilling over medium-high heat, or heat ridged grill pan over medium-high heat. Meanwhile, prepare couscous as label directs.

6 Grill chicken for 7 to 8 minutes, turning over once, until cooked through (165°F) and juices run clear. Grill reserved citrus slices as well, if desired. About 3 minutes before chicken is done, add snap peas to steamer; cook 2 to 3 minutes or until tender-crisp.

7 Fluff couscous and spoon onto large platter; top with chicken and snap peas. Drizzle sauce over all. Garnish with citrus slices.

SERVES 4 ABOUT 400 CALORIES, 46G PROTEIN, 33G CARBOHYDRATE, 9G FAT (1G SATURATED), 6G FIBER, 365MG SODIUM

Chicken with Tex-Mex Salsa

 **PREP** 10 MINUTES
TOTAL 40 MINUTES

½ cup minced white onion

1 jalapeño

3 cloves garlic, unpeeled

1 can (14.5 ounces) fire-roasted diced tomatoes, drained well

¼ cup packed fresh cilantro leaves, chopped

1 tablespoon lime juice

1 teaspoon salt

½ teaspoon freshly ground black pepper

1 whole chicken (3 to 3½ pounds), cut into 8 pieces

1 Prepare outdoor grill for direct grilling over medium heat.

2 In small bowl, soak onion in cold water. Wrap jalapeño and garlic in foil. Grill 17 minutes or until vegetables are charred and blackened in spots. Cool. Remove stem, skin, and seeds from jalapeño. Peel garlic; chop. Transfer jalapeño and garlic to food processor along with tomatoes, cilantro, lime juice, and ½ teaspoon salt. Pulse until finely chopped. Drain onion and stir into mixture.

3 Sprinkle remaining ½ teaspoon salt and pepper all over chicken. Grill, skin side down, covered for 15 to 20 minutes, turning over once, until cooked through (165°F), juices run clear, and skin is browned and crisp. Transfer chicken pieces to platter as they are done.

4 Serve chicken with salsa.

SERVES 4 ABOUT 425 CALORIES, 43G PROTEIN, 7G CARBOHYDRATE, 24G TOTAL FAT (7G SATURATED), 1G FIBER, 870MG SODIUM

Classic Barbecued Chicken

Proceed as directed for Chicken with Tex-Mex Salsa but omit salsa. Before grilling chicken make a BBQ sauce. In 3-quart saucepan, combine ⅓ **cup tomato paste, ⅓ cup water, 2 tablespoons brown sugar, 2 tablespoons molasses, 2 tablespoons apple cider vinegar, 2 teaspoons Worcestershire sauce, 1 teaspoon soy sauce, 1 teaspoon Dijon mustard, ¼ teaspoon crushed red pepper flakes, and ¼ teaspoon each salt and pepper**; stir until well combined. Heat to boiling on high, then reduce heat to maintain steady simmer. Cook sauce 30 minutes or until thickened, stirring occasionally. Grill chicken as directed and as soon as it comes off grill, transfer to large bowl and toss with barbecue sauce until evenly coated.

SERVES 4 ABOUT 475 CALORIES, 43G PROTEIN, 20G CARBOHYDRATE, 24G TOTAL FAT (7G SATURATED), 1G FIBER, 875MG SODIUM

Tangy Spicy Chicken

Proceed as directed for Chicken with Tex-Mex Salsa but omit salsa. Before grilling chicken make a tangy sauce. In large bowl, combine ½ **cup finely chopped red onion, ¼ cup honey, ¼ cup cayenne pepper sauce,** and **1 tablespoon apple cider vinegar**. Grill chicken as directed and as soon as it comes off grill, transfer to large bowl and toss with sauce until evenly coated.

SERVES 4 ABOUT 470 CALORIES, 43G PROTEIN, 20G CARBOHYDRATE, 24G TOTAL FAT (7G SATURATED), 1G FIBER, 925MG SODIUM

Lemon-Rosemary Chicken and Potatoes

PREP 10 MINUTES
TOTAL 40 MINUTES

- 4 medium red potatoes, thinly sliced
- Salt
- 4 large skinless, boneless chicken thighs
- 4 tablespoons butter, melted
- 2 teaspoons freshly ground black pepper
- Lemon slices
- 4 sprigs fresh rosemary

Foil packets

(see page 163) are a foolproof way to cook on the grill. Make sure to use **heavy-duty foil** to prevent rips and leaks. Also, always fold the excess foil rather than scrunch—it is a better way to prevent leaking and make sure everything stays inside.

1 On each of 4 foil sheets, arrange potato slices, overlapping slightly, and sprinkle with pinch of salt. Place chicken thighs on top. Drizzle each with melted butter; season each with ½ teaspoon salt and pepper. Top each with lemon slices and fresh rosemary. Seal packets.

2 On the grill, cook 30 minutes or until potatoes are tender.

SERVES 4 ABOUT 370 CALORIES, 21G PROTEIN, 36G CARBOHYDRATE, 16G FAT (8G SATURATED), 4G FIBER, 925MG SODIUM

Port and Black Currant-Glazed Chicken Thighs

PREP 15 MINUTES
TOTAL 30 MINUTES PLUS MARINATING

⅓ cup ruby port

¼ cup Dijon mustard

½ teaspoon salt

¼ teaspoon coarsely ground black pepper

2 tablespoons chopped fresh tarragon

8 medium skin-on, bone-in chicken thighs (5 ounces each), skin removed

¼ cup black currant jelly

1 In large bowl, with wire whisk, mix port, mustard, salt, pepper, and 1 tablespoon tarragon until blended. Transfer 3 tablespoons marinade to small bowl and set aside.

2 Add chicken to marinade in large bowl; toss until evenly coated. Cover bowl and let stand 15 minutes at room temperature or 30 minutes in refrigerator.

3 Prepare outdoor grill for direct grilling over medium heat.

4 Meanwhile, whisk black currant jelly into marinade in small bowl until blended; set aside.

5 Grill chicken for 25 minutes, turning over once, until cooked through (165°F). Brush jelly mixture all over chicken; grill 1 to 2 minutes longer, turning once, until glazed. Transfer chicken to platter; sprinkle with remaining 1 tablespoon tarragon.

SERVES 4 ABOUT 280 CALORIES, 28G PROTEIN, 15G CARBOHYDRATE, 12G FAT (3G SATURATED), 0G FIBER, 290MG SODIUM

Tandoori Chicken with Mango Chutney

PREP 20 MINUTES
TOTAL 50 MINUTES PLUS MARINATING

3 tablespoons plain low-fat yogurt

1 tablespoon paprika

1½ teaspoons ground cumin

1½ teaspoons ground coriander

½ teaspoon cayenne pepper

1 clove garlic, crushed with press

4½ teaspoons grated peeled fresh ginger

¾ teaspoon salt

4 medium skin-on, bone-in chicken breast halves (8 ounces each), skin removed

2 firm-ripe mangoes

1 tablespoon brown sugar

1 tablespoon apple cider vinegar

1 small green onion, thinly sliced

Cooked basmati rice (optional)

1 In small bowl, mix yogurt, paprika, cumin, coriander, cayenne, garlic, 4 teaspoons ginger, and ½ teaspoon salt until blended. Pour yogurt marinade into large resealable plastic bag; add chicken, turning to coat. Seal bag, pressing out excess air. Place bag on plate and refrigerate chicken at least 1 hour or up to 4 hours.

2 Meanwhile, prepare outdoor grill for direct grilling over medium heat.

3 Peel mangoes and cut lengthwise, slicing fruit from each side of long flat seed, as close to seed as possible. Place mango pieces on hot grill grate and cook about 8 minutes, turning over once, until lightly charred and tender. Transfer mangoes to cutting board to cool.

4 Coarsely chop grilled mangoes and place in medium bowl. Add brown sugar, vinegar, green onion, remaining ¼ teaspoon salt, and remaining ½ teaspoon ginger; stir to combine.

5 Remove chicken from marinade (discard marinade). Grill chicken, covered, for 20 to 25 minutes, turning over once, until cooked through (165°F) and juices run clear. Place chicken on platter and serve with mango chutney and basmati rice if you like.

SERVES 4 ABOUT 210 CALORIES, 35G PROTEIN, 13G CARBOHYDRATE, 2G FAT (1G SATURATED), 2G FIBER, 450MG SODIUM

Drumsticks with Three Sauces

PREP 10 MINUTES
TOTAL 45 MINUTES

Choice of sauce (recipes follow)

12 chicken drumsticks (4 pounds total), skin removed (see Tip)

½ teaspoon kosher salt

½ teaspoon freshly ground black pepper

1 Prepare outdoor grill for direct grilling over medium heat.

2 Prepare sauce of choice.

3 Pat drumsticks dry with paper towels; season all over with salt and pepper. Grill for 30 to 35 minutes, turning occasionally, until cooked through (165°F). Brush sauce onto drumsticks during last 5 minutes of cooking, turning occasionally.

4 Transfer chicken to serving platter. Brush with sauce again before serving.

If you can't find skinless drumsticks in your supermarket, try this: Take the **drumstick** in one hand, and—using a paper towel—grasp the skin with the other. Pull the skin toward the bone end, twisting as necessary to fully free it. (This method works well with other chicken parts, too.)

Polynesian Drumsticks

In blender, puree **1 (8-ounce) can crushed pineapple in unsweetened juice**, **½ cup packed brown sugar**, **3 tablespoons soy sauce**, **1 tablespoon grated peeled fresh ginger**, and **1 clove crushed garlic** until smooth. Spoon ½ cup pineapple puree into large resealable plastic bag; reserve remaining puree for grilling. Add drumsticks to bag, turning to coat. Let stand at room temperature 15 minutes. Proceed with steps 3 and 4.

SERVES 4 ABOUT 260 CALORIES, 38G PROTEIN, 8G CARBOHYDRATE, 8G FAT (2G SATURATED), 0G FIBER, 385MG SODIUM

Garlicky Herb Sauce

In food processor, pulse together **1 cup parsley**, **½ cup fresh mint**, **½ cup olive oil**, **3 tablespoons lemon juice**, **2 anchovies**, **1 clove garlic**, and **¼ teaspoon kosher salt** until finely chopped, scraping down sides of bowl as necessary.

SERVES 4 ABOUT 580 CALORIES, 52G PROTEIN, 3G CARBOHYDRATE, 39G FAT (7G SATURATED), 1G FIBER, 711MG SODIUM

Coconut Curry Sauce

Microwave **¼ cup coconut cream** (from top of **1 can full-fat coconut milk**), **2 tablespoons brown sugar**, **1 tablespoon curry powder**, and **¼ teaspoon kosher salt** for 30 seconds, or until just runny enough to whisk. Serve chicken with lime wedges.

SERVES 4 ABOUT 400 CALORIES, 51G PROTEIN, 10G CARBOHYDRATE, 16G FAT (7G SATURATED), 1G FIBER, 631MG SODIUM

Sweet 'n' Tangy Sauce

Whisk together **½ cup apricot jam** and **½ cup grainy Dijon mustard**.

SERVES 4 ABOUT 450 CALORIES, 50G PROTEIN, 26G CARBOHYDRATE, 12G FAT (3G SATURATED), 0G FIBER, 1,241MG SODIUM

Harissa Chicken Kebabs

PREP 10 MINUTES
TOTAL 20 MINUTES

- ¼ cup harissa
- 2 tablespoons olive oil
- 2 tablespoons honey
- 1¼ pounds skinless, boneless chicken breasts, thinly sliced
- 1 can (15 ounces) chickpeas, rinsed and drained
- 1 cup quick-cooking bulgur, cooked
- ¾ cup finely chopped fresh parsley
- ½ teaspoon salt

IIIIIIIIIIIIIIIIIIIIIIIIIIIIIIIIIIIIIIIIII

What makes this dinner so heart-healthy? It is made with monounsaturated fat from **olive oil**; **lean protein** from **chickpeas** and **chicken**; and **fiber** from **whole grains**. And it's packed with flavor but limited in saturated fat and sodium.

1. Prepare outdoor grill for direct grilling over medium-high heat.

2. In large bowl, whisk harissa, olive oil, and honey; set half aside for serving.

3. To remaining harissa mixture, add chicken breasts, tossing; thread onto skewers. Grill for 6 minutes, turning over once, until cooked through.

4. Toss chickpeas with bulgur, parsley, and salt. Serve chicken on tabbouleh with reserved harissa sauce.

SERVES 4 ABOUT 495 CALORIES, 39G PROTEIN, 57G CARBOHYDRATE, 13G FAT (2G SATURATED FAT), 13G FIBER, 560MG SODIUM

Jerk Chicken Kebabs

PREP 15 MINUTES
TOTAL 25 MINUTES PLUS MARINATING

2 green onions, chopped

1 jalapeño, seeded and minced

1 tablespoon minced peeled fresh ginger

2 tablespoons white wine vinegar

2 tablespoons Worcestershire sauce

3 teaspoons vegetable oil

1 teaspoon ground allspice

1 teaspoon dried thyme

½ teaspoon plus ⅛ teaspoon salt

1 pound skinless, boneless chicken breasts, cut into 12 pieces

1 red bell pepper, cut into 1-inch pieces

1 green bell pepper, cut into 1-inch pieces

4 skewers (10-inch), preferably metal

1 In blender or food processor, process green onions, jalapeño, ginger, vinegar, Worcestershire, 2 teaspoons oil, allspice, thyme, and ½ teaspoon salt until paste forms.

2 Place chicken in small bowl or resealable plastic bag and add green-onion mixture, turning to coat chicken. Cover bowl or seal bag and marinate 1 hour in refrigerator.

3 Meanwhile, in small bowl, toss bell peppers with remaining 1 teaspoon oil and ⅛ teaspoon salt.

4 Prepare outdoor grill for direct grilling over medium heat. Alternately thread chicken and pepper pieces on each skewer.

5 Grill skewers, brushing kebabs with any remaining marinade, for 5 minutes; turn and cook about 5 minutes longer, until cooked through (165°F) and chicken loses its pink color throughout.

||||||||||||||||||||||||||||||||||||||||||

Jerk seasoning was originally used to season pork shoulder, which was "jerked" apart into shreds before serving.

SERVES 4 ABOUT 180 CALORIES, 27G PROTEIN, 6G CARBOHYDRATE, 5G FAT (1G SATURATED), 0G FIBER, 525MG SODIUM

Spiced Chicken Skewers

PREP 20 MINUTES

TOTAL 30 MINUTES PLUS
SOAKING SKEWERS

8 bamboo skewers (12-inch)

1 cup bulgur

1 pound skinless, boneless
chicken breasts, cut into
1-inch chunks

2 teaspoons chili powder

2 teaspoons extra-virgin
olive oil

½ teaspoon salt

½ teaspoon freshly ground
black pepper

2 pints cherry tomatoes

2 lemons

1 clove garlic, crushed with
press

1 cup chopped flat-leaf parsley
leaves

Charring makes the
tomatoes extra juicy and sweet.

1 Soak bamboo skewers in hot water at least
30 minutes. Prepare outdoor grill for direct grilling,
or heat large ridged grill pan over medium-high heat
until very hot.

2 In large microwave-safe bowl, combine bulgur and
1¾ cups water. Microwave on High 10 minutes or
until bulgur is tender and water is absorbed, stirring
mixture once.

3 In medium bowl, toss chicken with chili powder,
1 teaspoon oil, and ¼ teaspoon each salt and pepper
until well coated. Thread chicken and tomatoes
alternately onto skewers, spacing ¼ inch apart.

4 Grill chicken skewers 7 to 8 minutes, turning
occasionally, until chicken is cooked through (165°F)
and just loses pink color throughout.

5 Meanwhile, into bowl with bulgur, from 1 lemon,
finely grate 1 teaspoon zest and squeeze 3
tablespoons juice. Add crushed garlic, parsley,
remaining ¼ teaspoon salt, ¼ teaspoon pepper, and
1 teaspoon oil. Stir well.

6 Divide bulgur mixture and chicken skewers among
serving plates. Serve with remaining lemon, cut into
wedges.

SERVES 4 ABOUT 305 CALORIES, 29G PROTEIN, 37G CARBOHYDRATE, 6G TOTAL FAT (1G SATURATED), 10G FIBER,
390MG SODIUM

Pair this dish with
Feta-Dill Greek Salad
(page 25) and
**Onion Dip
with Naan Chips**
(page 37).
Quinoa Tabbouleh
(page 274) would also
make a nice pairing.

Chicken Souvlaki Skewers

 **PREP** 15 MINUTES
TOTAL 25 MINUTES

1 pound skinless, boneless chicken breasts, cut into 1-inch chunks

3 tablespoons olive oil

½ teaspoon ground coriander

½ teaspoon dried oregano

¾ teaspoon kosher salt

¾ teaspoon freshly ground black pepper

1 pint grape tomatoes

2 cloves garlic, chopped

3 tablespoons lemon juice, plus wedges for serving

½ head romaine lettuce, shredded

4 green onions, thinly sliced

½ cup fresh dill, chopped

4 pitas, warmed

1 Prepare outdoor grill for direct grilling over medium-high heat.

2 Toss chicken with 1 tablespoon oil, coriander, oregano, and ¼ teaspoon each salt and pepper. Thread onto skewers.

3 Place tomatoes and garlic on large piece heavy-duty foil. Sprinkle with 1 tablespoon oil and ¼ teaspoon each salt and pepper. Fold and crimp foil to form pouch.

4 Place pouch and skewers on grill. Cook 8 to 10 minutes, shaking pouch and turning skewers occasionally, until chicken is cooked through (165°F). Just before removing from grill, brush chicken with 1 tablespoon lemon juice.

5 Meanwhile, in bowl, toss lettuce, green onions, dill, remaining 2 tablespoons lemon juice, 1 tablespoon oil, and ¼ teaspoon each salt and pepper.

6 Serve chicken, tomatoes, and salad with pitas and lemon wedges.

SERVES 4 ABOUT 415 CALORIES, 30G PROTEIN, 42G CARBOHYDRATE, 14G FAT (2G SATURATED), 5G FIBER, 750MG SODIUM

Turkey Kebabs and Tomato Jam

 **PREP** 30 MINUTES
TOTAL 40 MINUTES PLUS
MARINATING

1 navel orange

1 tablespoon olive oil

1 onion, chopped

1 pound plum tomatoes
(about 7 large), seeded and
cut into ¼-inch dice

⅓ cup golden raisins

¼ teaspoon salt

¼ cup loosely packed fresh
cilantro leaves, chopped

1 clove garlic, crushed with
press

1 tablespoon olive oil

1½ teaspoons chili powder

¾ teaspoon paprika

¾ teaspoon salt

¼ teaspoon cayenne pepper

¼ teaspoon freshly ground
black pepper

2 pounds skinless, boneless
turkey breast, cut into
1½-inch cubes

4 skewers (12-inch), preferably
metal

Cilantro sprigs, for garnish

1 From orange, grate 1 teaspoon zest and squeeze ¼ cup juice. In 10-inch skillet, heat oil on medium-low. Add onion and cook about 5 minutes, stirring occasionally, until golden. Add tomatoes, raisins, salt, and orange zest and juice. Increase heat to medium-high; cook about 6 minutes, until tomatoes soften and liquid evaporates. Set skillet aside to cool; just before serving, stir chopped cilantro into jam.

2 In large resealable plastic bag, combine garlic, oil, chili powder, paprika, salt, cayenne, and black pepper. Add turkey to bag, tossing to coat with spice mixture. Seal bag, pressing out excess air. Place bag on plate; refrigerate at least 15 minutes or up to 1 hour.

3 Prepare outdoor grill for direct grilling over medium heat.

4 Thread turkey onto skewers. Grill skewers for about 10 minutes, turning over once, until cooked through (165°F).

5 To serve, place skewers on platter; garnish with cilantro sprigs. Serve with tomato jam.

SERVES 6 ABOUT 250 CALORIES, 35G PROTEIN, 14G CARBOHYDRATE, 6G FAT (1G SATURATED), 0G FIBER, 460MG SODIUM

Spiced Turkey Breasts

PREP 35 MINUTES
TOTAL 1 HOUR

- ¼ cup sugar
- ¼ cup kosher salt
- 2 tablespoons cracked black pepper
- 2 tablespoons ground ginger
- 1 tablespoon ground cinnamon
- 1 whole boneless turkey breast (about 4 pounds), skin removed and breast cut in half
- 4 cloves garlic, crushed with press
- 2 tablespoons honey
- 2 tablespoons Dijon mustard
- 1 chipotle chile in adobo sauce, minced
- 1 teaspoon balsamic vinegar
- Peach Salsa (optional; page 299)

Soaking a whole **turkey breast** overnight in a spiced salt solution (brine) produces exceptionally tender and flavorful meat. You can also brine a whole chicken before roasting.

1 In 2-quart saucepan, heat sugar, salt, pepper, ginger, cinnamon, and 1 cup water to boiling over high. Reduce heat to low; simmer 2 minutes. Remove from heat; stir in 3 cups ice water.

2 Place turkey breast in large resealable plastic bag; add brine and garlic. Seal bag, pressing out excess air. Place bag in bowl and refrigerate breast, turning occasionally, 24 hours.

3 Prepare outdoor grill for direct grilling over medium heat.

4 Meanwhile, in small bowl, stir honey, mustard, chipotle, and vinegar until blended; set aside.

5 Remove turkey from bag (discard brine and garlic). With paper towels, pat turkey dry and brush off most of pepper. Grill turkey, covered, for 20 minutes, turning once. Brush turkey with glaze and grill 5 to 10 minutes longer (depending on thickness of breast), basting and turning frequently, until cooked through (165°F). Transfer turkey to cutting board and let rest 10 minutes to set juices for easier slicing.

6 While turkey rests, prepare Peach Salsa, if desired.

7 Serve turkey hot, or cover and refrigerate to serve cold. Accompany with salsa.

SERVES 12 ABOUT 170 CALORIES, 34G PROTEIN, 4G CARBOHYDRATE, 1G FAT (0G SATURATED), 0G FIBER, 555MG SODIUM

Indian-Style Turkey Cutlets

PREP 15 MINUTES
TOTAL 20 MINUTES

2 large limes

⅓ cup plain low-fat yogurt

1 tablespoon vegetable oil

2 teaspoons minced peeled fresh ginger

1 teaspoon ground coriander

1 teaspoon ground cumin

1 teaspoon salt

1 clove garlic, crushed with press

6 turkey breast cutlets (4 ounces each)

1 Prepare outdoor grill for direct grilling over medium heat.

2 From 1 lime, grate 1 teaspoon zest and squeeze 1 tablespoon juice. Cut remaining lime into wedges; set aside.

3 In large bowl, mix lime zest and juice, yogurt, oil, ginger, coriander, cumin, salt, and garlic until blended.

4 Just before grilling, add turkey to bowl with yogurt mixture; stir to coat. (Do not let cutlets marinate in yogurt mixture; texture will become mealy.)

5 Grill cutlets 5 to 7 minutes, turning over once, until cooked through (165°F) and cutlets have just lost pink color throughout. Serve with lime wedges.

These are delicious with a squeeze of fresh lime or **ZIPPY PINEAPPLE SALSA** (page 297) alongside. For a festive presentation, set out bowls of yogurt, store-bought mango chutney, fluffy basmati rice, and chopped fresh cilantro.

SERVES 6 ABOUT 160 CALORIES, 29G PROTEIN, 3G CARBOHYDRATE, 3G FAT (1G SATURATED), 0G FIBER, 450MG SODIUM

Turkey Cutlets with Melon Salsa

PREP 20 MINUTES
TOTAL 25 MINUTES

2 limes

1½ cups chopped cantaloupe

1½ cups chopped honeydew melon

1 small Kirby (pickling) cucumber, shredded (½ cup)

1 jalapeño, seeded and finely chopped

¼ cup loosely packed fresh basil leaves, chopped

¼ teaspoon salt

¼ teaspoon coarsely ground black pepper

4 turkey breast cutlets (4 ounces each)

4 ounces thinly sliced prosciutto

1 Prepare outdoor grill for direct grilling over medium heat.

2 From 1 lime, grate 1 teaspoon zest and squeeze 2 tablespoons juice. Cut remaining lime into 4 wedges and set aside.

3 In medium bowl, combine lime juice, cantaloupe, honeydew, cucumber, jalapeño, basil, and salt.

4 Sprinkle turkey cutlets with lime zest and pepper. Wrap with prosciutto, pressing prosciutto firmly onto turkey.

5 Grill cutlets 5 to 7 minutes, turning over once, until cooked through (165°F) and turkey has just lost pink color throughout. Transfer to plate; serve with melon salsa and lime wedges.

SERVES 4 ABOUT 195 CALORIES, 35G PROTEIN, 3G CARBOHYDRATE, 4G FAT (1G SATURATED), 0G FIBER, 865MG SODIUM

Charcoal Turkey

PREP 15 MINUTES

TOTAL 2 HOURS 30 MINUTES
PLUS SOAKING AND
STANDING TIME

- 2 cups mesquite chips, soaked in water for 1 hour
- 1 whole turkey (12 pounds), fresh or frozen (thawed), neck and giblets removed
- 1 or 2 metal skewers (8-inch) and kitchen string or stuffing clamp
- 2 tablespoons vegetable oil
- 2 teaspoons dried rosemary, crumbled
- 2 teaspoons dried thyme
- 2 teaspoons salt
- ½ teaspoon ground black pepper
- Rosemary sprigs, for garnish

Pair the CHARCOAL TURKEY with **SRIRACHA-LIME SLAW** (page 259), **FLAME-ROASTED CHILES RELLENOS** (page 246), and **SWEET POTATOES** (page 244). A refreshing margarita is the perfect drink for this dinner with flare.

1 Fasten neck skin to turkey back with 1 or 2 skewers. With turkey breast side up, fold wings under back so they stay in place. Tie legs and tail together with string, or push drumsticks under band of skin, or use stuffing clamp. In cup, mix oil, dried rosemary, thyme, salt, and pepper; rub mixture all over turkey.

2 Place turkey, breast side up, on hot grill grate directly over foil pan. Cover grill and roast turkey 2 hours 15 minutes to 3 hours (11 to 13 minutes per pound for unstuffed bird), adding 8 briquettes to each side of pan every hour to maintain grill temperature. Turkey is done when thigh temperature reaches 175° to 180°F and juices run clear when thickest part of thigh is pierced with tip of knife; breast temperature should reach 165° to 170°F. (Upon standing, temperature will rise 5° to 10°F.)

3 When turkey is done, place on cutting board; let stand 15 minutes to allow juices to set for easier carving. Serve drippings with turkey.

SERVES 16 ABOUT 250 CALORIES, 43G PROTEIN, 0G CARBOHYDRATE, 8G FAT (2G SATURATED), 0G FIBER, 190MG SODIUM

Honey and Spice Hens

PREP 15 MINUTES
TOTAL 32 MINUTES

2 Cornish hens (1½ pounds each), fresh or frozen (thawed)

1¾ teaspoons Chinese five-spice powder

1¼ teaspoons salt

2 tablespoons honey

1 Prepare outdoor grill for direct grilling over medium heat.

2 Remove giblets and necks from hens; refrigerate to use in soup another day. With kitchen shears, cut each hen in half.

3 In cup, mix five-spice powder and salt. Rub mixture on hen halves.

4 Grill hen halves for about 30 minutes, turning hens occasionally, until cooked through (165°F) and juices run clear. Brush hens with honey; grill 2 to 3 minutes longer, until hens are golden.

SERVES 4 ABOUT 360 CALORIES, 38G PROTEIN, 9G CARBOHYDRATE, 19G TOTAL FAT (1G SATURATED), 0G FIBER, 755MG SODIUM

Meats

Steak on the grill is an indulgence: That combination of flame-charred outside and tender pink inside can't be beat. Plus, lamb and pork in all its forms—spareribs, tenderloins, and chops—are extremely versatile. These recipes are sure to be the star of any grilled meal.

A Guide to Grilling Beef, Pork, and Lamb

Whatever the cut, there's nothing better than the taste of juicy beef, pork, or lamb hot off the grill. So why fight it? Grab yourself a plate.

KNOW YOUR STEAK

Here are our favorite cuts of steak (plus one roast) for grilling.

PORTERHOUSE. This is one of the most popular cuts of steak, perhaps because it includes a generous section of tenderloin. This fine-grained steak with a characteristic portion of fat is usually cut nice and thick, which makes it perfect for grilling.

FILET MIGNON. This is the French term for tenderloin steaks cut from the center of the loin. These small, rich steaks are cut in thick individual portions that are a treat prepared on the grill.

SIRLOIN. The sirloin steak is large, which makes it suitable for families or parties. It is cut from the end of the short loin where it meets the rump and is typically between 1¾ and 2½ inches thick, although some sirloins are as thick as 3½ inches.

LONDON BROIL. This is not an individual cut of beef, but rather a term used to describe lean, flat steak with fibers that run lengthwise down the meat. It is most often cut from flank steak, although it may also be cut from top round, flat iron, or shell steak, all of which are relatively affordable.

FLANK. This is a lean, flat boneless cut that comes from the lower section of the short loin. Flank steak has a lovely flavor and tender texture that we like to accentuate by marinating. For best results, it should be grilled quickly, then sliced on a diagonal, across the grain.

FLAT IRON. Also known as "chuck top blade," the flat iron steak is cut from the chuck. This popular steak is a value cut and it's very good grilled.

BRISKET. The brisket is located in front of the foreshank and below the chuck. Although most commonly used for pot roast, it is also irresistible grilled. We precook brisket on the stovetop (up to two days ahead) before brushing it with sauce and giving it a turn on the grill. To serve, cut it across the grain.

KNOW YOUR PORK

Here are our top picks for grilled pork.

PORK TENDERLOIN. The tenderloin or fillet is one of our favorite cuts for grilling. Similar to beef tenderloin but smaller, it lies beneath the ribs and is tender, lean, and quick cooking. Be careful not to overcook it though; it will dry out. It can also be cut into medallions before grilling.

PORK CHOPS. Loin chops include a nice little nugget of tenderloin next to the T-bone and are juicy and flavorful. The meat from a rib chop is similar to a loin chop, but it has a longer rib bone and no tenderloin. They're incredibly tasty; if you like spareribs, you'll love these.

PORK RIBS. See "Rib Rules" on page 170 for an overview of different types of ribs.

KNOW YOUR LAMB

LEG OF LAMB. Butterflied leg of lamb is especially delicious prepared on the grill; ask your butcher to bone it and slit it open for you; see tip on Butterflied Moroccan Lamb (page 190). Lamb kebabs precut from the leg are so tender and flavorful, they don't require marinating.

LAMB SHOULDER CHOPS. The shoulder is flavorful and also more affordable than other cuts of lamb meat. Shoulder chops are excellent for grilling, especially in the springtime.

TEST KITCHEN HACK

Is That Steak Done Yet?

Try one of these three options to determine doneness.

1 Using an instant-read meat thermometer, check the steak's internal temperature.

2 Cut a small slit in the meat near the bone or near the center of a boneless steak. Rare steak will be bright red in the center and pinkish toward the surface; medium-rare, very pink in the center and slightly brown toward the surface; medium, light pink in the center with a brown outer portion; and well-done, uniformly brown throughout.

3 To test doneness without cutting the meat, compare it to the pad of skin on your palm below your thumb. Here's how: A rare steak feels soft and spongy and offers very little resistance when pressed, similar to a relaxed hand. A medium-rare steak is springy to the touch, as on a loosely fisted hand. Medium steak feels firm, with minimal give, like a tight fist.

Steak with Summer Farro Salad

PREP 20 MINUTES
TOTAL 35 MINUTES

- 1 cup farro
- 2 medium red or yellow bell peppers, quartered
- 5 tablespoons olive oil
- 1½ pounds boneless beef top loin steaks, thinly sliced
- 1¼ teaspoons salt
- 1½ cups corn kernels
- 4 cups kale leaves, ribs removed, chopped
- ¼ cup balsamic vinegar
- ¾ teaspoon freshly ground black pepper

1. Prepare outdoor grill for direct grilling over medium-high heat. Cook farro as label directs.

2. Toss bell peppers with 2 tablespoons olive oil. Season beef with ½ teaspoon salt. Grill steak and peppers, covered, 2 to 4 minutes per side, or until steak is cooked to desired doneness and peppers are charred. Chop peppers.

3. Toss farro with peppers, corn, kale, vinegar, pepper, and remaining 3 tablespoons olive oil and ¾ teaspoon salt. Thinly slice steak; serve over farro.

SERVES 6 ABOUT 420 CALORIES, 27G PROTEIN, 35G CARBOHYDRATE, 19G FAT (5G SATURATED), 5G FIBER, 540MG SODIUM

Red Wine and Rosemary Porterhouse

⏱ **PREP** 10 MINUTES
🕐 **TOTAL** 30 MINUTES

- ¼ cup dry red wine
- 1 tablespoon Worcestershire sauce
- 1 tablespoon tomato paste
- 1 tablespoon Dijon mustard
- 1 tablespoon balsamic vinegar
- 1 tablespoon fresh rosemary leaves
- 1 clove garlic
- 1 beef loin porterhouse or T-bone steak
- 1 lemon

This robust marinade can season a thick, juicy steak in 15 minutes. Marinate for up to 1 hour for more intense flavor. It's also good on lamb, pork, or poultry.

1 Prepare Red Wine Marinade: In small bowl, stir all marinade ingredients.

2 Place steak in large resealable plastic bag. Pour marinade over steak, turning to coat. Seal bag, pressing out excess air. Let stand at room temperature 15 minutes to marinate or refrigerate up to 1 hour, turning once.

3 Prepare outdoor grill for direct grilling over medium heat.

4 Remove steak from bag (discard marinade). Grill steak, turning once, for 15 to 20 minutes for medium-rare (145°F) or to desired doneness.

5 Thinly slice steak and serve with lemon wedges.

SERVES 4 ABOUT 245 CALORIES, 30G PROTEIN, 11G CARBOHYDRATE, 10G FAT (3G SATURATED), 1G FIBER, 204MG SODIUM

Barbecued Beef Brisket

PREP 3 HOURS 25 MINUTES
TOTAL 3 HOURS 45 MINUTES

- 1 beef brisket (4½ pounds), trimmed
- 1 medium onion, peeled and cut into quarters
- 1 large carrot, peeled and cut into 1½-inch lengths
- 1 bay leaf
- 1 teaspoon black peppercorns
- ¼ teaspoon allspice berries
- 1 recipe Chunky Barbecue Sauce (page 303)

1 In 8-quart Dutch oven, place brisket, onion, carrot, bay leaf, peppercorns, and allspice. Add enough water to cover and heat to boiling over high. Reduce heat to low, cover, and simmer about 3 hours, until meat is fork-tender and center of meat reaches 145°F.

2 When brisket is done, transfer to platter. If not serving right away, cover and refrigerate until ready to serve.

3 Prepare outdoor grill for direct grilling over medium heat.

4 Grill brisket for 10 minutes. Turn brisket over and grill 5 minutes. Spoon 1 cup barbecue sauce on top of brisket and cook until brisket is heated through, about 5 minutes longer. (Do not turn brisket after topping with sauce.) If you like, reheat remaining sauce in small saucepan on grill. Thinly slice brisket across grain and serve with sauce.

BBQ Brisket Taco

Serve sliced **Barbecued Beef Brisket** with flour or corn tortillas. Top with cilantro leaves, sliced radishes, cheese and Avocado Pico de Gallo (page 298). Serve with lime wedges.

SERVES 12 ABOUT 300 CALORIES, 27G PROTEIN, 18G CARBOHYDRATE, 12G FAT (4G SATURATED), 0G FIBER, 500MG SODIUM

Filet Mignon with Horseradish Salsa

PREP 15 MINUTES
TOTAL 25 MINUTES

1 pound tomatoes, cut into ½-inch pieces

1 cup loosely packed fresh parsley leaves, chopped

½ small red onion, minced

2 tablespoons prepared horseradish

1 tablespoon balsamic vinegar

1 tablespoon olive oil

½ teaspoon salt

1 teaspoon cracked black pepper

1 teaspoon olive oil

½ teaspoon salt

¼ teaspoon dried thyme

1 clove garlic, crushed with press

4 beef tenderloin steaks (filet mignon), 1 inch thick (6 ounces each)

1 In medium bowl, toss together tomatoes, parsley, onion, horseradish, vinegar, oil, and salt. Cover and refrigerate up to 2 hours.

2 Prepare outdoor grill for direct grilling over medium heat, or lightly spray large ridged grill pan with nonstick cooking spray, then place over medium heat until hot.

3 In cup, mix pepper, oil, salt, thyme, and garlic. Rub mixture all over steaks.

4 Grill steaks, turning over once, for 10 to 12 minutes for medium-rare (145°F) or to desired doneness. Serve steaks with salsa.

SERVES 4 ABOUT 330 CALORIES, 39G PROTEIN, 9G CARBOHYDRATE, 15G FAT (4G SATURATED), 0G FIBER, 710MG SODIUM

Sirloin with Tomato-Corn Salsa

 **PREP** 15 MINUTES
TOTAL 25 MINUTES PLUS
STANDING OR
CHILLING

1 pound tomatoes, cut into
½-inch pieces

1 cup fresh corn kernels (from
2 ears), cooked

1 cup loosely packed fresh
parsley leaves, chopped

¼ cup chopped red onion

1 tablespoon lemon juice

1 tablespoon plus 1 teaspoon
olive oil

1 teaspoon cracked black
pepper

½ teaspoon salt

¼ teaspoon dried thyme

1 clove garlic, crushed with
press

1¼ pounds beef sirloin steak,
1 inch thick (6 ounces each),
or 4 eye round steaks
(6 ounces each)

1 In medium bowl, combine tomatoes, corn, parsley,
onion, lemon juice, and 1 tablespoon olive oil; toss
well to combine. Set aside at room temperature for
1 hour or cover and refrigerate up to 4 hours.

2 Prepare outdoor grill for direct grilling over medium
heat.

3 In cup, combine remaining 1 teaspoon oil with
pepper, salt, thyme, and garlic. Rub mixture all over
steaks.

4 Grill steaks, turning over once, for 10 to 12 minutes
for medium or to desired doneness. Serve steaks with
corn salsa.

SERVES 4 ABOUT 455 CALORIES, 36G PROTEIN, 17G CARBOHYDRATE, 27G FAT (9G SATURATED), 3G FIBER, 487MG SODIUM

Steak with Kale and White Bean Mash

PREP 5 MINUTES
TOTAL 20 MINUTES

2 boneless beef top loin steaks, trimmed

Salt

Freshly ground black pepper

8 ounces parsnips, peeled and thinly sliced

1 bunch kale, chopped

2 cloves garlic, chopped

2 cans (15 ounces each) cannellini beans, rinsed and drained

2 tablespoons refrigerated pesto

1 Heat ridged grill pan over medium-high heat until very hot. Season steaks with ¼ teaspoon each salt and pepper. Grill 4 minutes per side for medium doneness. Transfer to cutting board; let stand 5 minutes.

2 Place parsnips and ½ cup water in microwave-safe bowl; cover with vented plastic. Microwave on High 5 minutes or until very tender.

3 Coat large saucepot with nonstick cooking spray; cook kale, garlic, and ¼ teaspoon salt on medium 5 minutes or until stems are tender.

4 Transfer parsnips to food processor along with cannellini beans. Pulse until combined but still chunky, scraping occasionally; stir into kale along with ⅛ teaspoon salt. Heat through.

5 Thinly slice steak; top with refrigerated pesto. Serve with mash.

SERVES 4 ABOUT 525 CALORIES, 43G PROTEIN, 50G CARBOHYDRATE, 18G FAT (5G SATURATED), 20G FIBER, 775MG SODIUM

Soy-Scallion Flank Steak

PREP 15 MINUTES
TOTAL 30 MINUTES

⅓ cup soy sauce

3 cloves garlic, crushed with press

2 tablespoons grated peeled fresh ginger (see Tip)

2 tablespoons rice vinegar

1 tablespoon toasted sesame oil

1 tablespoon sugar

½ teaspoon cayenne pepper

1 bunch green onions, thinly sliced

2½ pounds beef flank steak

2 tablespoons hot water

Use a spoon, not a vegetable peeler, next time you need **peeled ginger**. Use its edge or tip to scrape away the skin. You'll find that a spoon maneuvers better than a peeler around the rhizome's knobby ends. It also removes a thinner layer of skin, keeping more of the ginger for you to use.

1 In medium bowl, whisk soy sauce, garlic, ginger, vinegar, sesame oil, sugar, and cayenne until sugar dissolves. Measure out 2 tablespoons marinade and set aside. Transfer remaining marinade to large resealable plastic bag.

2 Set aside ¼ cup sliced green onions for garnish. Add remaining green onions and steak to bag, turning to coat. Seal bag, pressing out excess air. Place bag on plate and refrigerate 2 hours or overnight, turning over several times.

3 Prepare outdoor grill for direct grilling over medium heat.

4 Remove steak from marinade, scraping off excess solids (discard marinade). Grill, covered, for 12 to 14 minutes, turning over once, for medium-rare (145°F) or to desired doneness. Let steak stand 10 minutes to set juices before slicing.

5 In small bowl, combine hot water with reserved marinade; drizzle over steak to serve and sprinkle with reserved green onion.

SERVES 8 ABOUT 260 CALORIES, 34G PROTEIN, 1G CARBOHYDRATE, 12G FAT (5G SATURATED), 0G FIBER, 315MG SODIUM

Pastrami-Spiced Flank Steak

PREP 15 MINUTES
TOTAL 30 MINUTES PLUS
MARINATING AND
STANDING

1 tablespoon coriander seeds

1 tablespoon paprika

1 tablespoon cracked black pepper

2 teaspoons ground ginger

1½ teaspoons salt

1 teaspoon sugar

½ teaspoon crushed red pepper flakes

3 cloves garlic, crushed with press

1½ pounds beef flank steak, well trimmed

12 slices rye bread

Deli-style mustard

||||||||||||||||||||||||||||||||||

Grinding whole spices—as opposed to using the already ground versions—releases their flavorful oils, which makes the steak even tastier.

1 In mortar with pestle or in resealable plastic bag with rolling pin, crush coriander seeds (see Tip). In cup, mix coriander, paprika, black pepper, ginger, salt, sugar, and pepper flakes.

2 Rub garlic on both sides of steak, then pat steak with spice mixture. Place steak in large resealable plastic bag. Seal bag, pressing out excess air. Place bag on plate; refrigerate at least 2 hours or up to 24 hours.

3 Prepare outdoor grill for direct grilling over medium heat.

4 Grill steak, turning once, for 12 to 15 minutes for medium-rare (145°F) or to desired doneness.

5 Place bread slices on grill grate and toast, without turning, just until grill marks appear on underside of bread.

6 Transfer steak to cutting board and let stand 10 minutes to allow juices to set for easier slicing. Thinly slice steak across grain and serve with grilled rye bread and mustard.

SERVES 6 ABOUT 380 CALORIES, 33G PROTEIN, 35G CARBOHYDRATE, 12G FAT (4G SATURATED), 0G FIBER, 1,015MG SODIUM

Chimichurri Strip Steak

PREP 10 MINUTES
TOTAL 25 MINUTES

1 cup packed fresh parsley

1 cup packed fresh cilantro

1 clove garlic

3 tablespoons extra-virgin olive oil

2 tablespoons sherry vinegar

¼ teaspoon dried oregano

¼ teaspoon crushed red pepper flakes

Kosher salt

Freshly ground black pepper

4 New York beef strip steaks, 1 inch thick (10 ounces each)

Grilled Red Potatoes and Plum Tomatoes (recipe follows), optional

1 Prepare outdoor grill for direct grilling over medium-high heat.

2 In food processor, pulse parsley, cilantro, and garlic until finely chopped. Add oil, vinegar, oregano, pepper flakes, and ⅛ teaspoon each kosher salt and black pepper; pulse to blend.

3 Pat steaks dry. Season with ½ teaspoon each kosher salt and pepper. Grill, turning occasionally, 7 to 8 minutes for medium-rare (145°F) or to desired doneness. Transfer to wire rack. Let stand 5 minutes.

4 Stir meat juices into herb sauce. Slice steak; serve with sauce as well as grilled potatoes and tomatoes if desired.

SERVES 6 (steak and sauce only) ABOUT 445 CALORIES, 38G PROTEIN, 1G CARBOHYDRATE, 31G FAT (10G SATURATED), 1G FIBER, 285MG SODIUM

Red Potatoes

On large sheet heavy-duty foil, place **1½ pounds small red potatoes**, cut into halves; toss with **1 tablespoon olive oil** and **½ teaspoon each kosher salt and freshly ground black pepper**. Fold foil over; crimp edges to seal. Grill on medium-high 25 to 30 minutes, turning over once, until tender.

Plum Tomatoes

Cut **6 medium plum tomatoes** into halves. Brush cut sides lightly with **1 tablespoon olive oil** and sprinkle with **¼ teaspoon each kosher salt and freshly ground black pepper**. Grill 3 to 5 minutes per side, until lightly charred.

Flank Steak Fajitas

PREP 15 MINUTES
TOTAL 35 MINUTES

2 cloves garlic, chopped

1 pound beef flank steak

1 bunch radishes (10 ounces), trimmed and cut into quarters

⅜ teaspoon salt

¼ teaspoon ground black pepper

2 limes

½ cup reduced-fat sour cream

2 teaspoons vegetable oil

3 poblano peppers, seeded and thinly sliced

1 medium onion (6 to 8 ounces), thinly sliced

¼ cup water

8 fajita-size flour tortillas (6-inch), warmed

Using a grill pan on your stovetop, you can achieve the perfect doneness for the steaks and vegetables to fill these delicious **fajitas**.

1. Rub garlic all over steak and let stand at room temperature. In colander, toss radishes with ⅛ teaspoon salt. Set colander over bowl, cover, and refrigerate. Into small bowl, grate zest from 1 lime and cut lime into quarters; set aside. Stir sour cream into lime zest. Cover bowl and refrigerate.

2. Place ridged grill pan over medium-high heat until hot. Brush garlic off steak and discard. Squeeze juice from lime quarters all over steak, then sprinkle with ¼ teaspoon salt and pepper to season both sides. Brush 1 teaspoon oil onto pan, then add steak. Grill, turning over once, for 10 minutes for medium-rare (145°F) or to desired doneness. Transfer steak to cutting board; reduce heat to medium.

3. Brush remaining 1 teaspoon oil onto pan and add poblanos and onion. Cook 2 to 3 minutes or until onion browns, turning occasionally with spatula. Add ¼ cup water and cook 5 minutes longer or until vegetables are tender, stirring occasionally.

4. Cut steak across grain into thin slices. Cut remaining lime into wedges. Divide steak and vegetables among warm tortillas; top with lime sour cream. Serve with radish salad and lime wedges.

SERVES 4 ABOUT 525 CALORIES, 34G PROTEIN, 51G CARBOHYDRATE, 21G FAT (8G SATURATED), 4G FIBER, 625MG SODIUM

Flank Steak with Citrus-Dressed Salad

PREP 10 MINUTES
TOTAL 25 MINUTES PLUS STANDING

1 pound beef flank steak, well trimmed

½ teaspoon salt

¼ teaspoon coarsely ground black pepper

2 bags (10 ounces each) mixed salad greens

1 pint grape tomatoes

1 English (seedless) cucumber, not peeled, quartered lengthwise, then cut crosswise into ¼-inch-thick pieces

6 tablespoons bottled citrus dressing

1 Lightly spray ridged grill pan and place over medium heat until very hot but not smoking. Add steak; sprinkle evenly with salt and pepper. Grill steak, turning over once, for about 15 minutes for medium-rare (145°F) or to desired doneness.

2 Meanwhile, in large bowl, toss salad greens, tomatoes, cucumber, and ¼ cup citrus dressing.

3 Transfer steak to cutting board; let stand 10 minutes to allow juices to set for easier slicing. Thinly slice steak diagonally across the grain. Arrange steak slices on top of salad greens and drizzle with remaining 2 tablespoons dressing.

SERVES 4 ABOUT 315 CALORIES, 33G PROTEIN, 16G CARBOHYDRATE, 15G FAT (5G SATURATED), 0G FIBER, 580MG SODIUM

Steak with Broccolini-Radish Salad

PREP 10 MINUTES
TOTAL 25 MINUTES

2 boneless beef top loin steaks, 1¾ pounds (each 1½ inches thick)

1 teaspoon kosher salt

½ teaspoon ground black pepper

2 bunches broccolini, trimmed

2 tablespoons olive oil

2 tablespoons Dijon mustard

2 tablespoons lemon juice

1 tablespoon maple syrup

5 radishes, thinly sliced

2 green onions, thinly sliced

Need a place for steak to cool after coming off the fire? Fit a wire rack into a rimmed baking sheet to make a convenient cooling rack.

1 Prepare outdoor grill for direct grilling over medium-high heat.

2 Sprinkle steaks with ½ teaspoon each salt and pepper. Place steaks on hot grill rack. Grill, covered, for 5 minutes per side for medium-rare (145°F) or to desired doneness. Transfer to cutting board and let stand 10 minutes. Slice steak across the grain before serving.

3 In a large bowl, toss broccolini, 1 tablespoon olive oil, and ¼ teaspoon salt. Grill, covered and turning occasionally, for 4 minutes or until tender.

4 Meanwhile make dressing. In small bowl, whisk together mustard, lemon juice, maple syrup, and remaining 1 tablespoons oil and ¼ teaspoon salt.

5 Toss radishes, green onions, and broccolini with dressing. Serve with steak.

SERVES 4 ABOUT 410 CALORIES, 42G PROTEIN, 18G CARBOHYDRATE, 19G FAT (6G SATURATED), 5G FIBER, 810MG SODIUM

Chili Steak with Hawaiian Rice

PREP 5 MINUTES
TOTAL 20 MINUTES

1½ pounds skirt steak

2 teaspoons chili powder

1½ teaspoons grated lime zest

½ teaspoon salt

2 cups chopped fresh pineapple

1 cup packed fresh cilantro leaves, finely chopped

3 cups cooked white rice

Lime wedges, for garnish

1 Prepare outdoor grill for direct grilling over medium-high heat.

2 Rub skirt steak with chili powder, lime zest, and salt. Grill for 3 to 4 minutes per side or until desired doneness.

3 Transfer to cutting board and let stand 5 minutes. Meanwhile, toss pineapple with the cilantro leaves and white rice.

4 Thinly slice the steak and serve with rice. Garnish with lime wedges.

SERVES 4 ABOUT 500 CALORIES, 42G PROTEIN, 45G CARBOHYDRATE, 19G FAT (7G SATURATED), 2G FIBER, 430MG SODIUM

Spiced Steak and Green Onion Kebabs

⏱ **PREP** 5 MINUTES
TOTAL 20 MINUTES

1 tablespoon canola oil

2 teaspoons ground cumin

2 teaspoons ground coriander

1¼ pounds beef flank steak, cut into 1-inch chunks

6 green onions, cut into 2-inch lengths

½ teaspoon kosher salt

½ cup plain Greek yogurt

3 tablespoons chopped fresh mint

Naan or pitas, for serving

1 In small bowl, combine oil, cumin, and coriander. Thread steak and green onions onto skewers; brush with oil mixture and sprinkle with salt. Grill on medium for 7 minutes, turning occasionally.

2 Combine Greek yogurt and mint; serve with kebabs, microgreens, and toasted naan or fluffy pitas.

Swap in **4 teaspoons chili powder** or **4 teaspoons curry powder** for cumin and coriander mixture for a different flavor profile.

SERVES 4 ABOUT 300 CALORIES, 32G PROTEIN, 4G CARBOHYDRATE, 17G FAT (7G SATURATED), 2G FIBER, 440MG SODIUM

Sweet and Smoky Tri-Tip

PREP 5 MINUTES
TOTAL 50 MINUTES

1 tablespoon olive oil

1 tablespoon brown sugar

1 tablespoon ground cumin

1 tablespoon smoked paprika

1 teaspoon garlic powder

1 teaspoon onion powder

1 boneless beef tri-tip roast (about 2¼ pounds)

Tri-tip, the triangle of meat at the bottom of a sirloin, can also be referred to as a bottom sirloin roast or the triangle roast. It is tender and boneless and offers rich beef flavor along with versatility at an economical price.

1   Heat grill on medium.

2   In small bowl, combine oil, sugar, cumin, paprika, garlic powder, onion powder, 2 teaspoons salt and ½ teaspoon pepper. Rub all over tri-tip, which can be wrapped in plastic and refrigerated up to 1 day.

3   Grill beef 30 minutes or until 125°F on meat thermometer, turning over 3 times. Transfer to cutting board; let rest at least 10 minutes. Thinly slice against grain to serve.

SERVES 12 ABOUT 265 CALORIES, 28G PROTEIN, 3G CARBOHYDRATES, 15G FAT (5G SATURATED), 1G FIBER, 545MG SODIUM.

Asian Beef Kaboom Kebabs

PREP 10 MINUTES
TOTAL 20 MINUTES PLUS
MARINATING

½ cup packed fresh cilantro leaves

¼ cup soy sauce

2 tablespoons honey

2 tablespoons vegetable oil

1 tablespoon coriander seeds

1 clove garlic, peeled

2 teaspoons rice vinegar

1½ pounds beef top sirloin, trimmed and thinly sliced into 2-inch-long pieces

1 In blender or food processor, blend cilantro, soy sauce, honey, oil, coriander seeds, garlic, and vinegar until mostly smooth; transfer half to large bowl along with beef. Toss beef to coat. Reserve remaining marinade for basting. Marinate beef at least 30 minutes or up to 1 day, covered and refrigerated.

2 Prepare outdoor grill for direct grilling over medium-high heat.

3 Thread beef onto skewers. Grill for 6 to 7 minutes, turning and brushing with reserved marinade occasionally, until cooked through and charred in spots.

SERVES 8 ABOUT 150 CALORIES, 18G PROTEIN, 2G CARBOHYDRATE, 8G FAT (2G SATURATED), 0G FIBER, 110MG SODIUM

Jambalaya Kebabs

PREP 25 MINUTES
TOTAL 35 MINUTES

2 small zucchini (6 ounces each), cut diagonally into slices ¾ inch thick

1 red bell pepper, cut into 1¼-inch pieces

½ small Vidalia onion, cut into 4 wedges, each wedge held together with toothpick

1 tablespoon plus 1 teaspoon olive oil

2 teaspoons Cajun seasoning

16 ounces light kielbasa or other fully cooked smoked sausage, cut diagonally into 1-inch chunks

1 large stalk celery, chopped

1 package (8 to 9 ounces) white rice, fully cooked

1 medium tomato (6 to 8 ounces), chopped

1 Prepare outdoor grill for direct grilling over medium heat.

2 In large bowl, toss zucchini, bell pepper, onion, 1 tablespoon oil, and 1 teaspoon Cajun seasoning. Thread vegetables and kielbasa onto skewers.

3 Grill skewers, covered and turning occasionally, for 10 to 12 minutes, or until kielbasa browns and vegetables are tender-crisp. Remove skewers to platter; keep warm.

4 In nonstick 10-inch skillet, heat remaining 1 teaspoon oil over medium heat. Add celery and remaining 1 teaspoon Cajun seasoning. Cover and cook, stirring occasionally, about 5 minutes or until celery softens. Stir in rice, tomato, and 2 tablespoons water. Cover and cook until rice is hot, about 3 minutes. Serve rice with kebabs.

SERVES 4 ABOUT 405 CALORIES, 20G PROTEIN, 26G CARBOHYDRATE, 27G FAT (8G SATURATED), 0G FIBER, 1,310MG SODIUM

Oktoberfest Feast

 **PREP** 5 MINUTES
TOTAL 20 MINUTES

12 ounces kielbasa (smoked Polish sausage), sliced

1⅓ cups sauerkraut

1 small red onion, cut into wedges

1 apple, sliced

2 teaspoons caraway seeds

¼ cup beer

Rye toast

Spicy mustard

1 Prepare outdoor grill for direct grilling over medium heat.

2 In bowl, toss together kielbasa, sauerkraut, red onion, apple, and caraway seeds. Tear off four 18-inch-long foil sheets. Divide mixture among sheets; pour beer over each.

3 Seal packets. Grill foil packets for 15 minutes. Serve with rye toast and spicy mustard.

HOW TO COOK WITH FOIL

Foil packets are equivalent to one-pot meals on the grill. Follow these tips for quick and easy meals.

Use an 18 x 12-inch sheet of heavy-duty foil for each packet.

Seal in the flavor. Fold foil around food and tightly crimp the edges so steam and juices can't escape. Place food on one half of foil sheet and fold over unfilled half for easy preparation.

Transport packets easily. Place on large baking sheet to move them to and from the grill.

Grill or bake. The cooking time's the same! Plop the foil packet on a medium grill or set the oven at 425°F when outdoor grilling season is over.

Unwrap carefully. The steam inside will be hot, hot, hot!

SERVES 4 ABOUT 235 CALORIES, 15G PROTEIN, 13G CARBOHYDRATE, 15G FAT (6G SATURATED), 3G FIBER, 985MG SODIUM

For the best backyard barbecue ever serve this dish with **TROPICAL RADICCHIO SLAW** (page 257), **RAINBOW VEGGIE KABOBS** (page 235), and **HONEY-LIME RAMEN SALAD** (page 279).

Pinwheel Sausage and Mixed Grill

 **PREP** 5 MINUTES
TOTAL 25 MINUTES

Pinwheel sausages

Tropical Radicchio Slaw
(page 257)

Sweet Leeks and Fennel
Spread (page 300)

Triple Pepper Salsa
(page 301)

8 sausage buns

1 Prepare outdoor grill for direct grilling over medium heat. (Cooking at too high heat causes flare-ups and dries out the links.)

2 Grill sausages, covered and turning occasionally, for 15 to 20 minutes (under 165°F).

3 Prepare condiments: Tropical Radicchio Slaw, Sweet Leeks and Fennel Spread, and Triple Pepper Salsa. If not serving immediately, cover and refrigerate.

4 For hot, fluffy buns, stack on top of large sheet of foil; wrap tightly. Place in oven at 450°F for 12 minutes.

5 Serve sausages with buns and condiments.

SERVES 8 ABOUT 420 CALORIES, 14G PROTEIN, 31G CARBOHYDRATE, 25G FAT (8G SATURATED), 3G FIBER, 1,072MG SODIUM

Korean-Style Short Ribs

PREP 15 MINUTES
TOTAL 35 MINUTES PLUS MARINATING

4 pounds beef chuck short ribs, cut into 2-inch pieces

½ cup lower-sodium soy sauce

4 teaspoons minced peeled fresh ginger

2 teaspoons toasted sesame oil

3 large cloves garlic, minced

Marinating overnight makes these meaty ribs irresistible. Serve them with a **spicy cabbage slaw** or a **cool rice salad**. If you like, sprinkle them with sesame seeds and thinly sliced green onion just before serving.

1 With sharp knife, cut ¼-inch-deep slashes in meaty side of short ribs at ½-inch intervals.

2 In large resealable plastic bag, combine soy sauce, ginger, sesame oil, and garlic. Add short ribs, turning to coat. Seal bag, pressing out as much air as possible. Place bag on plate and refrigerate overnight, turning once.

3 Prepare outdoor grill for direct grilling over medium heat.

4 Lift ribs from bag and place on hot grill rack; brush with remaining marinade from bag. Grill, turning occasionally, for 20 to 25 minutes for medium-rare (145°F) or to desired doneness.

THE SKINNY ON BEEF RIBS

You know, it's not all about pork when you're talking ribs. Here are some tasty beef alternatives when you're looking for something a little different:

Beef back ribs are the large bones left when a standing rib roast is cut to make a boneless rib-eye roast. The ribs are trimmed and divided into single-rib portions.

Short ribs, cut from the shoulder, are rectangular. They contain a cross section of rib bones with alternating layers of lean meat and fat.

Flanken-style ribs are similar to short ribs (they're from the same area of the cow), but are cut across rather than between the ribs.

SERVES 6 ABOUT 745 CALORIES, 34G PROTEIN, 3G CARBOHYDRATE, 65G FAT (27G SATURATED), 0G FIBER, 880MG SODIUM

Ribs with Carolina Barbecue Sauce

 **PREP** 1 HOUR 50 MINUTES
TOTAL 2 HOURS PLUS
CHILLING

3 tablespoons paprika

½ teaspoon cayenne pepper

½ teaspoon celery salt

½ teaspoon mustard powder

½ teaspoon ground cumin

2 teaspoons plus 1 tablespoon brown sugar

1½ teaspoons kosher salt

2 teaspoons ground black pepper

2 racks St. Louis–style pork ribs (2 to 2½ pounds each)

1 cup boiling water

¾ cup apple cider vinegar

3 tablespoons ketchup

½ teaspoon crushed red pepper flakes

1. In bowl, combine paprika, cayenne, celery salt, mustard, cumin, 2 teaspoons brown sugar, salt, and pepper. In large roasting pan, place ribs side by side; rub with dry rub. Cover; refrigerate at least 1 hour or up to 1 day.

2. Preheat oven to 350°F. Uncover ribs and add boiling water to pan. Cover pan tightly with foil. Bake 1 hour 30 minutes or until tender. Uncover ribs.

3. Meanwhile, prepare outdoor grill for direct grilling over medium-low heat. In bowl, stir together vinegar, ketchup, pepper flakes, and remaining 1 tablespoon brown sugar.

4. Grill ribs, bone side down, for 5 minutes, brushing with sauce. Turn ribs over; grill for 5 minutes, brushing with sauce. Repeat.

SERVES 8 ABOUT 555 CALORIES, 39G PROTEIN, 6G CARBOHYDRATE, 41G FAT (15G SATURATED), 1G FIBER, 615MG SODIUM

Memphis Ribs

Prepare **Ribs with Carolina Barbecue Sauce**, but double amount of dry rub and omit vinegar sauce. Use half dry rub for marinating ribs. Substitute remaining dry rub for sauce, sprinkling over ribs while grilling.

Baby Back Ribs Supreme

PREP 1 HOUR 15 MINUTES
TOTAL 1 HOUR 30 MINUTES

4 teaspoons grated peeled fresh ginger

2 teaspoons grated lemon zest

¾ teaspoon salt

2 cloves garlic, crushed with press

4 racks pork baby back ribs (1 pound each)

2 cups boiling water

2 cups preferred barbecue sauce

Only fifteen minutes of grilling time! The trick: Steam the seasoned ribs for an hour in the oven up to two days before barbecuing. With both the ribs and the barbecue sauce prepared in advance, this could easily become a part of your summer weeknight repertoire.

1 Preheat oven to 350°F.

2 In cup, mix ginger, lemon zest, salt, and garlic until combined. Rub ginger mixture on ribs. Place ribs in large roasting pan (15½ x 11½ inches), overlapping slightly. Pour boiling water into roasting pan. Cover pan tightly with foil and oven-steam ribs for 1 hour.

3 Carefully remove foil from roasting pan (escaping steam is very hot). Remove ribs from pan (discard water). Ribs may be grilled immediately or refrigerated up to 2 days before grilling.

4 Prepare outdoor grill for direct grilling over medium heat.

5 Grill ribs, meat side up, for 5 minutes, turning over once. Turn ribs over, brush with barbecue sauce, and grill 5 minutes. Turn ribs over again, brush with more sauce, and grill 5 minutes longer. Cut racks into 2-rib portions; serve with remaining sauce.

SERVES 6 ABOUT 615 CALORIES, 36G PROTEIN, 16G CARBOHYDRATE, 44G FAT (16G SATURATED), 0G FIBER, 760MG SODIUM

Southern Smoked Pork Ribs

PREP 20 MINUTES

TOTAL 5 HOURS 20 MINUTES

- ¼ cup packed dark brown sugar
- 1 tablespoon freshly ground black pepper
- 1 tablespoon garlic powder
- 1 tablespoon ground cumin
- 1 tablespoon ground ginger
- 2 teaspoons kosher salt
- 2 slabs St. Louis–style pork ribs (about 3 pounds each)
- ¼ cup plus 1 cup apple cider vinegar
- 4 cups wood smoking chips

‖‖‖‖‖‖‖‖‖‖‖‖‖‖‖‖‖‖‖‖‖‖‖‖‖‖‖‖‖‖‖‖‖

If you prefer, you can use the same weight of **baby back ribs**, but reduce the cooking time to 3 hours.

1 In bowl, combine brown sugar, pepper, garlic powder, cumin, ginger, and salt. Discard membrane from back of pork ribs. Brush ribs with ¼ cup vinegar. Rub all over with spice mixture, packing to adhere.

2 Place smoking chips on a large sheet of foil; fold and crimp to seal. Poke holes all over. Place foil packet on 1 unlit burner underneath grill grates. Cover and heat all burners of grill on high until smoke appears.

3 Arrange ribs on side of grate over burners not covered by foil packet. Turn burners under ribs off. Reduce heat of burner under foil packet to low. Cook ribs 5 to 6 hours, or until tender but not falling off the bone, adjusting heat to maintain temperature of 250°F and brushing with remaining 1 cup vinegar every hour.

SERVES 10 ABOUT 500 CALORIES, 28G PROTEIN, 7G CARBOHYDRATE, 40G FAT (12G SATURATED), 1G FIBER, 520MG SODIUM

Sugar and Spice Rib Steaks

⏱ **PREP** 10 MINUTES
TOTAL 25 MINUTES PLUS
MARINATING AND
STANDING

4 teaspoons coarsely ground black pepper

1 tablespoon kosher salt

1 tablespoon garlic powder

1 tablespoon brown sugar

1 teaspoon hot paprika

3 bone-in beef rib steaks, 1¼ inches thick (1 pound each)

1 Prepare outdoor grill for direct grilling over medium-high heat.

2 Meanwhile, in small bowl, combine pepper, salt, garlic powder, brown sugar, and paprika. On waxed paper, sprinkle spice mixture over steaks, patting to coat both sides. Let stand 5 minutes.

3 Grill steaks for 1 minute on each side to sear. Cover grill and cook 10 to 12 minutes longer for medium-rare (145°F) or to desired doneness.

4 Transfer steaks to cutting board; let stand 10 minutes to set juices for easier slicing.

RIB RULES
||||||||||||||||||||||||||

Pork ribs are the quintessential grill food—part splurge, part fun, all finger-licking flavor. The different kinds are interchangeable, but here's a guide to the basics:

Spareribs, cut from the underbelly, are the least meaty and most fatty of all pork ribs: They contain long rib bones with a thin covering of meat on the outside and between the ribs. St. Louis-style ribs are a special cut of spareribs, from which the loose flap of meat known as the skirt and the rib tips are removed.

Back ribs, also known as loin back ribs and baby back ribs (when small) are short, easy to hold, and meatier than spareribs because they contain loin meat. We love baby back ribs on the grill.

Country-style ribs are cut from the shoulder of the loin and have the highest meat-to-bone ratio, with the least fat. They're sometimes mistaken for pork chops—you usually need a knife and fork to eat them.

SERVES 12 ABOUT 275 CALORIES, 29G PROTEIN, 4G CARBOHYDRATE, 15G FAT (6G SATURATED), 0G FIBER, 1,045MG SODIUM

Orange-Dijon Pork Spareribs

 **PREP** 20 MINUTES
TOTAL 1 HOUR 20 MINUTES

4 pounds pork spareribs, cut into 1- or 2-rib portions

1 cup sweet orange marmalade

¼ cup Dijon mustard

¼ cup packed brown sugar

1 teaspoon grated orange zest

1½ teaspoon salt

1 Early in day or one day ahead, precook spareribs: In 8-quart Dutch oven, place ribs and add enough water to cover. Heat to boiling over high. Reduce heat; cover and simmer for about 1 hour or until spareribs are tender. Transfer spareribs to platter; cover and refrigerate.

2 Prepare outdoor grill for direct grilling over medium heat.

3 Meanwhile, in a small bowl, combine remaining ingredients. Set sauce aside.

4 Grill cooked spareribs, turning frequently and brushing with sauce often, for about 20 minutes or until heated through.

Balsamic-Rosemary Sauce

In 1-quart saucepan, combine ⅓ **cup balsamic vinegar, 2 tablespoons brown sugar, 1 teaspoon salt,** and ½ **teaspoon freshly ground black pepper** and heat to boiling over medium. Cook about 15 minutes to reduce sauce to ⅓ cup, about 15 minutes. Stir in **1 teaspoon dried rosemary,** crumbled.

SERVES 8 ABOUT 485 CALORIES, 26G PROTEIN, 33G CARBOHYDRATE, 27G FAT (10G SATURATED), 0G FIBER, 723MG SODIUM

Baby Back Ribs with Mixed Berry Chipotle Glaze

PREP 30 MINUTES
TOTAL 2 HOUR 30 MINUTES

- 2 racks pork baby back ribs (2 pounds each)
- 1 tablespoon chipotle chile powder
- 1 tablespoon Old Bay seasoning
- 1¼ teaspoons salt
- ¾ cup packed brown sugar
- 1½ teaspoons garlic powder
- 3 cups mixed berries (raspberries, strawberries, blackberries, and/or blueberries)
- ½ cup ketchup
- 3 tablespoons cider vinegar
- 2 tablespoons chopped chipotle chiles in adobo sauce
- 1 tablespoon olive oil
- 1 medium onion, chopped

1 Pat ribs dry. In bowl, mix chipotle chile powder, Old Bay, 1 teaspoon salt, ½ cup brown sugar, and 1 teaspoon garlic powder. Rub all over ribs. Tightly wrap in foil; refrigerate ribs at least 2 hours or overnight.

2 Preheat oven to 350°F. Place wrapped ribs in rimmed baking sheet and bake 1 hour 30 minutes or until tender. Carefully unwrap; transfer ¼ cup collected juices to measuring cup; discard any remaining.

3 In food processor, pulse berries, ketchup, vinegar, chipotles, remaining ¼ teaspoon salt, ¼ cup brown sugar, and ½ teaspoon garlic powder, and reserved meat juices until smooth. Press through fine-mesh sieve into medium bowl; discard seeds.

4 In 4-quart saucepan, heat olive oil on medium-high. Add onion and cook 5 minutes or until soft, stirring occasionally. Add berry mixture, heat to boiling, then reduce heat and simmer 20 to 30 minutes, or until reduced by about one-third (to about 2 cups).

5 Prepare outdoor grill for direct grilling over medium-high heat.

6 Set aside half of berry glaze for serving. Grill ribs 8 to 10 minutes, basting with remaining glaze and turning over occasionally, until glossy. Transfer to platter; garnish with mixed berries. Serve with reserved glaze.

SERVES 8 ABOUT 365 CALORIES, 21G PROTEIN, 23G CARBOHYDRATE, 22G FAT (8G SATURATED), 2G FIBER, 760MG SODIUM

Plum and Pork Salad

PREP 5 MINUTES

TOTAL 25 MINUTES

1 pound pork tenderloin

2 teaspoons canola oil, plus more for brushing

Kosher salt

3 plums, cut into wedges

8 cups thinly sliced cabbage

¼ cup hot sauce

2 tablespoons brown sugar

2 cloves garlic, crushed with press

1 Prepare outdoor grill for direct grilling over medium-high heat.

2 Brush pork tenderloin with canola oil; sprinkle with ¼ teaspoon salt. Grill, covered, for 10 minutes, turning once.

3 Meanwhile, coat plums with oil. Grill, cut sides down, covered, for 3 to 5 minutes, turning once. Toss plums with cabbage, 2 teaspoons oil, and salt to taste; transfer to platter.

4 Whisk hot sauce with brown sugar and garlic cloves. Brush pork generously with hot-sauce mixture and grill, brushing and turning, for 6 to 8 minutes longer, or until cooked through. Slice pork; serve over plums and cabbage.

SERVES 4 ABOUT 265 CALORIES, 24G PROTEIN, 22G CARBOHYDRATE, 10G FAT (2G SATURATED), 4G FIBER, 875MG SODIUM

Pork Tenderloin with Lemon, Thyme and Garlic

PREP 15 MINUTES

TOTAL 1 HOUR 5 MINUTES
PLUS STANDING

- 3 to 4 lemons
- 4 **cloves garlic, crushed with press**
- 2 **tablespoons fresh thyme leaves, chopped**
- 1 **tablespoon olive oil**
- ½ **teaspoon salt**
- ½ **teaspoon coarsely ground black pepper**
- 1 **boneless pork loin roast (3 pounds), trimmed**

1 Prepare charcoal fire for indirect grilling with drip pan as manufacturer directs, or preheat gas grill for indirect grilling over medium heat.

2 From 1 or 2 lemons, grate 1 tablespoon zest and squeeze 1 tablespoon juice. Cut 2 lemons into 4 wedges each.

3 In small bowl, combine lemon zest and juice, garlic, thyme, olive oil, salt, and pepper.

4 Make 10 to 12 slits 1 inch long and ½ inch deep in pork. Rub pork all over with lemon mixture, pushing some into slits.

5 Place pork on grill grate over direct heat and grill 10 minutes, turning several times to sear all sides. Move pork to part of grate above drip pan on charcoal grill or away from heat source on gas grill; cover and cook about 40 minutes or until still slightly pink in center (145°F).

6 Transfer pork to cutting board; let stand 5 minutes to allow juices to set for easier slicing.

7 Serve sliced pork with lemon wedges and any juices from cutting board.

SERVES 8 ABOUT 350 CALORIES, 35G PROTEIN, 3G CARBOHYDRATE, 21G FAT (7G SATURATED), 0G FIBER, 240MG SODIUM

Hoisin-Honey-Glazed Pork with Pineapple

PREP 10 MINUTES
TOTAL 30 MINUTES PLUS STANDING

¼ cup hoisin sauce

1 tablespoon honey

1 tablespoon grated peeled fresh ginger

1 teaspoon toasted sesame oil

1 pork tenderloin (1½ pounds), trimmed

½ medium pineapple, skin removed

2 tablespoons brown sugar

When choosing a **pineapple**, pick one that is slightly soft, with a deep, sweet fragrance. Pineapples are harvested ripe and will not get any sweeter with time.

1 Prepare outdoor grill for direct grilling over medium heat.

2 In small bowl, combine hoisin sauce, honey, ginger, and sesame oil.

3 Grill pork, covered and turning over occasionally, for 18 to 20 minutes, or until browned outside and still slightly pink in center (145°F).

4 Meanwhile, with serrated knife, cut pineapple half into 4 wedges. Rub cut sides of pineapple with brown sugar.

5 Grill pineapple alongside pork about 5 minutes, turning over once, until browned on both sides. While pineapple is grilling, brush pork with hoisin-honey glaze and turn frequently.

6 Transfer pork to cutting board; let stand 5 minutes to allow juices to set for easier slicing. Transfer pineapple to platter. Thinly slice pork and serve with pineapple wedges.

SERVES 4 ABOUT 275 CALORIES, 31G PROTEIN, 23G CARBOHYDRATE, 6G FAT (2G SATURATED), 0G FIBER, 245MG SODIUM

Pineapple-Pork Tacos

PREP 15 MINUTES
TOTAL 25 MINUTES

1 canned chipotle chile plus
  2 tablespoons adobo sauce

3 tablespoons honey

2 cloves garlic, crushed with
  press

½ small pineapple, peeled and
  cut into ½-inch-thick slices

½ teaspoon salt

½ teaspoon freshly ground
  black pepper

1 pound boneless pork chops,
  ¾ inch thick

½ small white onion, sliced

¼ cup chopped fresh cilantro
  leaves

8 corn tortillas, warmed

1 Prepare outdoor grill for direct grilling over medium heat.

2 In blender, puree chipotle, adobo sauce, honey, garlic, half of pineapple slices, and ¼ teaspoon each salt and pepper. Pour ⅓ cup sauce into pie plate. Pour remainder into small bowl for serving and set aside.

3 Add pork to sauce in plate; turn to coat. Let stand. Grill onion and remaining pineapple 4 to 6 minutes, until tender, turning. Transfer to cutting board.

4 Grill pork, thinly coated with sauce, 6 to 8 minutes, turning over once, until meat just loses pink color (145°F).

5 Chop onion and pineapple; place in bowl. Stir in cilantro and remaining ¼ teaspoon each salt and pepper. Cut pork into chunks; place in tortillas with pineapple mixture. Serve with reserved sauce.

SERVES 4 ABOUT 430 CALORIES, 26G PROTEIN, 45G CARBOHYDRATE, 16G FAT (8G SATURATED), 0G FIBER, 450MG SODIUM

Jerk-Seasoned Pork Loin Cutlets

PREP 20 MINUTES
TOTAL 30 MINUTES

2 lemons

1 pound jicama, peeled and coarsely chopped

1 cup coarsely chopped fresh pineapple

1 cup canned black beans, rinsed and drained

1 medium yellow bell pepper, coarsely chopped

¼ cup loosely packed fresh mint leaves, chopped

Salt

4 boneless pork loin chops, 1 inch thick (5 ounces each), trimmed of fat

2 teaspoons jerk seasoning (see Tip)

Jerk seasoning

is a popular spice blend sold by many companies. Some, but not all blends, contain salt. **Choose one that's salt-free**—the spice combination in all brands is so flavorful, you won't even miss it.

1 Prepare outdoor grill for direct grilling over medium heat, or heat large ridged grill pan over medium heat until hot.

2 From 1 lemon, squeeze 2 tablespoons juice. Cut remaining lemon into 4 wedges; set aside. In large bowl, toss jicama, pineapple, beans, bell pepper, and mint with lemon juice and ¼ teaspoon salt.

3 Rub pork chops with jerk seasoning to coat both sides. (If seasoning is salt-free, also sprinkle meat with ¼ teaspoon salt.) Grill pork for 10 to 12 minutes, turning over once, until browned but still slightly pink in center (145°F).

4 Serve pork with jicama salad and lemon wedges.

SERVES 4 ABOUT 295 CALORIES, 35G PROTEIN, 24G CARBOHYDRATE, 7G FAT (2G SATURATED), 0G FIBER, 505MG SODIUM

Pork Tenderloin with Mustard Vinaigrette

PREP 5 MINUTES
TOTAL 35 MINUTES

- 12 ounces green beans
- 2 tablespoons olive oil
- 1 teaspoon salt
- 1¼ pounds pork tenderloin
- ½ teaspoon freshly ground black pepper
- 3 tablespoons no-salt-added grainy mustard
- 2 tablespoons red wine vinegar
- 1 small shallot, finely chopped
- 1 teaspoon mayonnaise
- 6 cups baby kale
- 1 pint grape tomatoes, cut into halves

1   Prepare outdoor grill for direct grilling over medium heat.

2   Toss green beans with 1 teaspoon olive oil and ¼ teaspoon salt; arrange on one half of large sheet heavy-duty foil. Fold foil over; crimp to seal tightly. Grill, covered, for 20 minutes or until tender.

3   Brush pork with 2 teaspoons olive oil; season with ½ teaspoon each salt and pepper. Grill, covered, turning occasionally, for 18 to 20 minutes, or until still slightly pink in center (145°F). Let rest 5 minutes; slice.

4   In bowl, whisk together mustard, vinegar, shallot, mayonnaise, and remaining 1 tablespoon olive oil and ¼ teaspoon salt.

5   Toss baby kale and grape tomatoes with half of vinaigrette. Serve with beans, pork, and remaining vinaigrette.

SERVES 4 ABOUT 290 CALORIES, 32G PROTEIN, 11G CARBOHYDRATE, 13G FAT (3G SATURATED), 5G FIBER, 595MG SODIUM

Pork Scaloppine with Mango Salsa

PREP 15 MINUTES
TOTAL 20 MINUTES

2 medium ears corn, shucked

4 thin boneless pork chops (about 5 ounces each)

1 tablespoon olive oil

1 teaspoon chili powder

Kosher salt

2 cans (15 ounces) black beans, rinsed and drained

1 mango, peeled and chopped

Freshly ground black pepper

Lime wedges, for garnish

1 Prepare outdoor grill for direct grilling over medium-high heat.

2 Grill corn 8 minutes, turning occasionally, until lightly charred; cut kernels off cobs.

3 Cover each pork chop with large sheet plastic wrap; with meat mallet or rolling pin, pound to ¼-inch thickness. Brush pork all over with olive oil; sprinkle with chili powder and ¼ teaspoon salt. Grill pork for 2 minutes per side.

4 Toss together black beans, mango, corn kernels, and ½ teaspoon each salt and pepper. Serve pork over salsa with lime wedges.

SERVES 4 ABOUT 480 CALORIES, 38G PROTEIN, 53G CARBOHYDRATE, 16G FAT (4G SATURATED), 13G FIBER, 870MG SODIUM

Fennel-Orange Pork with Vegetables

PREP 15 MINUTES

TOTAL 25 MINUTES

1 teaspoon fennel seeds

½ teaspoon dried thyme

¼ teaspoon coarsely ground black pepper

¾ teaspoon salt

1 teaspoon grated orange zest

4 pork rib or loin chops, 1 inch thick (6 ounces each), trimmed

2 heads radicchio di Treviso (4 ounces each), or 1 large round head radicchio (8 ounces)

2 large heads Belgian endive (5 ounces each)

1 tablespoon olive oil

1 tablespoon balsamic vinegar

1   Prepare outdoor grill for direct grilling over medium heat.

2   In mortar with pestle or in resealable plastic bag with rolling pin, crush fennel seeds with thyme, pepper, and ½ teaspoon salt. Stir orange zest into fennel-seed mixture. Rub both sides of pork chops with spice mixture.

3   Halve small heads radicchio lengthwise or cut large head into 8 wedges; cut endive head lengthwise into quarters. In medium bowl, mix oil, vinegar, and remaining ¼ teaspoon salt. Add radicchio and endive to bowl and gently toss to coat.

4   Grill pork chops for 5 minutes. Turn chops over and add vegetables to grill. Grill 5 to 7 minutes longer, or until chops have just a hint of pink color in center (145°F) and vegetables are browned.

5   Serve pork chops with grilled radicchio and endive.

SERVES 4 ABOUT 690 CALORIES, 37G PROTEIN, 38G CARBOHYDRATE, 43G FAT (16G SATURATED), 0G FIBER, 860MG SODIUM

Southern Peach Pork Chops

PREP 15 MINUTES
TOTAL 30 MINUTES

1 tablespoon curry powder

1 tablespoon brown sugar

1 tablespoon olive oil

½ teaspoon salt

¼ teaspoon ground cinnamon

　Pinch coarsely ground black pepper

1 clove garlic, crushed with press

4 pork loin chops, ¾ inch thick (5 ounces each)

4 large peaches, halved

½ cup peach or apricot jam or preserves

1 Prepare outdoor grill for direct grilling over medium heat.

2 In cup, stir curry powder, brown sugar, oil, salt, cinnamon, pepper, and garlic until blended. Rub curry mixture on both sides of pork chops.

3 Brush cut side of peach halves and one side of chops with some jam. Place peaches, jam side down, and chops, jam side up, on hot grill rack; grill 5 minutes. Turn chops and peaches over and brush grilled side of chops with some jam; grill 5 minutes longer.

4 Remove peaches from grill when browned; place on platter. Turn chops and brush with remaining jam; grill 2 to 3 minutes longer, or until browned on outside and still slightly pink inside (145°F). Place chops on platter with peaches.

Juicy summer peaches hot off the grill are perfect with tender, seared meat. Lightly brush the grill rack with oil to prevent the jam from sticking.

SERVES 4 ABOUT 500 CALORIES, 21G PROTEIN, 29G CARBOHYDRATE, 26G FAT (9G SATURATED), 0G FIBER, 360MG SODIUM

Spice-Rubbed Pork with Cucumber Salad

⏱ **PREP** 10 MINUTES
TOTAL 30 MINUTES

- 1 teaspoon mustard powder
- 2 teaspoons ground cumin
- ½ teaspoon crushed red pepper fakes
- ½ teaspoon salt
- 1½ pounds pork tenderloin
- 4 pieces store-bought cornbread
- ¼ cup ranch dressing
- 2 tablespoons milk
- 2 tablespoons snipped chives
- 1 teaspoon lemon juice
- ¼ teaspoon freshly ground black pepper
- 1 pound sugar snap peas, trimmed and sliced
- ½ medium seedless (English) cucumber, halved and sliced
- ½ cup coarsely grated radishes

1 Prepare outdoor grill for direct grilling over medium-high heat.

2 In small bowl, mix mustard, cumin, pepper flakes, and ½ teaspoon salt. Rub all over pork. Grill, covered, for 15 minutes, turning occasionally, until cooked through and still slightly pink in center (145°F). Add cornbread to hot grill 2 minutes before pork is done cooking; grill 1 minute per side or until toasted. Transfer pork and cornbread to cutting board; tent with foil.

3 Meanwhile, in large bowl, whisk dressing, milk, chives, lemon juice, and ¼ teaspoon pepper. Add snap peas, cucumber, and radishes and toss to combine.

4 Thinly slice pork. Divide among plates. Serve with snap pea–cucumber salad and grilled cornbread.

Mix it up with the different flavor variations like **Avocado-Lime**, **Spicy Chipotle** and **Green Goddess**, too!

SERVES 4 ABOUT 465 CALORIES, 41G PROTEIN, 33G CARBOHYDRATE, 19G FAT (4G SATURATED), 6G FIBER, 880MG SODIUM

Jerk Pork Chops with Pineapple

 **PREP** 10 MINUTES
TOTAL 20 MINUTES

1 tablespoon olive oil

1 tablespoon brown sugar

1 tablespoon jerk seasoning

½ teaspoon cayenne pepper

1 tablespoon grated lime zest

2 cloves garlic, crushed with press

4 pork chops

2 sweet potatoes, peeled and cut into slices ½ inch thick

1 pineapple, peeled and cut into slices ½ inch thick

4 green onions, chopped

Lime wedges, for serving

1 Prepare outdoor grill for direct grilling over medium-high heat.

2 In bowl, stir together olive oil, brown sugar, jerk seasoning, cayenne, lime zest, and garlic. Rub onto pork chops.

3 Spray sweet potatoes and pineapple slices with nonstick cooking spray.

4 Grill pork, pineapple, and sweet potatoes for 10 minutes, turning over once, until potatoes are tender and pork is still slightly pink in the center (145°F). Transfer to cutting board; cut potatoes and pineapple into wedges.

5 Divide pork chops, sweet potatoes, and pineapple among 4 plates. Sprinkle with green onions. Serve with lime wedges.

SERVES 4 ABOUT 440 CALORIES, 28G PROTEIN, 51G CARBOHYDRATE, 15G FAT (4G SATURATED), 4G FIBER, 310MG SODIUM

Italian Pork Chops

PREP 30 MINUTES
TOTAL 35 MINUTES

3 cups warm water

¼ cup salt, plus ¼ teaspoon salt

¼ cup packed brown sugar

4 bone-in, center-cut pork chops

¼ cup drained capers

3 cloves garlic, peeled

¾ cup chopped fresh basil

¾ cup chopped fresh parsley

¾ cup baby arugula, plus 4 cups baby arugula

¾ cup olive oil, plus 1 tablespoon olive oil

1 lemon

1   Prepare outdoor grill for indirect grilling on medium-high heat.

2   Prepare Brined Pork: In large bowl, stir together warm water, salt, and brown sugar. Add pork chops; soak 10 minutes.

3   Meanwhile, make Salsa Verde: In processor, pulse capers and garlic until finely chopped. Add basil, parsley, baby arugula, and olive oil; pulse until smooth.

4   Remove pork from brine; pat dry and brush all over with 1 tablespoon olive oil. Place over direct heat and grill for 4 to 6 minutes, or until marked. Move to cooler part of grill and cook 6 to 8 minutes more, turning once, until cooked through (140°F).

5   Halve 1 lemon. Squeeze juice from one half; cut remaining half into wedges. Toss baby arugula with lemon juice and salt.

6   Serve pork with salad, salsa verde, and lemon wedges.

SERVES 4 ABOUT 495 CALORIES, 38G PROTEIN, 4G CARBOHYDRATE, 36G FAT (8G SATURATED), 1G FIBER, 935MG SODIUM

Butterflied Moroccan Lamb

PREP 15 MINUTES
TOTAL 30 MINUTES PLUS MARINATING AND STANDING

⅓ cup loosely packed fresh cilantro leaves, chopped

¼ cup olive oil

2 tablespoons dried mint, crumbled

2 teaspoons ground coriander

1 teaspoon ground ginger

1 teaspoon salt

½ teaspoon coarsely ground black pepper

½ teaspoon chili powder

1 butterflied boneless leg of lamb (3½ pounds), trimmed (see Tip)

1 In small bowl, combine cilantro, oil, mint, coriander, ginger, salt, pepper, and chili powder.

2 Place lamb in 13 x 9-inch glass baking dish. Rub cilantro mixture on lamb to coat completely. Cover and refrigerate at least 1 hour or up to 4 hours.

3 Prepare outdoor grill for direct grilling over medium heat.

4 Grill lamb, covered, turning occasionally, for 15 to 25 minutes for medium-rare (145°F) or to desired doneness. Thickness of butterflied lamb will vary throughout; cut off sections of lamb as they are cooked and place on cutting board. Let stand 10 minutes to allow juices to set for easier slicing. Thinly slice lamb to serve.

Ask your butcher

to bone a 4½-pound **lamb leg** shank half and slit the meat lengthwise so that you can spread it open like a thick steak. (For a 3-pound boneless **leg of lamb**, ask your butcher to start with a 3½-pound **lamb leg shank**.)

SERVES 12 ABOUT 225 CALORIES, 28G PROTEIN, 1G CARBOHYDRATE, 12G FAT (3G SATURATED), 0G FIBER, 270MG SODIUM

Aromatic Lamb Leg

⏱ **PREP** 20 MINUTES
TOTAL 40 MINUTES

1 butterflied boneless (see Tip) leg of lamb (3 pounds), trimmed

3 cloves garlic, each halved and crushed with side of chef's knife

1 tablespoon olive oil

2 teaspoons fennel seeds, crushed

2 teaspoons cumin seeds, crushed

2 teaspoons coriander seeds, crushed

1½ teaspoons salt

Lemon wedges, for serving

1 Prepare outdoor grill for direct grilling over medium heat. Rub both sides of lamb with cut sides of garlic cloves; discard garlic.

2 In bowl, combine oil, fennel, cumin, coriander, and salt; rub on lamb.

3 Grill lamb, covered, turning occasionally, for 15 to 25 minutes, for medium-rare (145°F) or to desired doneness. Thickness of butterflied lamb will vary throughout; cut off sections of lamb as they are done and place on cutting board. Let stand 10 minutes to allow juices to set for easier slicing. Thinly slice the lamb and serve with lemon wedges.

Powdered spices are convenient, but when you're rubbing pork, beef, lamb, or poultry with a spice rub, the texture and flavor of crushed spices are ideal. Crush spices just before using them, so they retain their flavor and fragrance. Here's how: In a mortar with pestle or in a resealable plastic bag with rolling pin, mash the seeds until they are crushed into small pieces, then rub the spice mixture onto the meat, coating all sides for maximum flavor.

SERVES 8 ABOUT 265 CALORIES, 36G PROTEIN, 1G CARBOHYDRATE, 12G FAT (4G SATURATED), 0G FIBER, 525MG SODIUM

Spicy Garlic Lamb with Minted Cucumber Raita

PREP 30 MINUTES
TOTAL 45 MINUTES PLUS STANDING AND CHILLING

- 6 Kirby (pickling) cucumbers (1½ pounds)
- 1 teaspoon salt
- 2 cups plain low-fat yogurt
- ½ cup loosely packed fresh mint leaves, chopped
- 1½ teaspoons sugar
- 1 tablespoon fennel seeds
- 1 tablespoon mustard seeds
- 1 tablespoon cumin seeds
- 2 teaspoons salt
- 1 teaspoon black peppercorns
- 1 teaspoon dried thyme
- 3 whole cloves
- 3 cloves garlic, crushed with press
- 2 tablespoons lemon juice
- 1 butterflied boneless leg of lamb (3½ pounds), trimmed (see Tip, page 190)
- Mint sprigs, for garnish

1. With vegetable peeler, remove several strips of peel (but not all peel) from each cucumber. Halve each cucumber lengthwise; scoop out seeds; cut each piece lengthwise in half again, then crosswise into ½-inch-thick pieces. In medium bowl, toss cucumbers with ¼ teaspoon salt; let stand 10 minutes. Press cucumbers to remove as much liquid as possible. Stir in yogurt, mint, sugar, and remaining ¾ teaspoon salt. Cover and refrigerate until ready to serve or up to 6 hours.

2. Prepare outdoor grill for direct grilling over medium-low heat.

3. In spice grinder, blend fennel, mustard, cumin, salt, peppercorns, thyme, and cloves until finely ground. In small bowl, mix garlic and lemon juice with ground spices until blended. Rub spice mixture over both sides of lamb.

4. Grill lamb, covered, turning over once, for 15 to 25 minutes for medium-rare (145°F) or to desired doneness. Thickness of butterflied lamb will vary throughout; cut off sections of lamb as they are cooked and place on cutting board. Let stand 10 minutes. To serve, thinly slice, garnish with mint, and accompany with raita.

SERVES 8 ABOUT 335 CALORIES, 43G PROTEIN, 12G CARBOHYDRATE, 13G FAT (4G SATURATED), 0G FIBER, 935MG SODIUM

Lamb Chops with Spice Rub

⏱ **PREP** 5 MINUTES
⏱ **TOTAL** 15 MINUTES

4 lamb shoulder chops, ¾ inch thick (8 ounces each)

Choice of dry spice rub (pages 307–311)

Once your butcher has boned the **leg of lamb** for you, ask for the **lamb** bone. Use it to cook up some flavorful lamb broth for a tasty stew.

1 Prepare outdoor grill for direct grilling over medium heat.

2 In small bowl, combine rub ingredients; use to rub on lamb chops.

3 Grill chops for about 5 minutes per side for medium-rare (145°F) or to desired doneness.

SERVES 4 ABOUT 455 CALORIES, 57G PROTEIN, 2G CARBOHYDRATE, 22G FAT (8G SATURATED), 0G FIBER, 470MG SODIUM

Lamb Meatball and Pepper Skewers

PREP 10 MINUTES
TOTAL 35 MINUTES

½ cup fresh mint leaves, chopped

2 medium shallots, chopped

1 tablespoon fresh oregano leaves, chopped

½ teaspoon ground cumin

½ teaspoon smoked paprika

½ teaspoon salt

½ teaspoon freshly ground black pepper

1 pound ground lamb

2 bell peppers, chopped

2 pitas, toasted and cut into quarters

¼ cup pine-nut hummus

Sliced tomatoes, for serving

1 Prepare outdoor grill for direct grilling over medium heat.

2 In large bowl, combine mint, shallots, oregano, cumin, smoked paprika, salt, and pepper. Add ground lamb; mix just until combined.

3 With small scoop, form into 24 (1-inch) meatballs. Thread onto skewers, alternating with bell peppers.

4 Grill for 6 to 8 minutes, turning over once, until meatballs are cooked (165°F). Serve lamb with toasted pitas, hummus, and sliced tomatoes.

SERVES 4 ABOUT 385 CALORIES, 24G PROTEIN, 27G CARBOHYDRATE, 20G FAT (7G SATURATED), 4G FIBER, 580MG SODIUM

Fish and Shellfish

Fast-cooking and weeknight-friendly, fish and shellfish prepared on the grill are fork-tender in minutes. And the meals that follow are so pretty, they're great for entertaining, too.

A Guide to Grilling Seafood and Shellfish

> Grilling fish and seafood is a fantastic way to make eating this good-for-you protein irresistible.

FARM-RAISED SALMON. Farm-raised (usually Atlantic) salmon, with a rich, almost buttery texture and a milder flavor than its wilder sister, is mainly bred along the northeast coast of the United States or off the coast of Chile, first in freshwater hatcheries and then in pens suspended in the cold ocean water, where the fish have a chance to swim against currents and changing tides. Since farmed salmon is available all year, we generally use it in our recipes.

WILD SALMON, with a lean, firm texture and a more pronounced fish flavor, comes mostly from Alaska and is available only in summer months unless purchased frozen or canned. Alaska salmon is called "wild" because the fish swim freely in the Bering Sea, the Gulf of Alaska, and the waters of the northern Pacific. The five commercially sold varieties of wild Alaskan salmon are King (or Chinook), Sockeye (or Red or Blueback), Silver (or Coho), Chum, and Pink (which is primarily canned).

GOOD REASON TO EAT FISH. Despite their reputation for clogging arteries and packing on unwanted pounds, not all fats are villainous. Indeed, one type of polyunsaturated fat, omega-3, is thought to combat heart disease. Omega-3s help inhibit the formation of blood clots and reduce the incidence of heartbeat abnormalities. Preliminary studies also suggest that these fats possibly have a beneficial effect in the treatment of other disorders, ranging from asthma to rheumatoid arthritis. Where do you find omega-3s? In fish. And the oilier the fish (think salmon, mackerel, and sardines), the more omega-3 it contains.

SHRIMP SAVVY. You can buy shrimp year-round—95 percent of what's sold in the United States has been previously frozen. The color of shrimp can vary from light gray to brownish pink to red when they're raw, but when they're cooked, all will turn reddish. When buying raw shrimp, look for firm meat and shiny shells that feel full. Avoid black spots, which are a sign of aging. The heads are usually removed before shrimp are sold; if not, gently pull the head away from the body before shelling it. Buy about 4 ounces of shelled shrimp per serving.

GUIDE TO BUYING FISH

KEEP IT CLEAN. Shop in a well-maintained, reputable market. Don't buy fish that has a distinct "fishy" odor (fresh fish smells like a sea breeze).

BUYING FROZEN FISH? Select a brand that's well wrapped and rock hard, without any freezer burn.

WHEN BUYING WHOLE FISH, plan for 8 to 12 ounces per person. The fish should have bright, shiny eyes and scales that cling tightly to the skin.

THE BEST FILLETS AND STEAKS have a shiny, moist, translucent appearance; the flesh should be firm with no gaps between the flakes. There should be no browning or drying around the edges and no evidence of extra liquid. Purchase 8 ounces per person.

TEST KITCHEN HACK

How to Prepare Fish for the Grill

Thawing. Thaw frozen fish as slowly as possible to minimize bacteria growth. Let it sit in the refrigerator on a plate for about a day. If you're in a hurry, place well-wrapped fish in a bowl of cold water. Change the water every half hour until the fish is thawed (this will take one to two hours per pound of seafood). Be sure to cook it immediately.

Removing pin bones. Although fillets are often boneless, some may still have tiny bones near the head end as well as a row of bones down the center. They are easily removed with tweezers or needle-nose pliers.

Skinning. The skin of most fish is edible (and delicious when cooked to a crisp!), but you can easily skin a fillet if necessary. Place the fillet skin side down with the narrow end near you. At the edge of the narrow end, make a small cut through flesh to skin. Grab the skin and slip the knife blade between it and the fillet and, holding the blade almost parallel to work surface, use a gentle sawing motion to separate the skin from the flesh.

Honey-Ginger Planked Salmon

PREP 15 MINUTES
TOTAL 30 MINUTES PLUS
        SOAKING

1 large (15 x 7-inch) cedar
  grilling plank

1 pound lemons, plus slices for
  garnish

2 teaspoons grated peeled
  fresh ginger

½ teaspoon coarsely ground
  black pepper

1 large piece skin-on wild
  Alaskan salmon (about
  2 pounds)

¾ teaspoon salt

3 tablespoons lower-sodium
  soy sauce

2 tablespoons honey

1 tablespoon Sriracha sauce

1 clove garlic, crushed with
  press

4 cups packed arugula, plus
  more for garnish

4 mini cucumbers, thinly sliced

1¼ cups fresh corn kernels (from
  2 ears), cooked

½ cup loosely packed cilantro
  leaves

1 Soak grilling plank in water 1 to 2 hours. Prepare outdoor grill for direct grilling over medium heat.

2 From lemon, grate 1 teaspoon zest and squeeze ¼ cup juice; set juice aside. Combine zest with ginger and pepper; rub all over flesh side of salmon.

3 Place salmon on soaked plank skin side down; sprinkle with ½ teaspoon salt. Grill, covered, 20 to 25 minutes, until opaque throughout (145°F) or to desired doneness.

4 Meanwhile, in medium bowl, whisk soy sauce, honey, and Sriracha; set aside half. To remaining soy mixture, add garlic, reserved lemon juice, and remaining ¼ teaspoon salt; toss with arugula, cucumbers, corn, and cilantro.

5 Brush salmon with reserved soy mixture. Garnish with arugula and lemon slices. Serve with cucumber salad.

SERVES 8 ABOUT 190 CALORIES, 25G PROTEIN, 12G CARBOHYDRATE, 5G FAT (1G SATURATED), 1G FIBER, 530MG SODIUM

Spicy Salmon

PREP 10 MINUTES
TOTAL 25 MINUTES

4 salmon fillets (6 ounces each)

4 tablespoons hoisin sauce

½ teaspoon red pepper flakes

1½ pounds cauliflower florets

1 tablespoon oil

¼ teaspoon salt

¼ cup chopped peanuts, for garnish

Chopped fresh cilantro, for garnish

1 Prepare outdoor grill for direct grilling over medium heat.

2 Place salmon in centers of 4 foil sheets. Brush each with 1 tablespoon hoisin sauce; sprinkle each with ⅛ teaspoon pepper flakes.

3 Toss cauliflower with oil and salt. Arrange around each fillet. Seal packets. Grill 15 minutes or until cauliflower is tender. Garnish with peanuts and cilantro.

Lean protein and omega-3 fatty acids from salmon make this fish dish heart-healthy.

SERVES 4 ABOUT 410 CALORIES, 43G PROTEIN, 18G CARBOHYDRATE, 19G FAT (3G SATURATED), 5G FIBER, 535MG SODIUM

Honey-Lime Salmon

 **PREP** 15 MINUTES
TOTAL 25 MINUTES

- 3 tablespoons honey
- 1 teaspoon ground cumin
- 1 teaspoon ground coriander
- ¾ teaspoon salt
- ¾ teaspoon grated lime zest
- ¼ teaspoon coarsely ground black pepper
- 1 teaspoon very hot water
- 4 salmon fillets, ¾ inch thick (6 ounces each), skin removed
- 3 tablespoons chopped fresh cilantro
- Lime wedges, for garnish

1 In cup, mix honey, cumin, coriander, salt, lime zest, pepper, and water.

2 Prepare outdoor grill for direct grilling over medium heat.

3 Remove any pin bones from salmon with tweezers. Rub honey-spice mixture all over salmon. Grill salmon for about 10 minutes, carefully turning over once with wide spatula, just until salmon turns opaque throughout (145°F).

4 Sprinkle salmon with cilantro and serve with lime wedges.

SERVES 4 ABOUT 330 CALORIES, 30G PROTEIN, 13G CARBOHYDRATE, 17G FAT (3G SATURATED), 1G FIBER, 485MG SODIUM

Salmon BLTs with Lemon-Dill Mayonnaise

PREP 15 MINUTES
TOTAL 25 MINUTES

4 skin-on salmon fillets, 1 inch thick (6 ounces each)

¼ teaspoon salt

⅛ teaspoon coarsely ground black pepper

8 center slices (½ inch thick) country-style bread

1 recipe Lemon-Dill Mayonnaise (recipe follows)

4 romaine lettuce leaves

2 medium tomatoes (6 to 8 ounces each), sliced

6 slices bacon, cooked until crisp and broken in half

1. Prepare outdoor grill for direct grilling over medium heat.

2. Remove any pin bones from salmon with tweezers. Sprinkle salmon with salt and pepper.

3. Place salmon skin side down on grill grate. Cover and grill 10 to 12 minutes, without turning over, until salmon is opaque throughout (145°F). Meanwhile, grill bread next to salmon about 1 minute on each side, until lightly toasted.

4. Slide thin metal spatula between flesh and skin and lift fish, leaving skin on grill grate (discard skin).

5. Spread lemon-dill mayonnaise on 1 side of toasted bread slices. Place 1 lettuce leaf, folding to fit, on each of 4 bread slices. Top each with 2 or 3 tomato slices, 1 salmon fillet, 3 pieces bacon, and second bread slice.

Keeping the skin on the **salmon** fillets during grilling prevents them from falling apart.

SERVES 4 ABOUT 570 CALORIES, 44G PROTEIN, 41G CARBOHYDRATE, 24G FAT (5G SATURATED), 0G FIBER, 955MG SODIUM

Lemon-Dill Mayonnaise

In small bowl, stir ⅓ cup light mayonnaise, 2 teaspoons chopped fresh dill, and 1 teaspoon grated lemon zest until mixed. Refrigerate if not using right away.

Tarragon Salmon with Nectarine Salsa

 PREP 20 MINUTES

TOTAL 30 MINUTES

- 2 tablespoons chopped red onion
- 2 large nectarines, chopped
- 1 small red bell pepper, chopped
- 1 jalapeño, finely chopped
- 2 tablespoons lime juice
- 1 tablespoon chopped fresh cilantro
- ½ teaspoon salt
- ¼ teaspoon coarsely ground black pepper
- 1 tablespoon dried tarragon
- 4 skinless salmon fillets (6 ounces each; see Tip)
- 1 teaspoon olive oil

We love the ease of **salmon** fillets, but if you find it simplier to cook and turn **salmon** steaks, simply use the 10-minutes-per-inch-of-thickness rule as a guide for your cooking time.

1 In cup, place red onion; cover with cold water and let sit 10 minutes to reduce sharpness. In medium bowl, stir together nectarines, bell pepper, jalapeño, lime juice, cilantro, and ¼ teaspoon salt; set aside.

2 Prepare outdoor grill for direct grilling over medium heat.

3 In small bowl, combine tarragon, pepper, and remaining ¼ teaspoon salt. Remove any pin bones from salmon with tweezers. Brush salmon with oil and rub with tarragon mixture to coat both sides.

4 Grill salmon, covered, for 8 to 10 minutes, carefully turning over once with wide spatula, until opaque throughout (145°F). Transfer salmon to platter.

5 Drain onion well. Stir into nectarine mixture. Serve nectarine salsa with grilled salmon.

SERVES 4 ABOUT 305 CALORIES, 35G PROTEIN, 14G CARBOHYDRATE, 12G FAT (2G SATURATED), 0G FIBER, 365MG SODIUM

Salmon with Citrus-Spice Glaze

PREP 10 MINUTES
TOTAL 20 MINUTES

- 3 tablespoons dark brown sugar
- 2 tablespoons orange juice
- 1½ teaspoons smoked paprika
- ¼ teaspoon ground cumin
- ¼ teaspoon crushed red pepper flakes
- ¼ teaspoon salt
- ⅛ teaspoon freshly ground black pepper
- 4 center-cut skin-on salmon fillets (6 ounces each; see Tip)

We use skin-on **salmon** fillets to help us get the caramelized fish off the grill after cooking. The skin sticks to the grate, and the fish lifts easily off the skin. If you like to eat the **salmon** skin, use a spatula to remove it from the grill grate.

1 Prepare outdoor grill for direct grilling over medium heat.

2 In small bowl, stir brown sugar, orange juice, paprika, cumin, and pepper flakes until sugar dissolves.

3 Remove any pin bones from salmon with tweezers. Sprinkle salt and black pepper on flesh side of salmon.

4 Grill salmon, skin side up, 4 minutes, then carefully turn salmon over with wide spatula. Brush sugar mixture over salmon. Grill 4 to 5 minutes longer, continuously brushing with sugar mixture, until just opaque throughout (145°F).

5 Slide thin metal spatula between flesh and skin and lift fish, leaving skin on grill grate (discard skin).

SERVES 4 ABOUT 320 CALORIES, 39G PROTEIN, 12G CARBOHYDRATE, 13G FAT (2G SATURATED), 0G FIBER, 235MG SODIUM

Fish Packets with Caper Butter and Snap Peas

PREP 5 MINUTES
TOTAL 25 MINUTES

3 tablespoons softened butter

3 tablespoons capers, chopped

Kosher salt

1 pound sugar snap peas

1 lemon, thinly sliced

4 halibut or cod fillets
(5 ounces each)

Basil, for garnish

1 Prepare outdoor grill for direct grilling over medium heat.

2 Combine butter, capers, and ¼ teaspoon salt. Divide snap peas among 4 large sheets foil; sprinkle each with pinch of salt and top with 3 thin slices lemon.

3 Top peas with fish fillets. Sprinkle each fillet with pinch of salt and dot with caper butter. Fold and crimp foil edges to seal tightly. Grill, covered, for 12 minutes. Garnish with basil.

SERVES 4 ABOUT 260 CALORIES, 30G PROTEIN, 10G CARBOHYDRATE, 11G FAT (6G SATURATED), 3G FIBER, 690MG SODIUM

Thai Snapper in Foil Packets

PREP 30 MINUTES
TOTAL 40 MINUTES

- 3 tablespoons lime juice
- 1 tablespoon Asian fish sauce
- 1 tablespoon olive oil
- 1 teaspoon grated peeled fresh ginger
- ½ teaspoon sugar
- ½ teaspoon minced garlic
- 4 red snapper fillets (6 ounces each)
- 1 large carrot, cut into 2¼-inch-long matchsticks
- 1 large green onion, thinly sliced
- ¼ cup loosely packed fresh cilantro leaves

1 Prepare outdoor grill for direct grilling over medium heat.

2 In small bowl, mix lime juice, fish sauce, oil, ginger, sugar, and garlic.

3 Place fish on 4 sheets heavy-duty foil (see Tip). Top with carrot, green onion, and cilantro. Spoon lime juice mixture over snapper and vegetables. Seal packets.

4 Grill packets 8 minutes.

5 To serve, with kitchen shears, cut an "X" in top of each packet to allow steam to escape before carefully opening foil.

To make the perfect foil packet, refer to **"How to Cook with Foil,"** page 163.

SERVES 4 ABOUT 230 CALORIES, 36G PROTEIN, 5G CARBOHYDRATE, 6G FAT (1G SATURATED), 0G FIBER, 270MG SODIUM

Jerk Halibut with Sweet Potato Mash

PREP 35 MINUTES
TOTAL 45 MINUTES

2 pounds sweet potatoes, peeled and cut into 1-inch chunks

2 Granny Smith apples, peeled and cut into 8 wedges each

4 halibut steaks, 1½ inches thick (6 ounces each)

1 tablespoon jerk seasoning

1 bag (9 ounces) microwave-in-bag broccoli florets

½ teaspoon salt

¼ teaspoon coarsely ground black pepper

1 lime, cut into 4 wedges

1 In large pot with steamer basket, heat 1 inch water to boiling. Place potatoes and apples in steamer basket; cover and steam 20 minutes or until potatoes and apples are tender.

2 Meanwhile, grease large ridged grill pan; place over medium heat until hot. Rub halibut steaks with jerk seasoning on both sides. Grill halibut 6 to 8 minutes, turning over once, until opaque throughout (145°F) While halibut is cooking, microwave broccoli as label directs.

3 Place steamed potatoes and apples in bowl; mash with salt and pepper.

4 Serve halibut with lime wedges, mashed sweet potatoes, and broccoli.

SERVES 4 ABOUT 410 CALORIES, 40G PROTEIN, 53G CARBOHYDRATE, 5G FAT (1G SATURATED), 8G FIBER, 630MG SODIUM

Catfish with Chipotle Salsa over Polenta

 PREP 30 MINUTES
TOTAL 50 MINUTES

Nonstick cooking spray

4 large plum tomatoes (1 pound total), halved lengthwise

1 small red onion, cut crosswise into ½-inch-thick slices

4 catfish fillets (6 ounces each)

¾ teaspoon chipotle chile powder

¾ teaspoon salt

3 cups low-fat (1%) milk

1 can (14 to 14.5 ounces) reduced-sodium chicken broth (1¾ cups)

¾ cup instant polenta

1 cup fresh corn kernels (from 2 ears), or 1 cup frozen (thawed) corn kernels

2 teaspoons fresh lime juice

1 Preheat large ridged grill pan over medium-high heat. On sheet of waxed paper, place tomato halves and onion slices. Spray vegetables on both sides with nonstick cooking spray. Grill tomatoes and onion for about 10 minutes, turning over once, until lightly browned and softened. Transfer vegetables to cutting board.

2 While tomatoes and onion are cooking, place catfish fillets on same waxed paper. Sprinkle both sides with ½ teaspoon chipotle chile powder and ¼ teaspoon salt. Spray both sides with cooking spray. Grill catfish 7 to 8 minutes, turning over once, until it turns opaque throughout (145°F).

3 While catfish is cooking, prepare polenta: In 3-quart saucepan, combine milk, broth, and ¼ teaspoon salt; cover and heat to boiling over high. Uncover; slowly whisk in polenta and cook until mixture begins to thicken, stirring constantly. Reduce heat to low; cover saucepan and simmer 5 minutes, stirring occasionally. Stir in corn. Remove pan from heat.

4 Coarsely chop grilled tomatoes and onion; transfer to medium bowl. Stir in lime juice and remaining ¼ teaspoon chipotle chile powder and ¼ teaspoon salt.

5 To serve, divide polenta among 4 dinner plates; top with grilled catfish and tomato-chipotle salsa.

SERVES 4 ABOUT 480 CALORIES, 38G PROTEIN, 46G CARBOHYDRATE, 16G FAT (4G SATURATED), 0G FIBER, 980MG SODIUM

Spiced Tuna Steaks on Spinach Salad

PREP 25 MINUTES
TOTAL 35 MINUTES

- 1 tablespoon olive oil
- 1 teaspoon ground cumin
- 1 teaspoon ground coriander
- 1 teaspoon paprika
- 1 teaspoon grated lime zest
- ¾ teaspoon salt
- ½ teaspoon coarsely ground black pepper
- 4 tuna steaks, 1 inch thick (6 ounces each)
- ½ seedless English cucumber (8 ounces)
- 1 bunch radishes
- 2 tablespoons olive oil
- 2 tablespoons fresh lime juice
- 1 teaspoon sugar
- ¼ teaspoon ground cumin
- ¼ teaspoon salt
- ⅛ teaspoon coarsely ground black pepper
- 1 bag (6 ounces) baby spinach

1. In small bowl, stir together oil, cumin, coriander, paprika, lime zest, salt, and pepper until well blended. Rub spice mixture on both sides of tuna steaks.

2. Place large ridged grill pan over medium heat until hot but not smoking. Add tuna to pan and grill 8 to 10 minutes, turning over once, until opaque throughout (145°F). If you prefer seared tuna, grill about 2 minutes more per side. Transfer to cutting board.

3. Meanwhile, halve cucumber lengthwise, then thinly slice crosswise. Set aside 4 whole radishes with tops for garnish; thinly slice remainder of bunch.

4. In large bowl, whisk together oil, lime juice, sugar, cumin, salt, and pepper. Add cucumber, sliced radishes, and spinach; toss to coat.

5. Cut tuna steaks into ½-inch-thick slices. Arrange salad on dinner plates or large platter; top with tuna. Garnish with radishes.

SERVES 4 ABOUT 300 CALORIES, 42G PROTEIN, 5G CARBOHYDRATE, 12G FAT (2G SATURATED), 0G FIBER, 700MG SODIUM

Swordfish Kebabs

PREP 15 MINUTES
TOTAL 35 MINUTES

3 large ears corn, shucked

1 pound swordfish steak, skinned and cut into 1-inch chunks

4 ounces zucchini, sliced

1 tablespoon canola oil

2 teaspoons chili powder

Kosher salt

2 cans (15 ounces each) chickpeas, rinsed and drained

½ cup packed fresh mint leaves, chopped

3 tablespoons lime juice

1 tablespoon oil

1 Prepare outdoor grill for direct grilling over medium-high heat.

2 Grill corn 12 minutes, turning, until charred in spots.

3 Thread swordfish steak onto skewers. Brush fish and zucchini with canola oil; sprinkle with chili powder and ½ teaspoon salt. Grill fish and zucchini 6 minutes, turning once, until fish is opaque.

4 Cut corn off cobs, chop zucchini and toss with chickpeas, mint, lime juice, oil, and ¼ teaspoon salt. Serve with kebabs.

SERVES 4 ABOUT 500 CALORIES, 34G PROTEIN, 55G CARBOHYDRATE, 19G FAT (3G SATURATED), 12G FIBER, 735MG SODIUM

Mediterranean Sea Bass

PREP 10 MINUTES
TOTAL 25 MINUTES

1 small bunch fresh oregano

2 lemons

3 tablespoons olive oil

1 teaspoon ground coriander

1¼ teaspoons salt

2 whole sea bass (1½ pounds each), cleaned and scaled

¼ teaspoon ground black pepper

||||||||||||||||||||||||||||||||||||||

Sea bass is lovely on the grill; its firm white flesh holds up very well. If you can't get **sea bass**, substitute **red snapper** or **striped bass**.

1 Prepare outdoor grill for direct grilling over medium heat.

2 Meanwhile, set 2 large sprigs oregano aside; chop enough oregano leaves to make 1 tablespoon. From 1 lemon, grate 1 tablespoon zest and squeeze 2 tablespoons juice. Cut one half of remaining lemon into slices; cut other half into wedges for serving.

3 In small bowl, combine chopped oregano, lemon juice, lemon zest, oil, coriander, and ¼ teaspoon salt.

4 Rinse fish and pat dry with paper towels. Make three diagonal slashes in both sides of each fish. Sprinkle inside and out with pepper and remaining 1 teaspoon salt. Place lemon slices and reserved oregano sprigs inside fish cavities. Place fish in 13 x 9-inch glass baking dish. Set aside half of oil mixture. Rub remaining half of oil mixture on outside of both fish. Let stand 15 minutes at room temperature.

5 Remove fish from baking dish and place on grill. Cover and grill 12 to 14 minutes, turning over once, until just opaque throughout (145°F).

6 To serve, place 1 fish on cutting board. With knife, cut along backbone from head to tail. Slide wide metal spatula or cake server under front section of top fillet and lift off from backbone; transfer to platter. Gently pull out backbone and rib bones from bottom fillet and discard. Transfer bottom fillet to platter. Repeat with second fish. Drizzle fillets with remaining oil mixture. Serve with reserved lemon wedges.

SERVES 4 ABOUT 305 CALORIES, 40G PROTEIN, 1G CARBOHYDRATE, 15G FAT (3G SATURATED), 0G FIBER, 730MG SODIUM

Fish Tacos

PREP 15 MINUTES

TOTAL 25 MINUTES

1 lemon

2½ teaspoons vegetable oil

Salt

2 ears corn, shucked

1 avocado, halved and pitted

3 cloves garlic, crushed with press

½ teaspoon dried oregano

¼ teaspoon cayenne pepper

1 pound skinless tilapia fillets (see Tip)

12 corn tortillas

1 large tomato (10 to 12 ounces), finely chopped

Fresh cilantro leaves, for serving

Lime wedges, for serving

||||||||||||||||||||||||||||||||||||

Flounder, catfish, or any mild white fish would be a good substitute for the tilapia. Grill **fish fillets** 8 to 10 minutes per inch of thickness.

1 Prepare outdoor grill for direct grilling over medium-high heat.

2 From lemon, grate 2 teaspoons zest and squeeze 2 tablespoons juice.

3 Rub ½ teaspoon oil and pinch of salt all over corn and cut sides of avocado. On plate, combine garlic, oregano, cayenne, lemon zest, ¼ teaspoon salt, and remaining 2 teaspoons oil. Place fish on plate and rub mixture all over to coat.

4 Place fish, corn, and avocado, cut sides down, on hot grill grate. Grill fish 3 to 4 minutes, turning over once, until opaque throughout (145°F). Grill vegetables 5 minutes, turning corn occasionally, until charred.

5 Transfer fish, corn, and avocado to cutting board. Let cool while warming tortillas: Place tortillas on grill in single layer and cook 1 minute, turning once. Stack on large sheet of foil and wrap tightly.

6 Cut corn kernels from cobs. Peel and finely chop avocado. Break fish into large chunks. In large bowl, mix together tomato, corn, avocado, lemon juice, and ¼ teaspoon salt.

7 Divide fish and tomato mixture among tortillas and serve with cilantro and lime wedges.

SERVES 4 ABOUT 420 CALORIES, 31G PROTEIN, 49G CARBOHYDRATE, 13G FAT (2G SATURATED), 0G FIBER, 425MG SODIUM

For a Mexican-style grill-out fiesta, pair these tacos with **SWEET AND SPICED CHICKEN TACOS** (page 103), **BBQ BRISKET TACOS** (page 143) and **MEXICAN CORN** (page 239). To get the party started, **SMOKY GUACAMOLE** (page 23) is a great appetizer.

Citrus Shrimp Kaboom Kebabs

PREP 10 MINUTES
TOTAL 15 MINUTES

1 teaspoon smoked paprika

1 teaspoon salt

½ teaspoon ground cumin

3 small lemons, thinly sliced

3 small limes, thinly sliced

2 pounds shrimp, shelled and deveined

2 tablespoons olive oil

1 Prepare outdoor grill for direct grilling over medium-high heat.

2 In small bowl, combine paprika, salt, and cumin.

3 Alternating ingredients, thread shrimp, lemon slices, and lime slices onto skewers. Brush skewers on both sides with olive oil and sprinkle lightly with seasoned salt mixture.

4 Grill 4 to 5 minutes, turning over once halfway through, until shrimp are opaque.

SERVES 5 ABOUT 175 CALORIES, 45G PROTEIN, 6G CARBOHYDRATE, 6G FAT (1G SATURATED), 1G FIBER, 1,182MG SODIUM

Zesty Shrimp Tacos

Prepare **Citrusy Shrimp Kaboom Kebabs**. Use shrimp to fill warmed **corn tortillas**. Top with **cilantro**, **radishes**, **lime wedges**, **Cotija cheese**, and **salsa**.

SERVES 5 ABOUT 365 CALORIES, 51G PROTEIN, 35G CARBOHYDRATE, 12G FAT (4G SATURATED), 5G FIBER, 1,859MG SODIUM

Shrimp and Mango Skewers

⏱ **PREP** 20 MINUTES
⏱ **TOTAL** 25 MINUTES

12 skewers (12-inch), preferably metal

1 lime

1 cup plain low-fat yogurt

½ cup packed fresh mint leaves, finely chopped

1 teaspoon curry powder

¼ teaspoon salt

¼ teaspoon freshly ground black pepper

1 cup whole wheat couscous

5 ounces baby spinach

1 pound shelled and deveined shrimp (26/30 count)

2 mangoes (see tip), peeled and cut into 1-inch chunks

To tell if a **mango** is ripe, squeeze gently—it should yield slightly.

1 Prepare outdoor grill for direct grilling over medium-high heat.

2 From lime, grate 1 teaspoon zest and squeeze 2 teaspoons juice into medium bowl; stir in yogurt, half of chopped mint, curry powder, salt, and pepper.

3 In 4-quart saucepan, heat 1¼ cups water to boiling over high heat. Stir in couscous. Cover and remove from heat. Let stand 5 minutes; fluff with fork. Lay spinach on top of couscous; cover and let stand another 5 minutes.

4 Meanwhile, thread shrimp and mango chunks alternately onto skewers. Place half of yogurt mixture in small bowl; set aside for serving. Brush remaining mixture all over shrimp and mango. Grill 5 to 7 minutes, turning over once, until shrimp turn opaque.

5 Toss spinach and couscous until combined; transfer to large platter. Top with shrimp skewers. Drizzle reserved yogurt mixture over shrimp. Garnish with remaining mint.

SERVES 4 ABOUT 410 CALORIES, 28G PROTEIN, 73G CARBOHYDRATE, 3G FAT (1G SATURATED), 11G FIBER, 890MG SODIUM

Spicy Shrimp

PREP 5 MINUTES
TOTAL 10 MINUTES

1 pound large shrimp
1 teaspoon olive oil
¼ teaspoon cayenne pepper
⅛ teaspoon salt

1 Prepare outdoor grill for direct grilling over medium-high heat.

2 In a large bowl, toss shrimp with oil, cayenne, and salt to coat. Grill 3 to 5 minutes, turning once, until opaque throughout. Transfer shrimp to plate and let cool 5 minutes.

SERVES 4 ABOUT 77 CALORIES, 28G PROTEIN, 0G CARBOHYDRATE, 1G FAT (0G SATURATED), 0G FIBER, 527MG SODIUM

Shrimp Salad with Nectarines

Place **2 nectarines** on grill alongside Spicy Grilled Shrimp; cook 4 minutes, turning once. In a large bowl combine **6 ounces mixed baby greens, ½ cup fresh basil leaves**, and ⅓ cup Classic Vinaigrette (below). Toss to coat. Divide greens evenly among 4 serving plates and top each salad with shrimp, nectarines, **1 avocado** (sliced), and ¼ **cup sliced almonds**. This salad can also be served with grilled chicken as a substitute for shrimp.

Classic Vinaigrette

In a medium bowl, whisk together ¼ **cup red wine vinegar, 1 tablespoon Dijon mustard, ¼ teaspoon salt**, and ¼ teaspoon freshly ground black pepper. Continue whisking and add ½ **cup extra-virgin olive oil** in slow, steady stream. Whisk until well blended and emulsified. Cover and refrigerate up to 3 days.

These shrimp taste like pure summer. Throw them onto **FETA-DILL GREEK SALAD** (page 25) for added protein or eat them straight with **CHILE-LIME CORN** (page 237) on the side for a complete meal.

Old Bay Peel 'n' Eat Shrimp

PREP 5 MINUTES
TOTAL 5 MINUTES

1½ pounds shell-on deveined shrimp (16/20 count)

1 tablespoon olive oil

3 teaspoons Old Bay seasoning

¼ cup chopped fresh parsley

1 Prepare outdoor grill for direct grilling over high heat.

2 Toss shrimp with olive oil and 1½ teaspoons Old Bay seasoning.

3 Thread shrimp onto skewers and grill 3 to 5 minutes, turning over once, until opaque.

4 Remove shrimp from skewers and transfer to large bowl. Sprinkle with parsley and 1½ teaspoons Old Bay seasoning; toss to combine. Serve immediately.

SERVES 4 ABOUT 160 CALORIES, 27G PROTEIN, 0G CARBOHYDRATE, 5G FAT (1G SATURATED), 0G FIBER, 790MG SODIUM

Cocktail Sauce

Puree tomatoes as in **Homemade Ketchup** (page 289). In step 2, cook **2 cloves garlic**, chopped, with onion. In step 4, stir in **½ cup prepared horseradish** and **2 tablespoons lemon juice** after pureeing.

Shrimp with Asian BBQ Sauce

PREP 15 MINUTES
TOTAL 20 MINUTES

Romaine lettuce leaves

1¼ pounds large shrimp, shelled and deveined, tail left on

4 skewers (10- to 12-inch), preferably metal

⅓ cup hoisin sauce

3 tablespoons ketchup

1½ teaspoons grated peeled fresh ginger

¼ teaspoon Chinese five-spice powder

2 tablespoons rice vinegar

2 tablespoons water

1 Prepare outdoor grill for direct grilling over medium heat.

2 Arrange romaine on platter and set aside. Shell and devein shrimp, leaving tail shell on, if you like. Thread shrimp on skewers.

3 In small bowl, stir together hoisin sauce, ketchup, ginger, five-spice powder, and 1 tablespoon vinegar. Measure out ¼ cup barbecue sauce and transfer to ramekin; stir in 2 tablespoons water and remaining 1 tablespoon vinegar and set aside to use as dipping sauce.

4 Brush shrimp with some barbecue sauce from bowl. Grill shrimp 2 minutes. Brush with some sauce; turn, brush with remaining sauce, and grill 1 to 2 minutes longer, until opaque throughout.

5 Serve shrimp on skewers over romaine with reserved dipping sauce.

SERVES 4 ABOUT 185 CALORIES, 25G PROTEIN, 13G CARBOHYDRATE, 3G FAT (1G SATURATED), 0G FIBER, 540MG SODIUM

Cajun Shrimp with Rémoulade

 **PREP** 25 MINUTES
TOTAL 30 MINUTES

2 lemons

½ cup light mayonnaise

2 tablespoons ketchup

2 tablespoons minced celery

1 tablespoon coarse-grained Dijon mustard

1 tablespoon minced fresh parsley

½ teaspoon plus 1 tablespoon Cajun seasoning (see Tip)

1 green onion, minced

1 tablespoon olive oil

1¼ pounds large shrimp, shelled and deveined, tail left on

||||||||||||||||||||||||||||||||||||

Cajun seasoning
mixes vary among manufacturers, especially with regard to **salt** content. Add **salt** to taste if necessary.

1 Prepare outdoor grill for direct grilling over medium-high heat.

2 From 1 lemon, grate 2 teaspoons zest and squeeze 2 teaspoons juice; cut remaining lemon into wedges and set aside for serving.

3 In small bowl, combine mayonnaise, ketchup, celery, mustard, parsley, lemon juice, ½ teaspoon Cajun seasoning, and green onion. Cover and refrigerate up to 3 days if not serving right away.

4 In medium bowl, mix remaining 1 tablespoon Cajun seasoning, oil, and lemon zest. Add shrimp and toss until evenly coated.

5 Place shrimp on hot grill grated (or hot grill topper) and grill 4 to 5 minutes, turning once, until opaque throughout.

6 Transfer shrimp to platter; serve with sauce and lemon wedges.

SERVES 4 ABOUT 155 CALORIES, 24G PROTEIN, 2G CARBOHYDRATE, 5G FAT (1G SATURATED), 0G FIBER, 575MG SODIUM

New England Lobster Bake

PREP 10 MINUTES
TOTAL 1 HOUR

3 pounds red potatoes, quartered

4 lobsters (1½ to 2 pounds each)

2 pounds andouille or linguiça sausage

3 pounds littleneck clams, scrubbed

6 ears corn, shucked and halved

Drawn Butter

Lemon wedges

8 dinner rolls

1 Steam potatoes in 1 inch simmering water in a large pot for 20 to 30 minutes.

2 In very large covered pot, heat 1 inch water to boiling on high. Add 2 lobsters. Cover, reduce heat to medium, and cook 15 to 17 minutes, or until antennae come off easily when firmly tugged. Transfer to ice bath or sink and rinse with cold water until cool. Repeat with 2 more lobsters.

3 Prepare outdoor grill for direct grilling over medium heat.

4 Grill sausage 15 minutes, turning occasionally, until grill marks appear. Transfer to cutting board. Let stand 10 minutes. Cut into 3-inch lengths.

5 Grill clams, covered, 8 to 10 minutes (do not turn over), just until they open.

6 Steam corn in 1 inch simmering water in large pot, 8 to 10 minutes.

7 Arrange large sheets kraft paper or newspaper on outdoor serving table. Place potatoes, lobsters, sausages, clams, and corn in center. Serve with drawn butter, lemon wedges, and dinner rolls.

SERVES 8 ABOUT 1,030 CALORIES, 56G PROTEIN, 66G CARBOHYDRATE, 61G FAT (33G SATURATED), 5G FIBER, 1,837MG SODIUM

Drawn Butter

In small saucepan, heat **1 pound butter** on low about 15 minutes, until milk solids foam at the top and watery whey sinks to bottom. Let cool. Skim the foam off top and pour clear butter into serving bowl, leaving solids in pan to discard.

Scallop and Cherry Tomato Skewers

PREP 15 MINUTES
TOTAL 30 MINUTES

16 large sea scallops
   (1¼ pounds)

 1 lemon

 2 tablespoons olive oil

 2 tablespoons Dijon mustard

 ⅛ teaspoon salt

24 cherry tomatoes

 8 skewers (8-inch), preferably
   metal

1 Prepare outdoor grill for direct grilling over medium heat.

2 Meanwhile, pull off and discard tough crescent-shaped side muscle, if any, from each scallop. Rinse scallops well to remove sand from crevices and pat dry with paper towels.

3 From lemon, grate 1½ teaspoons zest and squeeze 1 tablespoon juice. In small bowl, whisk lemon zest and juice, oil, mustard, and salt until blended; set aside.

4 Thread 3 tomatoes and 2 scallops alternately on each skewer, beginning and ending with tomatoes.

5 Brush scallops and tomatoes with half of Dijon mixture. Grill 7 to 9 minutes, turning several times. Brush with remaining Dijon mixture, and grill 5 minutes longer or until scallops are just opaque throughout.

SERVES 4 ABOUT 215 CALORIES, 25G PROTEIN, 9G CARBOHYDRATE, 9G FAT (1G SATURATED), 0G FIBER, 355MG SODIUM

Bacon-Wrapped Scallops

 **PREP** 15 MINUTES
TOTAL 30 MINUTES

16 large sea scallops
(1¼ pounds)

4 ears corn, shucked

4 slices bacon

4 metal skewers

¼ teaspoon freshly ground
black pepper

2 medium tomatoes (6 to
8 ounces each), chopped

2 nectarines, chopped

¼ cup chopped fresh basil
leaves

2 tablespoons lemon juice

Pinch cayenne pepper

¼ teaspoon salt

1 Prepare outdoor grill for direct grilling over medium-high heat.

2 Pull off and discard tough crescent-shaped muscle, if any, from each scallop. Rinse scallops well to remove sand from crevices and pat dry with paper towels.

3 Grill corn 10 minutes, turning occasionally, until browned. Meanwhile, on microwave-safe plate, place bacon between paper towels. Microwave on High 1 minute.

4 Press 4 scallops together, flat sides down, in single layer; wrap 1 slice bacon around all 4 scallops. Insert skewer through overlapping ends of bacon, pressing through to other side of scallops. Repeat with remaining scallops and bacon. Sprinkle black pepper on scallops.

5 Grill, covered, 5 to 7 minutes, turning over once, until just opaque throughout.

6 Cut corn kernels off cobs and place in large bowl. Stir in tomatoes, nectarines, basil, lemon juice, cayenne, and salt. Serve with scallops.

SERVES 4 ABOUT 215 CALORIES, 16G PROTEIN, 30G CARBOHYDRATE, 5G FAT (1G SATURATED), 4G FIBER, 290MG SODIUM

Squid with Peppers and Arugula

PREP 15 MINUTES
TOTAL 30 MINUTES

1½ pounds cleaned squid

1 clove garlic, crushed with press

2 tablespoons plus 2 teaspoons olive oil

½ teaspoon salt

¼ teaspoon coarsely ground black pepper

4 medium bell peppers (red, orange, and/or yellow), quartered lengthwise

2 lemons, each halved

5 ounces baby arugula

Squid can turn chewy if it's not cooked properly. To ensure a tender result, remove each piece from the grill just as it becomes opaque.

1 With kitchen shears, cut each squid body lengthwise down 1 side and open flat. Cut large tentacles in half. Rinse squid with cold water and pat dry with paper towels. Transfer squid to bowl; add garlic, 1 tablespoon oil, ¼ teaspoon salt, and pepper and toss to coat; set aside.

2 Prepare outdoor grill for direct grilling over medium-high heat, or heat ridged grill pan over medium-high heat until very hot.

3 In large bowl, toss peppers with 2 teaspoons oil. Grill 10 to 15 minutes, turning once, until charred and tender. Place lemon halves, cut sides down, on grill with peppers and cook about 5 minutes or until marks appear and lemons soften. Transfer peppers to large bowl. Set lemon halves aside.

4 Place squid on grill pan and cook 1 to 2 minutes, turning over once, just until opaque throughout. Add squid to peppers in bowl and toss with remaining 1 tablespoon oil and ¼ teaspoon salt.

5 Arrange arugula on platter; top with squid mixture. Serve with grilled lemons to squeeze over servings.

SERVES 4 ABOUT 300 CALORIES, 30G PROTEIN, 23G CARBOHYDRATE, 12G FAT (2G SATURATED), 0G FIBER, 380MG SODIUM

Garlicky Clams and Mussels

PREP 20 MINUTES
TOTAL 30 MINUTES

4 tablespoons butter, cut into pieces

2 tablespoons olive oil

3 cloves garlic, minced

¼ cup minced shallots

½ cup dry white wine

¼ teaspoon crushed red pepper flakes

2 pounds mussels, scrubbed, beards removed

2 dozen littleneck clams, scrubbed

⅔ cup loosely packed fresh parsley leaves, coarsely chopped

Lemon and/or lime wedges, for serving

French bread slices, optional

1 Prepare outdoor grill for direct grilling over medium-high heat.

2 Place butter and oil in large disposable foil roasting pan (about 16 x 12½ inches). Place pan on hot grill and heat until butter has melted. Remove pan from grill. Stir in garlic, shallot, wine, and pepper flakes. Add mussels and clams, spreading out to an even layer. Cover pan tightly with foil.

3 Return pan to grill. Cover grill and cook 8 to 10 minutes, or until mussels and clams open.

4 Discard any mussels or clams that have not opened. Sprinkle with parsley and serve with citrus wedges and French bread.

Buy your **shellfish** from a reputable purveyor and plan to serve them the day of purchase. If you're not cooking right away, store them in a large bowl covered with a wet towel (not in plastic) in the refrigerator until the grill is ready.

SERVES 4 ABOUT 360 CALORIES, 28G PROTEIN, 10G CARBOHYDRATE, 22G FAT (14G SATURATED), 0G FIBER, 408MG SODIUM

Vegetables and Sides

Grilling brings out the best of any veggie's flavor. And you can't have a barbecue without classic sides, along with creative takes on them, too. The recipes that follow could be the main event or a delicious component to your next grilled meal.

A Guide to Grilling Vegetables

Grilling turns simple vegetables into the stars of the plate. Smoke and heat concentrate flavors and add depth to everything from corn to zucchini. Preheat the grill to medium-high.

VEGETABLE	PREPARATION	SEASONING	GRILLING TIME
8 ears corn	Soak 15 minutes, then remove silk from tops only or remove husks and silk.	Brush with 1 tablespoon oil.	20–30 minutes with husks; 12–15 minutes, turning occasionally, without husks
1½-pound eggplant	Cut crosswise into ½-inch-thick slices.	Brush with ¼ cup oil.	11–13 minutes per side
4 heads Belgian endive	Halve lengthwise.	Brush with 1 tablespoon oil.	10–12 minutes per side
2 medium fennel bulbs (1 pound each)	Cut lengthwise into ¼-inch-thick slices.	Brush with 4 teaspoons oil.	6–8 minutes per side
6 medium leeks	Remove dark green tops; blanch and halve lengthwise.	Toss with 1 tablespoon oil.	11–13 minutes per side
8 ounces large white mushrooms	Trim and thread onto skewers.	Brush with 2 teaspoons oil.	3 minutes per side, turning several times
4 large portobello mushrooms	Remove stems.	Brush with 4 teaspoons oil.	3–4 minutes per side
4 medium red or white onions	Slice into ½-inch-thick slices; secure with skewers.	Brush with 4 teaspoons oil.	12–14 minutes per side
2 bunches small green onions	Trim root ends and tops.	Toss with 4 teaspoons oil.	2–4 minutes, turning several times
4 red, green, or yellow bell peppers	Cut lengthwise into quarters; discard seeds.		10–12 minutes per side
4 medium yellow squash or zucchini	Cut lengthwise into ¼-inch-thick slabs.	Brush with 4 teaspoons oil.	5 minutes per side
4 medium tomatoes (6 to 8 ounces each)	Halve horizontally (through equator).	Brush cut sides with 2 tablespoons oil.	14–17 minutes per side

Buying and Storing Vegetables

When buying vegetables, appearance is usually the best indication of freshness. Avoid bruised vegetables or those with soft spots. Leafy tops should be crisp. Prepackaged vegetables in bags might appear to save time but aren't always a good choice because you can't inspect them thoroughly. Some vegetables are covered with a thin edible wax coating that seals in their moisture and gives them a fake sheen.

Refrigeration is the key to keeping most vegetables in prime condition. Store them in the coolest part of the refrigerator or in the crisper drawer. Don't store vegetables in zip-tight plastic bags, as the condensation that forms encourages rapid decay. The exception is leafy greens. Store them, loosely wrapped in paper towels, in a plastic bag, pressing out all the air. Mushrooms should be kept in a brown paper bag in the refrigerator, but store potatoes, onions, garlic, and winter squash in a dark, well-ventilated place at cool room temperature.

Preparing Vegetables

Wash vegetables briefly under cold running water just before use. If necessary, a gentle scrub with a soft vegetable brush will remove any surface dirt. When washing leafy greens, swish them around in a large bowl of cool water, changing the water several times. Cut or peel vegetables as close to serving time as possible. Once the skin on vegetables is broken, they begin to lose valuable nutrients. Some vegetables, such as artichokes, discolor when their cut surfaces are exposed to air. To prevent this, rub the cut surfaces with the cut side of a lemon half.

Not all vegetables require peeling, but you may want to peel if the outer skin is tough or unpleasant tasting. It is important to remove as thin a layer of peel as possible; a vegetable peeler is the best choice. Vegetables should be cut into uniform pieces to ensure even cooking on the grill.

Rainbow Veggie Kebabs

PREP 20 MINUTES
TOTAL 30 MINUTES

1 teaspoon ground cumin

½ teaspoon ground coriander

½ teaspoon smoked paprika

1 teaspoon salt

2 pounds small green and yellow summer squash, cut into 1-inch chunks

6 tablespoons olive oil

1 pint grape tomatoes

12 ounces small broccoli florets

8 ounces cremini or white mushrooms, halved if large

1 lime

Don't want to grill? Roast the veggies instead: Toss with all of the oil and spices on large, rimmed baking sheets, then **pop in the oven** at 425°F for 15 to 20 minutes. Squeeze lime over veggies before serving.

1 Prepare outdoor grill for direct grilling over medium heat.

2 In small bowl, combine cumin, coriander, paprika, and salt; set spice mixture aside.

3 In large bowl, toss squash and tomatoes with 2 tablespoons oil. In another bowl, toss broccoli with 1 tablespoon oil. In third bowl, toss mushrooms with 1 tablespoon oil. Thread vegetables onto skewers.

4 Grill broccoli and mushrooms 6 to 10 minutes, turning over once. Grill squash and tomatoes 6 to 8 minutes, turning over once. Transfer skewers to a large platter or cutting board and squeeze lime juice all over vegetables. Drizzle with remaining 2 tablespoons oil, then sprinkle all over with half of spice mixture. Cover platter tightly with foil; let stand, covered, at least 5 minutes before serving. Sprinkle with additional spice mixture, if desired.

SERVES 10 ABOUT 110 CALORIES, 3G PROTEIN, 8G CARBOHYDRATE, 9G FAT (1G SATURATED), 3G FIBER, 210MG SODIUM

Perfectly Grilled Corn

PREP 25 MINUTES
TOTAL 40 MINUTES

8 ears corn, with husks

Choice of topping (recipes follow)

1 Pull husks to stalk end of corn without removing; pull off silks. Return husks to original position; tie with kitchen string.

2 In large saucepot or baking pan, soak corn in cold water for 10 minutes. (Soaking corn this way helps keep husks from burning on grill.)

3 Prepare outdoor grill for direct grilling over medium-high heat.

4 Grill corn for 15 minutes, turning occasionally, until tender. Peel back husks; spread with topping of choice.

Cilantro-Lime Butter

In a food processor combine **6 tablespoons softened butter**, **1 tablespoon lime juice**, **¼ cup packed fresh cilantro leaves**, and **¼ cup packed fresh parsley leaves**. Pulse until combined well. Brush on corn.

SERVES 8 ABOUT 165 CALORIES, 3G PROTEIN, 19G CARBOHYDRATE, 10G FAT (5G SATURATED), 2G FIBER, 85MG SODIUM

Horseradish-Cheddar Topping

Stir together **⅓ cup light mayonnaise** and **2 tablespoons prepared horseradish** (well drained). Brush on corn and sprinkle with **1 cup shredded Cheddar cheese**.

SERVES 8 ABOUT 180 CALORIES, 7G PROTEIN, 21G CARBOHYDRATE, 9G FAT (3G SATURATED), 2G FIBER, 186MG SODIUM

Bruschetta Topping

Stir together **2 very-ripe medium tomatoes** (coarsely grated), **2 tablespoons finely grated Parmesan cheese**, **2 tablespoons chopped fresh basil**, and **¼ teaspoon salt**. Spoon evenly over corn.

SERVES 8 ABOUT 100 CALORIES, 3G PROTEIN, 20G CARBOHYDRATE, 1G FAT (0G SATURATED), 20G FIBER, 110MG SODIUM

Taco-Style Topping

In microwave-safe bowl, combine **4 tablespoons butter**, **2 teaspoons chili powder**, **1 teaspoon ground cumin**, **¼ teaspoon garlic powder**, and **¼ teaspoon salt**. Microwave in 30-second intervals until melted. Brush on corn.

SERVES 8 ABOUT 140 CALORIES, 3G PROTEIN, 19G CARBOHYDRATE, 7G FAT (4G SATURATED), 2G FIBER, 153MG SODIUM

Cheesy Garlic-Bacon Topping

In a small bowl, stir **¾ cup garlic-and-herb spreadable cheese** (about one 5-ounce package), softened. To coat, use **4 slices bacon**, cooked and crumbled and **¼ cup snipped chives**. Spread evenly over corn.

SERVES 8 ABOUT 160 CALORIES, 5G PROTEIN, 20G CARBOHYDRATE, 8G FAT (3G SATURATED), 2G FIBER, 131MG SODIUM

Chile-Lime Corn

Brush corn with **2 tablespoons olive oil**. Grill according to Perfectly Grilled Corn instructions. Brush with **1 cup Spicy Cilantro Pesto** (page 295) and sprinkle with **½ cup grated pecorino** before serving.

SERVES 8 ABOUT 355 CALORIES, 8G PROTEIN, 21G CARBOHYDRATE, 29G FAT (5G SATURATED), 3G FIBER, 308MG SODIUM

Mexican Corn

PREP 15 MINUTES
TOTAL 25 MINUTES

6 ears corn, with husks

¼ cup mayonnaise

1 tablespoon lime juice

½ teaspoon chili powder

½ teaspoon smoked paprika

¼ teaspoon salt

¾ cup crumbled Cotija or finely grated Parmesan cheese

1. Pull husks to stalk end of corn without removing; pull off silks. Return husks to original position; tie with kitchen string.

2. Prepare outdoor grill for direct grilling over medium heat.

3. Rinse corn in cold water until husks are thoroughly wet. Grill corn 10 minutes, turning occasionally, until slightly charred. Transfer to cutting board; let cool slightly.

4. While corn cooks, whisk together mayonnaise, lime juice, chili powder, smoked paprika, and ¼ teaspoon salt.

5. Brush mayonnaise mixture all over cooked corn. Place cheese in shallow dish. Roll corn in cheese, pressing to adhere.

SERVES 6 ABOUT 205 CALORIES, 6G PROTEIN, 20G CARBOHYDRATE, 13G FAT (4G SATURATED), 2G FIBER, 375MG SODIUM

Asparagus and Shiitake Tacos

PREP 15 MINUTES
TOTAL 20 MINUTES

3 tablespoons canola oil

4 cloves garlic, crushed with press

1 teaspoon chipotle chile powder

½ teaspoon kosher salt

1 pound asparagus, trimmed

8 ounces shiitake mushrooms, stems discarded

1 bunch green onions, trimmed

8 corn tortillas, warmed

1 cup homemade or prepared guacamole

Lime wedges, cilantro sprigs, and hot sauce, for serving

1 Prepare outdoor grill for direct grilling over medium heat.

2 In a large baking dish, combine oil, garlic, chipotle powder, and salt. Add asparagus, shiitakes, and green onions; toss to coat. Grill asparagus 5 to 6 minutes, turning occasionally, until tender and lightly charred. Grill shiitakes and green onions 4 to 5 minutes, turning occasionally, until lightly charred. Transfer vegetables to cutting board.

3 Cut asparagus and green onions into 2-inch lengths and slice shiitakes. Serve with corn tortillas, guacamole, lime wedges, cilantro, and hot sauce.

SERVES 4 ABOUT 350 CALORIES, 7G PROTEIN, 36G CARBOHYDRATE, 21G FAT (2G SATURATED), 11G FIBER, 445MG SODIUM

Herbed Potato Packets

 **PREP** 15 MINUTES
TOTAL 45 MINUTES

- 2 tablespoons olive oil
- 2 cloves garlic, crushed with press
- 1 tablespoon chopped fresh thyme leaves
- ¼ cup loosely packed fresh parsley leaves, chopped
- ½ teaspoon salt
- ¼ teaspoon coarsely ground black pepper
- 2 pounds medium red potatoes, cut into 1-inch chunks

1 Prepare outdoor grill for direct grilling over medium heat.

2 In large bowl, combine oil, garlic, thyme, parsley, salt, and pepper. Add potatoes and toss until coated.

3 Cut two 20 x 18-inch sheets heavy-duty foil. Layer both pieces foil to make double-thickness sheet. Spray with nonstick cooking spray. Place potato mixture on center of stacked foil. Bring long sides of foil up and over potato mixture and fold several times to seal well. Fold ends to seal in juices, making sure not to fold in too far—leave room for heat circulation inside.

4 Place foil packet on grill, cover, and cook potatoes 30 minutes, turning packet over once, until fork-tender.

5 To serve, carefully open one end of foil packet to allow steam to escape, then open top of packet. Transfer potatoes to a serving bowl.

SERVES 6 ABOUT 155 CALORIES, 3G PROTEIN, 31G CARBOHYDRATE, 2G FAT (0G SATURATED), 0G FIBER, 205MG SODIUM

Lemon-Garlic Potato Packets

Prepare grill as directed in **Herbed Potato Packets**. In large bowl, toss together **2 pounds red potatoes** (cut into 1-inch chunks), **12 whole peeled garlic cloves, 2 tablespoons olive oil, 1½ teaspoons grated lemon zest, 1 teaspoon salt**, and **¼ teaspoon coarsely ground black pepper**. Proceed with step 3 of recipe.

SERVES 6 ABOUT 140 CALORIES, 3G PROTEIN, 25G CARBOHYDRATE, 4G FAT (1G SATURATED), 0G FIBER, 275MG SODIUM

Chili Potato Packets

Prepare grill as directed in **Herbed Potato Packets**. In large bowl, toss together **2 pounds red potatoes** (cut into 1-inch chunks), **1 large red bell pepper** (cut into 1-inch pieces), **1 coarsely chopped onion, 2 tablespoons olive oil, 1 tablespoon chili powder, 1 teaspoon salt**, and **¼ teaspoon cayenne pepper**. Proceed with step 3 of recipe.

SERVES 6 ABOUT 145 CALORIES, 4G PROTEIN, 26G CARBOHYDRATE, 4G FAT (1G SATURATED), 0G FIBER, 285MG SODIUM

Rosemary Potato Packets

Prepare grill as directed in **Herbed Potato Packets**. In large bowl, toss together **2 pounds red potatoes** (cut into 1-inch chunks), **1 tablespoon olive oil, 1 tablespoon fresh rosemary leaves** (chopped), **1 teaspoon grated orange zest, 1 teaspoon salt**, and **¼ teaspoon coarsely ground black pepper**. Proceed with step 3 of recipe.

SERVES 6 ABOUT 135 CALORIES, 3G PROTEIN, 28G CARBOHYDRATE, 2G FAT (0G SATURATED), 0G FIBER, 300MG SODIUM

Sweet Potatoes

2½ pounds sweet potatoes
(5 medium), peeled if you
like and cut into ½-inch-thick
diagonal slices

1 tablespoon olive oil

¼ teaspoon salt

¼ teaspoon coarsely ground
black pepper

Parsley sprigs, for garnish

Steaming sweet potatoes
until they are just tender before
putting them on the grill ensures
that their insides will be soft
and cooked through while their
outsides get quickly crisped.

1 In large pot with steamer basket, heat 1 inch water to boiling. Place sweet potatoes in steamer basket; cover and steam 12 to 15 minutes or until sweet potatoes are fork-tender; do not overcook. (Potatoes can be steamed a day ahead and refrigerated until ready to grill.)

2 Prepare outdoor grill for direct grilling over medium heat.

3 Transfer potato slices to large rimmed baking sheet; brush with oil and sprinkle with salt and pepper. Place potato slices directly on hot grill grate. Cover and cook 10 to 12 minutes, turning slices over once with large metal spatula, until lightly charred and tender.

4 Transfer potatoes to serving bowl; garnish with parsley.

SERVES 8 ABOUT 245 CALORIES, 3G PROTEIN, 50G CARBOHYDRATE, 4G FAT (1G SATURATED), 6G FIBER, 170MG SODIUM

Charbroiled Portobellos

PREP 7 MINUTES

TOTAL 20 MINUTES

8 large portobello mushrooms (2½ pounds total), stems discarded

¼ cup olive oil

¼ cup balsamic vinegar

1 teaspoon sugar

½ teaspoon dried rosemary

½ teaspoon salt

¼ teaspoon freshly ground black pepper

Steaming the **mushrooms** speeds up grilling and requires less **olive oil.**

1 Preheat oven to 400°F.

2 Place rack in large roasting pan (17 x 11½ inches). Pour in enough boiling water to cover bottom of pan without touching top of rack. Place mushrooms, stemmed side down, on rack; cover with foil and steam in oven 20 minutes.

3 Meanwhile, in large resealable plastic bag, combine oil, vinegar, sugar, rosemary, salt, and pepper.

4 Pat mushrooms dry with paper towels. Place in bag with oil mixture, turning to coat. Seal bag, pressing out excess air. Place bag on plate; marinate 2 hours at room temperature, turning bag occasionally.

5 Meanwhile, prepare outdoor grill for direct grilling over medium heat.

6 Remove mushrooms from marinade; reserve marinade. Place mushrooms, stemmed side down, on hot grill grate. Grill about 8 minutes, turning once and basting frequently with marinade, until browned.

SERVES 8 ABOUT 90 CALORIES, 2G PROTEIN, 6G CARBOHYDRATE, 7G FAT (1G SATURATED), 0G FIBER, 140MG SODIUM

Flame-Roasted Chiles Rellenos

🕐 **PREP** 20 MINUTES
TOTAL 40 MINUTES

6 medium poblano chiles
(4 ounces each)

6 ounces Monterey Jack
cheese, shredded (1½ cups)

1 cup fresh corn kernels (from
2 ears)

½ cup loosely packed fresh
cilantro leaves, chopped

If you prefer hotter
flavor, after grilling
and before filling the
chiles, remove the
seeds and ribs but
don't rinse the insides.
Serve the chiles with
salsa if you like, but be
aware that poblanos
can sometimes be very
hot; choose your salsa
accordingly. If you
have access to a Latin
American market, look
for **queso blanco** and
use it in place of the
Monterey Jack.

1 Prepare outdoor grill for direct grilling over medium
heat.

2 Place whole chiles on hot grill grate and grill 10 to
15 minutes, turning occasionally, until blistered and
blackened on all sides. Keep grill hot.

3 Transfer chiles to large sheet of foil. Wrap them, seal
tightly, and allow to steam at room temperature until
cool enough to handle, about 15 minutes.

4 Meanwhile, in medium bowl, combine Jack cheese,
corn, and cilantro.

5 Remove chiles from foil. Cut 2-inch lengthwise slit in
side of each chile, being careful not to cut through
top or bottom. Under cold running water, gently peel
off skin. Remove seeds and ribs from opening; rinse
with running water. Pat chiles dry with paper towels.

6 With spoon, fill each chile with about ½ cup cheese
mixture. Gently reshape chiles to close opening.

7 Cut two 18-inch square sheets heavy-duty foil. Place
3 filled chiles in single layer on each sheet of foil.
Bring two sides of foil up and fold several times to
seal. Fold over ends to seal in juices. (Chiles can be
prepared to this point and refrigerated up to 6 hours
before grilling.)

8 Place foil packets on hot grill and cook about
10 minutes or until heated through and cheese has
melted.

SERVES 6 ABOUT 160 CALORIES, 9G PROTEIN, 13G CARBOHYDRATE, 9G FAT (5G SATURATED), 0G FIBER, 160MG SODIUM

Smoky Eggplant Parmesan

PREP 25 MINUTES
TOTAL 40 MINUTES

- 1 medium-large eggplant (1½ pounds), cut lengthwise into 4 slabs
- 1 tablespoon plus 1 teaspoon olive oil
- ½ teaspoon salt
- ¼ teaspoon coarsely ground black pepper
- 4 ounces mozzarella cheese, shredded (1 cup)
- ¼ cup freshly grated Parmesan cheese
- ½ cup loosely packed fresh basil leaves, thinly sliced
- 2 medium tomatoes (6 to 8 ounces each), each cut into 4 slices

1. Prepare outdoor grill for direct grilling over medium heat.

2. Lightly brush eggplant slices with oil and sprinkle with salt and pepper. In small bowl, mix mozzarella, Parmesan, and basil; set aside.

3. Grill eggplant slices 10 to 12 minutes, turning over once, until tender and lightly browned. Top with tomato slices and cheese mixture. Cover grill and cook 1 to 2 minutes to melt cheese and warm tomato slices.

Grilling gives **eggplant** a smoky flavor, and eliminating the frying makes this outdoor version of **Eggplant Parmesan** light and fresh tasting. Use freshly grated Parmesan cheese and the ripest summer tomatoes you can find for this flavorful twist on the traditional dish.

SERVES 4 ABOUT 205 CALORIES, 10G PROTEIN, 15G CARBOHYDRATE, 13G FAT (5G SATURATED), 0G FIBER, 500MG SODIUM

Mixed-Vegetable Bagna Cauda

PREP 30 MINUTES
TOTAL 45 MINUTES

¼ cup olive oil

5 canned anchovy fillets, minced

2 cloves garlic, minced

½ teaspoon grated lemon zest

½ teaspoon salt

¼ teaspoon coarsely ground black pepper

3 large Yukon Gold potatoes (8 ounces each), not peeled, cut lengthwise into ½-inch-thick slices

2 tablespoons fresh lemon juice

1 tablespoon olive oil

4 small zucchini (6 ounces each), each cut lengthwise into 3 pieces

3 medium heads Belgian endive, halved lengthwise

2 large red bell peppers, halved lengthwise

1 large yellow bell pepper, halved lengthwise

2 bunches green onions

2 tablespoons chopped fresh parsley, for garnish

1 In small bowl, whisk together oil, anchovies, garlic, lemon zest, salt, and pepper; set Bagna Cauda aside.

2 In deep 12-inch skillet, combine potato slices with enough water to cover and heat to boiling. Reduce heat to low, cover, and simmer 8 to 12 minutes, or until tender. With slotted spoon, remove potatoes to paper towels to drain; pat dry.

3 Prepare outdoor grill for direct grilling over medium heat.

4 In small bowl, mix lemon juice and oil. Brush cooked potato slices and all other vegetables with lemon mixture on one side. Working in batches, grill vegetables 5 to 15 minutes (depending on vegetable), turning over once and brushing with remaining lemon mixture, until browned and tender.

5 Transfer vegetables to large platter as pieces are done. Stir Bagna Cauda and pour over vegetables. Sprinkle with parsley for garnish.

SERVES 10 ABOUT 200 CALORIES, 4G PROTEIN, 18G CARBOHYDRATE, 7G FAT (1G SATURATED), 0G FIBER, 195MG SODIUM

Crumb-Topped Tomatoes

PREP 15 MINUTES
TOTAL 25 MINUTES

- 2 tablespoons butter
- 1 cup fresh bread crumbs (about 2 slices firm white bread)
- 1 clove garlic, crushed with press
- 2 tablespoons chopped fresh parsley
- ½ teaspoon salt
- ½ teaspoon coarsely ground black pepper
- 8 large plum tomatoes

1 Prepare outdoor grill for direct grilling over medium heat.

2 To make fresh bread crumbs, tear bread into large pieces and process in a food processor with the knife blade attached to form crumbs. Brown breadcrumbs in a nonstick skillet.

3 In 10-inch skillet, melt butter over low heat. Add bread crumbs and cook, stirring, until lightly browned. Stir in garlic; cook 30 seconds. Remove skillet from heat; stir in parsley, salt, and pepper.

4 Halve each tomato horizontally (through equator). Top each tomato half with some crumb mixture. Place tomatoes on hot grill grate and grill 8 to 10 minutes, until hot but not mushy.

HEIRLOOM TOMATOES

They may not be uniformly beautiful, but heirloom tomatoes have great flavor, texture, and aroma. Look for these variations.

Brandywine. One of the most common varieties sold, this descendant of Amish cultivars is reddish-pink, with a sweet and creamy interior. It makes an excellent stuffing tomato.

Cherokee Purple. This tomato, attributed to the Cherokee tribe, dates back to the 1800s. With a dusky-rose-to-purple exterior and smoky-sweet, deep-red flesh, it's a delectable T in a BLT sandwich.

Green Zebra. A Zebra weighs about 3 ounces and resembles a tiny, round watermelon with yellow and green stripes. Its pleasant tang and lemony essence add zip to salsa verde.

SERVES 8 ABOUT 40 CALORIES, 1G PROTEIN, 3G CARBOHYDRATE, 3G FAT (2G SATURATED), 0G FIBER, 191MG SODIUM

Veggie Muffaletta

PREP 5 MINUTES
TOTAL 25 MINUTES

2 large bell peppers, cut into sixths

1 small eggplant, thinly sliced

3 tablespoons olive oil

¼ teaspoon kosher salt

1 medium loaf round country bread

1 cup giardiniera (see Tip), drained and chopped

4 ounces thinly sliced provolone

3 tablespoons olive tapenade

Pronounced "jahr-dee-NYAY-rah," this secret ingredient is an Italian mix of pickled vegetables (typically carrots, cauliflower, and peppers). Look for it next to the pickled peppers on store shelves or make your own (see page 263).

1 Prepare outdoor grill for direct grilling over medium heat.

2 Toss peppers and eggplant with olive oil and salt. Grill 8 to 10 minutes, turning over once, until tender and lightly charred.

3 Slice top 1½ inches off bread; remove inside of loaf, leaving 1-inch wall. In cavity of bread, layer giardiniera, grilled eggplant, provolone, and grilled peppers. Spread olive tapenade on underside of bread "lid." Place on top of loaf, pressing down firmly. Cut into sixths to serve.

SERVES 6 ABOUT 385 CALORIES, 10G PROTEIN, 38G CARBOHYDRATE, 22G FAT (4G SATURATED), 3G FIBER, 930MG SODIUM

Soba Salad with Grilled Tofu

PREP 10 MINUTES
TOTAL 25 MINUTES

12 ounces extra-firm tofu
   Kosher salt
   Freshly ground black pepper
8 ounces soba noodles
5 ounces baby spinach
¼ cup ponzu sauce
6 radishes, thinly sliced
¼ cup peanuts, chopped

Can't find
ponzu sauce in the
supermarket? Make
your own ponzu with
3 tablespoons soy
sauce and 1 tablespoon
lime juice.

1 Prepare outdoor grill for direct grilling over medium-high heat.

2 Cut tofu horizontally into slices ½ inch thick; press dry with paper towels. Season with salt and pepper. Grill, covered, for 10 to 15 minutes, turning once. Cut into bite-size pieces.

3 Meanwhile, place baby spinach in colander in sink. Cook soba noodles as label directs and drain hot noodles directly over spinach. Rinse with cold water; drain well. Toss with ponzu sauce, radishes, and grilled tofu. Top with peanuts.

SERVES 4 ABOUT 360 CALORIES, 18G PROTEIN, 51G CARBOHYDRATE, 10G FAT (1G SATURATED), 6G FIBER, 775MG SODIUM

Hoisin-Ginger-Glazed Tofu and Veggies

PREP 25 MINUTES
TOTAL 40 MINUTES

½ cup hoisin sauce

2 cloves garlic, crushed with press

1 tablespoon vegetable oil

1 tablespoon lower-sodium soy sauce

1 tablespoon grated peeled fresh ginger

1 tablespoon seasoned rice vinegar

⅛ teaspoon cayenne pepper

1 package (15 ounces) extra-firm tofu, cut horizontally into 4 pieces, then cut crosswise in half

2 medium zucchini (8 to 10 ounces each), each cut lengthwise into 4 slabs, then cut crosswise in half

1 large red bell pepper, cut lengthwise into quarters

1 bunch green onions, trimmed

1 teaspoon vegetable oil

Be sure to buy extra-firm **tofu**; other varieties will fall apart on the grill.

1 Prepare outdoor grill for direct grilling over medium heat.

2 Make Hoisin-Ginger Glaze: In small bowl, whisk together hoisin sauce, garlic, oil, soy sauce, ginger, vinegar, and cayenne until well blended.

3 Prepare Tofu and Veggies: Place tofu on paper towels; pat dry with additional paper towels. Arrange tofu on large plate and brush both sides with half of glaze. Spoon remaining half of glaze into medium bowl; add zucchini and bell pepper. Gently toss vegetables to coat with glaze. On another plate, rub green onions with oil.

4 Grill tofu, zucchini, and bell peppers for 6 minutes, gently turning over once with wide metal spatula. Transfer tofu to platter; keep warm. Continue cooking vegetables, transferring pieces to platter with tofu when done, about 5 minutes longer or until tender and browned.

5 Grill green onions during last minute of cooking time; transfer to platter.

SERVES 4 ABOUT 245 CALORIES, 15G PROTEIN, 22G CARBOHYDRATE, 11G FAT (1G SATURATED), 0G FIBER, 615MG SODIUM

Parisian Potato Salad

PREP 20 MINUTES
TOTAL 45 MINUTES

- 3 pounds Yukon Gold potatoes, peeled and cut into 1-inch chunks
- ¾ cup plain, unsweetened Greek yogurt
- 3 tablespoons extra-virgin olive oil
- 2 tablespoons grainy mustard
- 1 teaspoon salt, plus more for salting the water
- 1 teaspoon pepper
- 4 stalks celery, thinly sliced
- ½ cup cornichon pickles, drained and thinly sliced
- ½ small red onion, very thinly sliced
- 5 large hard-cooked eggs, coarsely chopped
- ¼ cup finely chopped parsley

1 To a large saucepot of salted water, add potatoes. Partially cover; heat to boiling on high. Reduce heat to maintain simmer. Cook 12 to 15 minutes or until potatoes are tender. Drain well; let cool 10 minutes.

2 Meanwhile, in a large bowl, stir yogurt, oil, mustard, salt, and pepper. Add potatoes to dressing; toss until well-coated.

3 Fold in celery, pickles, and red onion. Then gently fold in eggs and parsley. Serve immediately or refrigerate, covered, up to 1 day.

SERVES 10 ABOUT 215 CALORIES, 8G PROTEIN, 26G CARBOHYDRATE, 9G FAT (3G SATURATED), 2G FIBER, 410MG SODIUM

Tropical Radicchio Slaw

PREP 5 MINUTES
TOTAL 15 MINUTES

- 2 medium heads radicchio, quartered through stem ends
- 2 tablespoons vegetable oil
- 2 cups finely chopped fresh pineapple
- ¼ cup packed fresh basil leaves, chopped
- 2 tablespoons orange juice
- ½ teaspoon kosher salt
- ½ teaspoon freshly ground black pepper

1 Prepare outdoor grill for direct grilling over medium heat.

2 Brush cut sides of radicchio with vegetable oil. Place on grill grate cut sides down, cover, and grill for 8 minutes, turning once to other cut side. Transfer to cutting board; cool.

3 Slice radicchio very thinly; toss with pineapple, basil, orange juice, salt, and pepper. Serve immediately or refrigerate, covered, up to 1 day.

SERVES 12 ABOUT 40 CALORIES, 0G PROTEIN, 5G CARBOHYDRATE, 2G FAT (0G SATURATED), 1G FIBER, 85MG SODIUM

Awetastic Slaw

PREP 5 MINUTES
TOTAL 15 MINUTES

6 cups thinly sliced cabbage

2 cups shredded carrots

1 small red bell pepper, thinly sliced

1 small yellow bell pepper, thinly sliced

3 stalks celery, thinly sliced on an angle

Choice of dressing (recipes follow)

In very large bowl, combine cabbage, carrots, bell peppers, and celery. Toss well with choice of dressing. Can be made up to 1 day ahead, covered and refrigerated.

SERVES 12 ABOUT 17 CALORIES, 1G PROTEIN, 4G CARBOHYDRATE, 0G FAT (0G SATURATED), 1G FIBER, 21MG SODIUM

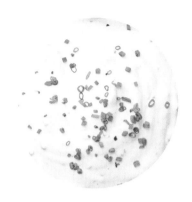

Creamy Herb Dressing

Whisk together ½ cup mayonnaise, ¼ cup sour cream, 2 tablespoons lemon juice, 2 tablespoons snipped chives, 1 teaspoon finely grated lemon zest, and ½ teaspoon celery salt.

SERVES 12 ABOUT 70 CALORIES, 0G PROTEIN, 0G CARBOHYDRATE, 7G FAT (1G SATURATED), 0G FIBER, 110MG SODIUM

Sriracha-Lime Dressing

Whisk **2 green onions** (finely chopped), ¼ cup soy sauce, 3 tablespoons lime juice, 1½ tablespoons Sriracha sauce, 2 tablespoons black or white sesame seeds, and ½ teaspoon sugar.

SERVES 12 ABOUT 15 CALORIES, 1G PROTEIN, 2G CARBOHYDRATE, 1G FAT (0G SATURATED), 0G FIBER, 345MG SODIUM

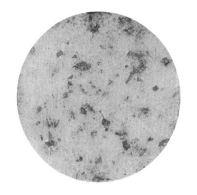

Garlicky Mustard Dressing

Whisk ⅓ cup apple cider vinegar, ⅓ cup extra-virgin olive oil, 2 tablespoons spicy brown mustard, 2 tablespoons finely chopped fresh parsley, 1 clove garlic (crushed with press), ½ teaspoon kosher salt, and ½ teaspoon freshly ground black pepper.

SERVES 12 ABOUT 60 CALORIES, 0G PROTEIN, 0G CARBOHYDRATE, 6G FAT (1G SATURATED), 0G FIBER, 106MG SODIUM

Classic Coleslaw

PREP 20 MINUTES

TOTAL 1 HOUR 20 MINUTES

- 2 tablespoons olive or vegetable oil
- 2 tablespoons red wine vinegar
- 1 tablespoon sugar
- 1 teaspoon salt
- ½ teaspoon caraway seeds, or ¼ teaspoon celery seeds, crushed
- 1 small head green cabbage (1½ pounds), quartered, cored, and thinly sliced, tough ribs discarded (6 cups)
- 1 large red bell pepper, cut into 2 x ¼-inch strips

IIIIIIIIIIIIIIIIIIIIIIIIIIIIIIIIIIIII

This coleslaw flavored with **caraway seeds** is best when thoroughly chilled.

In large bowl, whisk together oil, vinegar, sugar, salt, and caraway seeds until blended. Add cabbage and bell pepper; toss to coat. Cover and refrigerate at least 1 hour or up to 6 hours to blend flavors.

SERVES 6 ABOUT 75 CALORIES, 1G PROTEIN, 8G CARBOHYDRATE, 5G FAT (1G SATURATED), 0G FIBER, 405MG SODIUM

Red Pepper Relish

TOTAL 30 MINUTES PLUS COOLING

In 2-quart saucepan, heat ½ cup red wine vinegar and ¼ cup sugar to boiling on high. Add 2 finely chopped red bell peppers, ½ cup finely chopped sweet onion, 1 teaspoon mustard seeds, and ¼ teaspoon salt. Adjust heat to maintain simmer. Cook 20 minutes or until peppers are just tender. Cool slightly. Can be refrigerated, covered, up to 3 days.

SERVES 8 ABOUT 45 CALORIES, 1G PROTEIN, 10G CARBOHYDRATE, 0G FAT (0G SATURATED), 1G FIBER, 75MG SODIUM

Apple Sauerkraut

TOTAL 10 MINUTES PLUS STANDING

In large bowl, combine 8 cups very thinly sliced cabbage, 1 Granny Smith apple, cut into thin matchsticks, ⅓ cup rice vinegar, 1 teaspoon lower-sodium fish sauce, ½ teaspoon caraway seeds, and 1 teaspoon salt. Let stand 3 hours, stirring occasionally. Can be refrigerated, covered, up to 3 days.

SERVES 12 ABOUT 25 CALORIES, 1G PROTEIN, 6G CARBOHYDRATE, 0G FAT (0G SATURATED), 2G FIBER, 230MG SODIUM

Quick Sauerkraut

TOTAL 20 MINUTES PLUS STORING

Make brine as directed in **Classic Dill Pickles**, (page 263) but use **rice vinegar** instead of white vinegar. In step 2, replace cucumbers with **2 cups packed thinly sliced cabbage** and **1 small onion**, thinly sliced. Replace dill with **4 star anises** and **2 teaspoons mustard seeds**.

SERVES 6 ABOUT 10 CALORIES, 0G PROTEIN, 2G CARBOHYDRATE, 0G FAT (0G SATURATED), 0G FIBER, 323MG SODIUM

Classic Dill Pickles

PREP 10 MINUTES
TOTAL 20 MINUTES PLUS
STORING

1¼ cups distilled white vinegar

4 cloves garlic, smashed and peeled

3 tablespoons sugar

2 tablespoons kosher salt

1 pound Kirby (pickling) cucumbers, quartered lengthwise

3 sprigs fresh dill

1 In small pot, combine vinegar, 1 cup water, garlic, sugar, and salt. Heat on medium until sugar dissolves, stirring.

2 Arrange cucumber spears and dill in 32-ounce jar; pour warm brine over cucumbers to cover. (Can be made in 2 or more smaller jars as long as there's enough brine to cover.) Let cool slightly.

3 Replace lid and refrigerate at least 4 hours or up to 2 weeks.

SERVES 6 ABOUT 10 CALORIES, 0G PROTEIN, 2G CARBOHYDRATE, 0G FAT (0G SATURATED), 0G FIBER, 240MG SODIUM

Spicy Beans

Make brine as directed in **Classic Dill Pickles**, but use **cider vinegar** instead of white vinegar. In step 2, replace cucumbers with **12 ounces green beans**. Replace dill with **2 teaspoons crushed red pepper flakes**. In step 3, refrigerate at least 1 day.

Giardiniera

Make brine as directed in **Classic Dill Pickles**. In step 2, replace cucumbers with **3 cups total sliced carrots, small cauliflower florets,** and **chopped red bell peppers**. Replace dill with **2 sprigs rosemary**. In step 3, refrigerate at least 1 day.

Campfire Baked Beans

 PREP 5 MINUTES
TOTAL 1 HOUR 15 MINUTES

6 slices bacon

1 onion, chopped

1 green bell pepper, chopped

¼ teaspoon kosher salt

3 cans (15 ounces each) navy beans, rinsed and drained

1¼ cups Homemade Ketchup (page 289)

¼ cup molasses

4 teaspoons mustard powder

½ teaspoon freshly ground black pepper

1 Preheat oven to 325°F.

2 In a 12-inch ovenproof skillet, cook bacon on medium heat until fat is rendered. Transfer to plate; coarsely crumble.

3 To skillet, add onion, bell pepper, and salt. Cook for 8 minutes.

4 Off heat, stir in bacon, navy beans, Homemade Ketchup, molasses, mustard powder, and black pepper. Cover and bake for 1 hour.

SERVES 8 ABOUT 225 CALORIES, 11G PROTEIN, 45G CARBOHYDRATE, 2G TOTAL FAT (0G SATURATED), 8G FIBER, 532MG SODIUM

Six-Bean Salad with Tomato Vinaigrette

PREP 20 MINUTES
TOTAL 30 MINUTES

1 teaspoon salt

8 ounces green beans, cut into 1-inch pieces

8 ounces wax beans, cut into 1-inch pieces

1 can (15 to 19 ounces) chickpeas, rinsed and drained

1 can (15 to 19 ounces) black beans or black soybeans, rinsed and drained

1 can (15 to 19 ounces) red kidney beans, rinsed and drained

1½ cups (half of 16-ounce bag) frozen (thawed) shelled edamame

1 small tomato (4 ounces), coarsely chopped

1 small shallot, coarsely chopped

¼ cup extra-virgin olive oil

2 tablespoons red wine vinegar

1 tablespoon Dijon mustard

½ teaspoon salt

¼ teaspoon ground black pepper

1 In 12-inch skillet, heat 1 inch water with salt to boiling on high. Add green and wax beans; return water to a boil. Reduce heat to low; simmer 6 to 8 minutes, or until beans are tender-crisp. Drain beans. Rinse with cold running water to stop cooking; drain again. Transfer beans to large serving bowl.

2 Add canned beans and edamame to bowl with green and wax beans.

3 Prepare Tomato Vinaigrette: In blender, combine tomato, shallot, oil, vinegar, mustard, salt, and pepper. Blend until smooth.

4 Add vinaigrette to beans in bowl. Toss until beans are evenly coated with vinaigrette. Cover and refrigerate at least 1 hour to blend flavors or up to 8 hours.

SERVES 18 ABOUT 130 CALORIES, 7G PROTEIN, 17G CARBOHYDRATE, 4G FAT (0G SATURATED), 6G FIBER, 230MG SODIUM

Fried Green Tomatoes

PREP 20 MINUTES
TOTAL 25 MINUTES

6 slices bacon

1 large egg white

¼ teaspoon salt

½ cup cornmeal

¼ teaspoon coarsely ground black pepper

3 medium green tomatoes (6 to 8 ounces each), cut into scant ½-inch-thick slices

Here's a classic Southern way to use a bumper crop of unripened **tomatoes**. Serve them as a side dish, substitute them for fresh tomato in a BLT, or use them as a creative burger topping.

1 In 12-inch skillet, cook bacon over medium heat until browned. With tongs, transfer bacon to paper towels to drain; crumble. Set aside skillet with bacon drippings.

2 In pie plate, beat egg white and salt. On waxed paper, combine cornmeal and pepper. Dip tomatoes in egg mixture to coat both sides, then dip into cornmeal mixture, pressing so mixture adheres. Place on waxed paper.

3 Heat bacon drippings in skillet on medium-high. In batches, cook tomatoes about 1½ minutes per side, until coating is golden brown, transferring to paper towels to drain.

4 Transfer tomatoes to platter and top with bacon. Serve hot.

SERVES 6 ABOUT 190 CALORIES, 4G PROTEIN, 14G CARBOHYDRATE, 13G FAT (5G SATURATED), 0G FIBER, 270MG SODIUM

Garlic and Herb Bread

PREP 10 MINUTES
TOTAL 20 MINUTES

5 tablespoons soft spreadable cheese with garlic and herbs

½ long loaf (16 ounces) French or Italian bread, halved lengthwise

1 plum tomato, seeded and chopped

1 Prepare outdoor grill for direct grilling over medium heat.

2 Evenly spread cheese on cut sides of bread. Sprinkle bottom half of bread with tomato. Replace top half of bread. Wrap bread tightly in heavy-duty foil.

3 Grill foil-wrapped bread, covered, for 10 minutes, turning over once halfway through.

4 Transfer bread to cutting board. To serve, carefully remove foil. With serrated knife, cut bread crosswise into slices.

SERVES 6 ABOUT 155 CALORIES, 4G PROTEIN, 20G CARBOHYDRATE, 7G FAT (4G SATURATED), 0G FIBER, 305MG SODIUM

Basil-Romano Bread

Prepare grill as for **Grilled Garlic and Herb Bread**. In step 2, brush cut sides of bread with **2 tablespoons bottled Italian salad dressing**. Sprinkle bottom half of bread with **⅓ cup torn fresh basil leaves** and **¼ cup freshly grated Pecorino Romano cheese**. Wrap and grill as directed.

Horseradish-Chive Bread

Prepare grill as for **Grilled Garlic and Herb Bread**. In step 2, in small bowl, combine **2 tablespoons light mayonnaise**, **1 tablespoon prepared horseradish** (well drained), and **1 tablespoon snipped chives**. Spread mayonnaise mixture on cut sides of bread. Wrap and grill as directed.

Sweet 'n' Tangy Pasta Salad

PREP 5 MINUTES
TOTAL 10 MINUTES

1 cup mayonnaise

½ cup balsamic vinegar

¼ cup extra-virgin olive oil

2 cloves garlic, crushed with press

Kosher salt

Freshly ground black pepper

1 pound rotini, cooked, slightly cooled

3 stalks celery, thinly sliced

3 carrots, shredded

1 red bell pepper, chopped

5 ounces arugula

2 cans (15 ounces each) cannellini beans, rinsed and drained

1 In small container, combine mayo, vinegar, oil, garlic, salt, and pepper in small container. Close the container and shake until mixed.

2 In a large bowl, combine rotini, celery, carrots, bell pepper, arugula, and cannellini beans.

3 Add the dressing and toss to combine.

SERVES 12 ABOUT 290 CALORIES, 11G PROTEIN, 46G CARBOHYDRATE, 8G FAT (1G SATURATED), 9G FIBER, 285MG SODIUM

Farmer's Pasta Salad

PREP 25 MINUTES
TOTAL 45 MINUTES

1 pound campanelle or penne pasta

½ small red onion, very thinly sliced

½ pound green beans

1 teaspoon plus ¼ cup extra-virgin olive oil

Salt

4 large ears corn, shucked

⅓ cup sherry vinegar

¼ cup lemon juice

1 clove garlic, crushed with press

¼ teaspoon freshly ground black pepper

12 ounces multicolored cherry tomatoes, halved

¼ cup fresh basil leaves, finely chopped

1 Cook pasta as label directs. In medium bowl, soak onion in ice water at least 30 minutes.

2 Prepare outdoor grill for direct grilling over medium-high heat.

3 Pull out 30 x 12-inch sheet heavy-duty foil. In large bowl, toss green beans with 1 teaspoon oil and ⅛ teaspoon salt. Place beans in center of foil. Crimp edges of foil to seal tightly. Grill 15 minutes, turning over once halfway through. Grill corn 8 to 10 minutes, turning occasionally, until charred in spots.

4 Transfer bean packet and corn to cutting board; let cool. In large bowl, whisk together vinegar, lemon juice, garlic, remaining ¼ cup oil, ¾ teaspoon salt, and black pepper. Add cooked pasta and tomatoes to bowl, tossing to combine.

5 When cool enough to handle, slice beans into 2-inch lengths and cut corn kernels off cob; add to bowl with pasta along with basil, tossing until well combined. Drain soaked onions well. Pat dry with paper towel and add to pasta, tossing. Pasta can be covered and refrigerated up to 1 day ahead.

SERVES 8 ABOUT 345 CALORIES, 12G PROTEIN, 59G CARBOHYDRATE, 10G TOTAL FAT (1G SATURATED), 7G FIBER, 239MG SODIUM

Quinoa Tabbouleh Salad

⏱ **PREP** 20 MINUTES
🕐 **TOTAL** 40 MINUTES

1½ cups quinoa, rinsed

1 cup packed fresh mint leaves

1 cup packed fresh parsley leaves

¼ cup lemon juice

¼ cup extra-virgin olive oil

½ teaspoon salt

½ teaspoon freshly ground black pepper

1 can (15 ounces) chickpeas, rinsed and drained

12 ounces tomatoes, seeded and chopped

4 ounces feta cheese, cut into ½-inch cubes

Refrigerate and serve this salad cold. It would also pair well with **grilled chicken** like **Spiced Chicken Skewers** (page 127).

1 Cook quinoa as label directs; spread on a large platter to cool completely.

2 Meanwhile, in food processor, pulse mint, parsley, lemon juice, oil, salt, and pepper until very finely chopped, occasionally scraping down side of bowl.

3 Transfer herb mixture to large bowl. Add chickpeas, tomatoes, feta, and cooked quinoa; toss to combine.

SERVES 12 ABOUT 190 CALORIES, 7G PROTEIN, 22G CARBOHYDRATE, 9G TOTAL FAT (3G SATURATED), 4G FIBER, 240MG SODIUM

Orzo Salad with Grape Tomatoes, Feta and Mint

PREP 10 MINUTES
TOTAL 20 MINUTES

- 1 lemon
- 2 cups orzo pasta (12 ounces)
- 1 tablespoon olive oil
- 1 pint grape tomatoes
- 1 cup crumbled feta cheese (4 ounces)
- ⅓ cup pitted Kalamata olives, sliced
- ⅓ cup loosely packed fresh mint leaves, chopped
- ¼ teaspoon coarsely ground black pepper

1 From lemon, grate 1 teaspoon zest and squeeze 1 tablespoon juice; set aside.

2 Cook orzo as label directs. Reserving ¼ cup cooking water, drain.

3 Meanwhile, in 12-inch skillet, heat oil on medium until hot. Add tomatoes; cook 5 to 6 minutes, shaking pan occasionally, until skins split. Remove skillet from heat.

4 Add drained orzo and reserved cooking water to tomatoes in skillet; stir in lemon zest and juice, feta, olives, mint, and pepper.

5 Serve salad hot, chilled, or at room temperature.

SERVES 6 ABOUT 305 CALORIES, 11G PROTEIN, 47G CARBOHYDRATE, 8G FAT (4G SATURATED), 3G FIBER, 385MG SODIUM

Veggie Couscous Salad

PREP 5 MINUTES
TOTAL 25 MINUTES

- 2 medium red bell peppers, quartered
- 2 portobello mushroom caps
- 2 lemons, halved
- 5 tablespoons extra-virgin olive oil
- ¾ teaspoon kosher salt
- 5 ounces arugula
- 4 ounces pecorino cheese
- 1 cup couscous, cooked
- ¼ teaspoon freshly ground black pepper

1 Prepare outdoor grill for direct grilling over medium-high heat.

2 Brush bell peppers, portobello mushroom caps, and lemons with 2 tablespoons olive oil. Sprinkle with ½ teaspoon salt. Grill mushrooms 15 minutes, turning once, until tender. Grill lemons, cut sides down, 8 minutes or until charred. Grill peppers 6 minutes, turning once, until softened.

3 Combine arugula, pecorino cheese, couscous, pepper, and remaining 3 tablespoons olive oil and ¼ teaspoon salt. Thinly slice peppers and chop mushrooms; add to arugula along with juice from lemons. Toss well.

SERVES 4 ABOUT 450 CALORIES, 19G PROTEIN, 42G CARBOHYDRATE, 23G FAT (7G SATURATED), 5G FIBER, 920MG SODIUM

Honey-Lime Ramen Salad

 **PREP** 20 MINUTES
TOTAL 30 MINUTES

8 ounces Chinese curly egg noodles (or ramen noodles)

¼ cup tahini

3 tablespoons soy sauce

3 tablespoons lime juice

1 tablespoon honey

2 cloves garlic, crushed with press

1 large seedless (English) cucumber, chopped

1 pint grape tomatoes, halved

3 cups thinly sliced napa or savoy cabbage

¼ cup finely chopped fresh cilantro

1 Cook noodles as label directs.

2 Meanwhile, in a large bowl, whisk together tahini, soy sauce, lime juice, honey, and garlic until smooth. Add cucumber, tomatoes, and cabbage; toss to coat well.

3 Drain noodles and rinse with cold water. Drain once more, shaking off as much excess water as possible. Add to bowl with vegetables along with cilantro. Toss until well combined. Serve immediately or refrigerate, covered, up to 1 day.

SERVES 8 ABOUT 180 CALORIES, 7G PROTEIN, 28G CARBOHYDRATE, 5G FAT (1G SATURATED), 3G FIBER, 340MG SODIUM

Asian Sesame Zucchini Noodles

 **PREP** 5 MINUTES
TOTAL 15 MINUTES

¼ cup packed fresh cilantro, finely chopped

3 tablespoons seasoned rice vinegar

1 tablespoon toasted sesame oil

2 cloves garlic, crushed with press

2 teaspoons crushed red pepper flakes

2 teaspoons sugar

½ teaspoon salt

3 medium zucchini, spiralized

1 In a large bowl, whisk cilantro, vinegar, sesame oil, garlic, pepper flakes, sugar, and salt.

2 Add zucchini; toss until well combined. Serve immediately.

A spiralizer will turn fresh zucchinis into noodles. If you don't own a spiralizer, use a hand-held julienne slicer or purchase premade zucchini noodles at the supermarket.

SERVES 4 ABOUT 85 CALORIES, 2G PROTEIN, 12G CARBOHYDRATE, 4G FAT (1G SATURATED), 2G FIBER, 575MG SODIUM

Sauces, Marinades, and Rubs

Salsas, sauces, and sides are the finishing touches that make grilled meals finger-lickin' good. Indulge in the options that follow and make your meals sing!

Supporting Acts: Sauces, Marinades, and Rubs

Flame and flavor go together! So rub, marinate, glaze, or sauce your way to delicious meals on the grill.

Here are four ways to leave boring barbecues behind:

PREMADE SEASONING BLENDS. We sampled dozens of these in our test kitchens; some favorites are Thai, Cajun, jerk, and garam masala seasoning mixes, available in jars in the spice aisle.

HOMEMADE RUBS. In addition to the rub recipes in this chapter (pages 308–311), use the ideas below to come up with your own blends. Mix the spices together in a cup, then toss the seasoning with shrimp or scallops or rub it into the poultry or meat of your choice.

- Ground cumin, chili powder, cayenne pepper
- Ground coriander, ground cumin, crushed fennel seeds, coarsely ground black pepper
- Crumbled dried rosemary, dried thyme, dried oregano

MARINADES. Whisk the marinade ingredients in a large bowl; add steak, pork tenderloin, or chicken quarters, turning to coat, and let stand at least fifteen minutes before grilling.

- Grated fresh ginger, lemon juice, soy sauce
- Ground coriander, cumin, minced garlic, plain nonfat yogurt
- Minced shallot, coarse-grained mustard, red wine vinegar

GLAZES. Whisk the glaze ingredients together in a small bowl, then brush the mixture liberally over beef, pork, or poultry during the last few minutes the meat is on the grill.

- Crushed red pepper flakes, ground ginger, balsamic vinegar, apricot jam
- Chinese five-spice powder, lime juice, honey
- Sliced green onion, hoisin sauce, seasoned rice vinegar

THE BEST WAY TO MARINATE

WE LOVE THE EASE OF RESEALABLE PLASTIC BAGS. Simply add the marinade ingredients, then the meat or poultry, press out excess air in the bag and zip to seal. Squish the bag all around so the marinade coats the meat. Then put the bag on a plate in the fridge and turn it over occasionally. If you use a bowl or pan instead of a bag, be sure it's made of a nonreactive material (glass, ceramic, or stainless steel).

PLAY IT SAFE. Don't marinate meat, poultry, or seafood at room temperature for longer than thirty minutes. If the recipe calls for longer marinating, refrigerate it. Also, to avoid contamination, never let marinade in which you've soaked raw meat, fish, or poultry (or the dish it's been sitting in) come into contact with cooked food. Discard the marinade after using it or boil it for at least two minutes.

IF A RECIPE CALLS FOR BASTING WITH MARINADE, baste periodically throughout grilling, so there's enough time for the marinade to cook through.

HOW LONG SHOULD YOU MARINATE? For the best, fullest flavor, most meat and poultry need one to three hours; seafood takes fifteen to thirty minutes. But the more acidic the marinade—the greater the percentage of vinegar, citrus juice, or yogurt—the less time needed to marinate. (Leaving meat or seafood in a highly acidic marinade for too long can alter its texture, leaving it unpleasantly mushy.) Marinades penetrate about ½ inch (from all sides), so don't expect really thick cuts of meat to pick up flavor in the center.

Best-Ever Ranch Dressing

PREP 10 MINUTES
TOTAL 10 MINUTES

¾ cup buttermilk

½ cup mayonnaise

⅓ cup plain Greek yogurt

2 tablespoons lemon juice

1 tablespoon Dijon mustard

1 clove garlic, peeled but whole

Pinch sugar

¾ teaspoon kosher salt

¼ teaspoon freshly ground black pepper

½ cup loosely packed fresh parsley

2 tablespoons snipped chives

1 In a blender, puree buttermilk, mayonnaise, yogurt, lemon juice, mustard, garlic, sugar, salt, and pepper until smooth.

2 Add fresh parsley and chives; pulse until just finely chopped. Keeps for up to 2 weeks in fridge. Dressing might separate; stir before using. **Makes about 2¼ cups.**

EACH TABLESPOON ABOUT 25 CALORIES, 0G PROTEIN, 1G CARBOHYDRATE, 3G FAT (0G SATURATED), 0G FIBER, 77MG SODIUM

Avocado-Lime Dressing

In step 1 of **Ranch Dressing**, replace lemon juice with **3 tablespoons lime juice** and replace salt with **3 tablespoons soy sauce**; replace yogurt and mustard with **1 small avocado**. **Makes about 2 cups.**

Spicy Chipotle Ranch

In step 1 of **Ranch Dressing**, add **2 small chipotles in adobo sauce**. In step 2, replace parsley with **cilantro**. **Makes about 2⅓ cups.**

Green Goddess Dressing

In step 1 of **Ranch Dressing**, add **4 anchovies (or 2 teaspoons anchovy paste)**. In step 2, add **¼ cup packed basil** and **3 tablespoons fresh tarragon**. **Makes about 2⅓ cups.**

Use the Homemade Ketchup in the cocktail sauce recipe served with **OLD BAY PEEL 'N' EAT SHRIMP** (page 221).

Homemade Ketchup

PREP 5 MINUTES
TOTAL 1 HOUR

1 can (28 ounces) whole, peeled tomatoes

2 teaspoons canola oil

1 small onion, chopped

⅛ teaspoon ground cloves

¼ teaspoon freshly ground black pepper

⅓ cup packed brown sugar

⅓ cup apple cider vinegar

3 tablespoons tomato paste

1 tablespoon soy sauce

1 In blender, puree tomatoes until smooth.

2 In medium pot, heat canola oil on medium. Add onion; cook 6 minutes or until browned. Add clove and pepper; cook 1 minute.

3 Add brown sugar, vinegar, tomato paste, soy sauce, and pureed tomatoes. Heat to boiling on high. Reduce heat to medium-low; simmer 50 minutes or until thickened, stirring occasionally.

4 Cool slightly. In a blender, puree until smooth. Refrigerate until cold. Keeps for 3 weeks in fridge.

Makes about 2½ cups.

EACH TABLESPOON ABOUT 15 CALORIES, 0G PROTEIN, 3G CARBOHYDRATE, 0G FAT (0G SATURATED), 0G FIBER, 58MG SODIUM

Pineapple-Chipotle Ketchup

Puree tomatoes as in **Homemade Ketchup.** In step 2, add **1 cup pineapple chunks** to onion and cook 10 minutes. In step 3, add **1 chipotle chile in adobo sauce** along with pureed tomatoes.

Cilantro-Ginger Ketchup

Puree tomatoes as in **Homemade Ketchup.** In step 2, cook **2 tablespoons finely chopped fresh ginger** and **½ teaspoon ground cumin** with onion. In step 4, stir in **½ cup chopped cilantro** after pureeing.

Homemade Mayonnaise

 **PREP** 5 MINUTES
TOTAL 5 MINUTES

1 large egg yolk

2 teaspoons white wine vinegar

1 teaspoon Dijon mustard

¼ teaspoon salt

1 cup vegetable oil

2 teaspoons lemon juice

1 In medium bowl, with hand mixer on medium, beat egg yolk with vinegar, mustard, and salt until smooth.

2 With mixer running, slowly drizzle in vegetable oil drop by drop, stopping and scraping occasionally.

3 Stir in lemon juice. Keeps up to 1 week in refrigerator. **Makes about 1 cup.**

EACH TABLESPOON ABOUT 130 CALORIES, 0G PROTEIN, 0G CARBOHYDRATE, 14G FAT (1G SATURATED), 0G FIBER, 44MG SODIUM

Gingery Mayo

Stir together ½ cup Homemade Mayonnaise, 2 tablespoons Sriracha sauce, 2 teaspoons soy sauce, 1 teaspoon grated peeled fresh ginger until well mixed. **Makes about ½ cup.**

EACH TABLESPOON ABOUT 130 CALORIES, 0G PROTEIN, 1G CARBOHYDRATE, 14G FAT (1G SATURATED), 0G FIBER, 193MG SODIUM

Reuben Mayo

Stir together ⅓ cup Homemade Mayo, ¼ cup sauerkraut, 2 tablespoons relish, 1 tablespoon ketchup, 1 tablespoon brown spicy mustard, ¼ teaspoon garlic powder. **Makes about ½ cup.**

EACH TABLESPOON ABOUT 60 CALORIES, 0G PROTEIN, 1G CARBOHYDRATE, 6G FAT (1G SATURATED), 0G FIBER, 84MG SODIUM

Horseradish-Mustard Mayo

In small serving bowl, stir together ¼ cup Homemade Mayonnaise, 1 tablespoon undrained prepared horseradish, and 2 teaspoons coarse-grained Dijon mustard. **Makes about ½ cup.**

EACH TABLESPOON ABOUT 45 CALORIES, 0G PROTEIN, 1G CARBOHYDRATE, 4G FAT (1G SATURATED), 0G FIBER, 105MG SODIUM

Bacon-Chipotle Mayo

Place **2 slices bacon** between two paper towels on microwave-safe plate. Microwave on High 1½ to 2 minutes, until well browned. Cool until crisp, then crumble bacon and place in small serving bowl. Stir in ¼ cup Homemade Mayonnaise and **1 teaspoon canned chipotle chile puree** until blended. **Makes about ⅓ cup.**

EACH TABLESPOON ABOUT 55 CALORIES, 1G PROTEIN, 1G CARBOHYDRATE, 5G FAT (1G SATURATED), 0G FIBER, 135MG SODIUM

Onion-Thyme Mayo

Prepare outdoor grill for direct grilling over medium heat. Grill **1 medium onion**, cut crosswise into ½-inch-thick slices 8 to 10 minutes, turning over once, until tender and browned on both sides. Transfer to cutting board; coarsely chop. Place onion in small serving bowl; stir in ¼ cup Homemade Mayonnaise and **1 teaspoon chopped thyme** until blended. **Makes about ½ cup.**

EACH TABLESPOON ABOUT 30 CALORIES, 0G PROTEIN, 2G CARBOHYDRATE, 3G FAT (1G SATURATED), 0G FIBER, 60MG SODIUM

Creole Sauce

PREP 10 MINUTES

TOTAL 25 MINUTES

1 teaspoon olive oil

2 stalks celery, finely chopped

1 medium onion, finely chopped

1 small green bell pepper, finely chopped

¼ teaspoon salt

¼ teaspoon freshly ground black pepper

2 cloves garlic, finely chopped

⅛ teaspoon thyme

¾ pound tomatoes, chopped

2 tablespoons Worcestershire sauce

½ cup loosely packed parsley leaves, finely chopped

1 In 4-quart saucepot, heat oil on medium. Add celery, onion, bell pepper, salt, and pepper. Cook, stirring often, for 12 minutes or until tender.

2 Add garlic and thyme; cook 1 minute, stirring. Add tomatoes and ¼ cup water. Heat to simmering; cook, stirring occasionally, for 10 minutes or until tomatoes have broken down. Stir in Worcestershire sauce and parsley. Serve warm or at room temperature. **Makes about 2 cups.**

EACH ¼ CUP ABOUT 35 CALORIES, 1G PROTEIN, 5G CARBOHYDRATE, 2G FAT (0G SATURATED), 1G FIBER, 105 MG SODIUM

Miami Mojo Sauce

PREP 5 MINUTES
TOTAL 15 MINUTES

¼ cup olive oil

3 cloves garlic, sliced

½ teaspoon dried oregano

½ cup fresh orange juice

¼ cup fresh lime juice

¼ teaspoon ground cumin

1 cup packed fresh cilantro leaves

1 In 8-inch skillet, combine oil, garlic, and oregano. Cook on medium-low 5 minutes or until garlic is golden brown. Remove from heat; cool slightly.

2 In food processor, pulse garlic-oil mixture with orange juice, lime juice, and ground cumin until smooth. Add cilantro; pulse just until finely chopped, stopping and scraping bowl occasionally. **Makes about 1 cup.**

Serve these sauces with **SWEET AND SMOKEY TRI TIP** (page 162) or **GRILLED CHICKEN WITH WHITE BBQ SAUCE** (page 105)

EACH 2 TABLESPOONS ABOUT 70 CALORIES, 3G CARBOHYDRATE, 7G FAT (1G SATURATED), 0G FIBER, 125MG SODIUM

Homemade Pesto

PREP 5 MINUTES
TOTAL 5 MINUTES

3 cups loosely packed fresh basil leaves

1 large clove garlic, crushed with press

½ cup olive oil

¼ cup grated Parmesan cheese

¼ cup toasted pine nuts

2 teaspoons lemon juice

¼ teaspoon freshly ground black pepper

In food processor or blender, pulse basil, garlic, olive oil, Parmesan, pine nuts, lemon juice, and pepper until smooth. Keeps up to 3 days in refrigerator.

EACH TABLESPOON ABOUT 110 CALORIES, 1G PROTEIN, 1G CARBOHYDRATE, 11G FAT (2G SATURATED), 0G FIBER, 31MG SODIUM

Smoky Almond Pesto

In **Homemade Pesto,** replace basil with **parsley,** pine nuts with **blanched almonds,** and Parmesan with **Manchego.** Add ½ cup roasted red peppers and 1 teaspoon smoked paprika.

Spicy Cilantro Pesto

In **Homemade Pesto,** replace half of basil with **cilantro.** Omit Parmesan and replace pine nuts with **roasted unsalted peanuts.** Replace lemon juice with **1 tablespoon lime juice.** Add 1 teaspoon toasted sesame oil, 1 teaspoon grated fresh ginger, 1 small serrano chile (seeded and chopped), and ½ teaspoon salt.

Hazelnut-Arugula Pesto

In **Homemade Pesto,** replace basil with 2½ cups **arugula** and ½ cup parsley. Replace pine nuts with **hazelnuts.** Add **pinch nutmeg.**

Salsa Fresca

PREP 10 MINUTES
TOTAL 10 MINUTES

- 1 pound tomatoes, chopped
- ¼ cup chopped sweet onion
- ¼ cup fresh cilantro leaves
- 2 tablespoons lime juice
- 1 jalapeño, seeded and minced
- ½ teaspoon salt
- ⅛ teaspoon coarsely ground black pepper

In medium bowl, gently stir together tomatoes, onion, cilantro, lime juice, jalapeño, salt, and pepper. Cover and refrigerate at least 1 hour to blend flavors, or up to 8 hours. Drain before serving if chilled longer than 1 hour. **Makes about 3 cups.**

EACH ¼ CUP ABOUT 10 CALORIES, 0G PROTEIN, 2G CARBOHYDRATE, 0G FAT (0G SATURATED), 1G FIBER, 99MG SODIUM

Green Tomato Salsa

PREP 15 MINUTES
TOTAL 15 MINUTES PLUS CHILLING

- 8 ounces green tomatoes (2 small), chopped
- 8 ounces ripe red tomatoes (2 small), chopped
- 1 cup fresh corn kernels (from 2 ears)
- ¼ cup snipped chives
- 2 tablespoons fresh lemon juice
- ½ teaspoon salt
- ⅛ teaspoon coarsely ground black pepper

In medium bowl, gently stir tomatoes with corn, chives, lemon juice, salt, and pepper. Cover and refrigerate at least 1 hour to blend flavors, or up to 8 hours. Drain before serving if chilled longer than 1 hour. **Makes about 3½ cups.**

EACH ½ CUP ABOUT 20 CALORIES, 0G PROTEIN, 4G CARBOHYDRATE, 0G FAT (0G SATURATED), 1G FIBER, 90MG SODIUM

Southwestern Corn Salsa

PREP 10 MINUTES
TOTAL 10 MINUTES

2 limes

4 cups fresh corn kernels (from 8 ears)

⅓ cup finely chopped red bell pepper

1 jalapeño, seeded and minced

1 green onion, thinly sliced

½ cup loosely packed fresh cilantro leaves, chopped

½ teaspoon salt

⅛ teaspoon coarsely ground black pepper

⅛ teaspoon ground cumin

1 From 2 limes, grate ½ teaspoon zest and squeeze 3 tablespoons juice; place in medium bowl.

2 Add corn, bell pepper, jalapeño, green onion, cilantro, salt, black pepper, and cumin. Toss well to combine. If not serving right away, cover and refrigerate up to 12 hours. **Makes about 4½ cups.**

Want to add a little smoky flavor to this salsa? Use leftover grilled corn in this recipe for a great charred combo.

EACH ¼ CUP ABOUT 35 CALORIES, 1G PROTEIN, 8G CARBOHYDRATE, 0G FAT (0G SATURATED), 0G FIBER, 80MG SODIUM

Avocado Pico de Gallo

PREP 15 MINUTES
TOTAL 15 MINUTES

- 2 medium avocados, halved, pitted, peeled, and cut into ½-inch chunks
- 2 plum tomatoes, seeded and coarsely chopped
- 1 jalapeño, chopped
- ⅓ cup chopped sweet onion, such as Vidalia or Maui
- ¼ cup loosely packed fresh cilantro leaves, chopped
- 2 tablespoons lime juice
- ½ teaspoon kosher salt

In medium bowl, combine avocados, tomatoes, jalapeño, onion, cilantro, lime juice, and salt. Serve immediately or store, covered, in the refrigerator up to 4 hours. **Makes about 2¾ cups.**

Have leftover avocados? Throw them on the grill and make **Smoky Guacamole** (page 23)

EACH ¼ CUP ABOUT 60 CALORIES, 1G PROTEIN, 4G CARBOHYDRATE, 5G FAT (1G SATURATED), 2G FIBER, 95MG SODIUM

Peach Salsa

PREP 10 MINUTES
TOTAL 10 MINUTES

- 1¾ pounds peaches (5 medium), peeled and cut into ½-inch chunks
- 2 tablespoons finely chopped red onion
- 1 tablespoon chopped fresh mint
- 1 teaspoon minced seeded jalapeño
- 1 tablespoon lime juice
- ⅛ teaspoon salt

In medium bowl, gently stir together peaches, onion, mint, jalapeño, lime juice, and salt until well mixed. Cover and refrigerate 1 hour to blend flavors or up to 2 days. **Makes about 2 cups.**

EACH ¼ CUP ABOUT 25 CALORIES, 1G PROTEIN, 6G CARBOHYDRATE, 0G FAT (0G SATURATED), 0G FIBER, 55MG SODIUM

Triple Pepper Salsa

PREP 5 MINUTES
TOTAL 20 MINUTES

1 medium red bell pepper,
cut into sixths

1 medium green bell pepper,
cut into sixths

2 jalapeños, halved and seeded

2 tablespoons olive oil

3 medium plum tomatoes,
finely chopped

2 green onions, finely chopped

1 tablespoon lime juice

½ teaspoon kosher salt

1 Prepare outdoor grill for direct grilling over medium heat.

2 Toss together bell peppers, jalapeño, and olive oil. Grill for 10 minutes, turning once, until tender and lightly charred.

3 Finely chop peppers and toss with tomatoes, green onions, lime juice, and salt. Serve immediately or refrigerate, covered, up to 1 day. **Makes about 3½ cups.**

EACH ¼ CUP ABOUT 30 CALORIES, 0G PROTEIN, 2G CARBOHYDRATE, 2G FAT (0G SATURATED), 1G FIBER, 80MG SODIUM

Sweet Leeks and Fennel Spread

 **PREP** 5 MINUTES
TOTAL 40 MINUTES

1 tablespoon olive oil

2 medium leeks, thinly sliced

1 large fennel bulb, cored and thinly sliced

¼ teaspoon kosher salt

¼ teaspoon sugar

1 cup Dijon mustard

1 In a 12-inch skillet, heat oil on medium-low. Add leeks, fennel, salt, and sugar. Cover and cook 20 to 30 minutes, stirring occasionally, until very soft. Remove from heat.

2 Stir in mustard. Serve immediately or refrigerate, covered, up to 3 days. **Makes about 3 cups**.

EACH 2 TABLESPOONS ABOUT 20 CALORIES, 0G PROTEIN, 3G CARBOHYDRATE, 3G FAT (0G SATURATED), 1G FIBER, 180MG SODIUM

Chunky Barbecue Sauce

PREP 10 MINUTES
TOTAL 20 MINUTES

1 tablespoon vegetable oil

1 large onion, chopped

3 cloves garlic, minced

2 tablespoons minced peeled fresh ginger

1 teaspoon ground cumin

1 can (14.5 ounces) tomatoes in puree, chopped, puree reserved

1 bottle (12 ounces) chili sauce

⅓ cup apple cider vinegar

2 tablespoons brown sugar

2 tablespoons light (mild) molasses

2 teaspoons mustard powder

1 tablespoon cornstarch

1 In 12-inch skillet, heat oil on medium until hot. Add onion and cook about 10 minutes, stirring occasionally, until tender. Add garlic and ginger and cook, stirring, 1 minute. Stir in cumin. Stir in tomatoes, reserved puree, chili sauce, vinegar, brown sugar, molasses, and mustard; heat to boiling over high. Reduce heat to medium-high and cook, uncovered, 5 minutes, stirring occasionally.

2 In cup, mix cornstarch and 2 tablespoons water until blended. Stir into sauce and cook 1 to 2 minutes longer, until sauce boils and thickens. If not using right away, refrigerate in an airtight container up to 1 week or freeze up to 2 months. **Makes about 4 cups.**

EACH ½ CUP ABOUT 120 CALORIES, 2G PROTEIN, 25G CARBOHYDRATE, 2G FAT (0G SATURATED), 0G FIBER, 655MG SODIUM

Mouthwatering Marinades

These marinades will seep into chicken, pork, beef or vegetables for delicious flavor.

Soy Marinade

PREP 10 MINUTES
TOTAL 10 MINUTES

⅓ cup soy sauce

3 tablespoons seasoned rice vinegar

2 tablespoons brown sugar

2 tablespoons minced peeled fresh ginger

1 tablespoon vegetable oil

2 cloves garlic, crushed with press

2 green onions, thinly sliced

½ teaspoon toasted sesame oil

¼ teaspoon crushed red pepper flakes

In medium bowl, stir together soy sauce, vinegar, brown sugar, ginger, oil, garlic, green onions, sesame oil, and pepper flakes. **Makes about 1 cup.**

EACH TABLESPOON ABOUT 30 CALORIES, 1G PROTEIN, 4G CARBOHYDRATE, 1G FAT (0G SATURATED), 0G FIBER, 530MG SODIUM

This wonderful combination of Asian flavors turns **chicken** or **pork** into a scrumptious supper with no muss, no fuss. Simply let the meat marinate from one to four hours, then grill.

Spiced Yogurt Marinade

PREP 5 MINUTES
TOTAL 5 MINUTES

⅔ cup Greek yogurt

3 tablespoons lemon juice

3 tablespoons olive oil

2 tablespoons harissa

2 teaspoons ground cumin

½ teaspoon apple pie spice

1¼ teaspoons salt

Stir together yogurt, lemon juice, olive oil, harissa, cumin, apple pie spice, and salt. **Makes about 1 cup.**

EACH TABLESPOON ABOUT 35 CALORIES, 1G PROTEIN, 1G CARBOHYDRATE, 3G FAT (1G SATURATED), 0G FIBER, 196MG SODIUM

Toss Spiced Yogurt Marinade with 2½ pounds lamb chunks or thin slices top sirloin beef. Marinate at least 2 hours or up to 4 hours in refrigerator. Wipe off excess marinade before threading onto skewers and grilling.

Sweet Italian Marinade

PREP 10 MINUTES
TOTAL 10 MINUTES

2 tablespoons white wine vinegar

1 tablespoon vegetable oil

2 teaspoons dried oregano

1½ teaspoons salt

½ cup chopped roasted red pepper

¼ cup packed fresh basil

1 medium shallot, chopped

In food processor, pulse vinegar, oil, oregano, and salt until combined. Add roasted red pepper, basil, and shallot; pulse until finely chopped. **Makes about ⅔ cup.**

EACH TABLESPOON ABOUT 15 CALORIES, 0G PROTEIN, 1G CARBOHYDRATE, 1G FAT (0G SATURATED), 1G FIBER, 312MG SODIUM

||||||||||||||||||||||||||||||||||||||||||

Toss Sweet Italian Marinade with 2½ pounds skinless, boneless chicken breasts or pork tenderloin. Marinate at least 3 hours or up to 6 hours in refrigerator before grilling. It's also great on any veggies!

Gochujang-Ginger Marinade

PREP 10 MINUTES
TOTAL 10 MINUTES

¼ cup soy sauce

3 tablespoons gochujang (Korean red pepper paste)

1 tablespoon brown sugar

1 tablespoon toasted sesame oil

2 cloves garlic, crushed with press

1 teaspoon ground ginger

In bowl, whisk together soy sauce, gochujang, brown sugar, sesame oil, garlic, and ground ginger until smooth. **Makes about ½ cup.**

EACH TABLESPOON ABOUT 45 CALORIES, 1G PROTEIN, 6G CARBOHYDRATE, 2G FAT (0G SATURATED), 0G FIBER, 631MG SODIUM

||||||||||||||||||||||||||||||||||||||||||

Toss Gochujang-Ginger Marinade with 2 pounds skirt, hanger, or flank steak, or 3 pounds chicken parts. Marinate at least 1 hour or up to 3 hours before grilling.

Great Glazes

Honey-Mustard Glaze

PREP 1 MINUTE
TOTAL 2 MINUTES

- 2 tablespoons coarse-grained mustard
- 2 tablespoons honey
- ½ teaspoon dried thyme, or 2 teaspoons minced fresh thyme

In small microwave-safe bowl, stir mustard, honey, and thyme until blended. Microwave, uncovered, on High 30 seconds, stirring once. **Makes about ¼ cup.**

EACH TABLESPOON ABOUT 40 CALORIES, 0G PROTEIN, 10G CARBOHYDRATE, 0G FAT (0G SATURATED), 0G FIBER, 180MG SODIUM

Apricot-Ginger Glaze

PREP 1 MINUTE
TOTAL 2 MINUTES

- 2 tablespoons apricot jam
- 2 tablespoons prepared horseradish
- ½ teaspoon ground ginger

In small microwave-safe bowl, stir jam, horseradish, and ginger until blended. Microwave, uncovered, on High 30 seconds, stirring once. **Makes about ¼ cup.**

EACH TABLESPOON ABOUT 30 CALORIES, 0G PROTEIN, 7G CARBOHYDRATE, 0G FAT (0G SATURATED), 0G FIBER, 28MG SODIUM

Brush Apricot-Ginger **Glaze** on poultry or pork.

Moroccan-Spice Glaze

TOTAL 5 MINUTES

3 tablespoons honey

1 tablespoon lemon juice

½ teaspoon ground cinnamon

½ teaspoon ground cumin

In small microwave-safe bowl, stir honey, lemon juice, cinnamon, and cumin until blended. Microwave, uncovered, on High 1 minute, stirring once. **Makes about ¼ cup.**

EACH TABLESPOON ABOUT 50 CALORIES, 0G PROTEIN, 14G CARBOHYDRATE, 0G FAT (0G SATURATED), 0G FIBER, 1MG SODIUM

||||||||||||||||||||||||||||||||||||||||||||||||

Try Moroccan-Spice Glaze on lamb or chicken.

Hoisin and Five-Spice Glaze

TOTAL 5 MINUTES

¼ cup hoisin sauce

2 tablespoons soy sauce

1 teaspoon Chinese five-spice powder

In small microwave-safe bowl, stir together hoisin and soy sauces with five-spice powder. Cook, uncovered, in microwave oven on High 30 seconds, stirring once. **Makes about ¼ cup.**

EACH TABLESPOON ABOUT 45 CALORIES, 2G PROTEIN, 8G CARBOHYDRATE, 0G FAT (0G SATURATED), 0G FIBER, 710G SODIUM

||||||||||||||||||||||||||||||||||||||||||||||||

Brush Hoisin and Five-Spice Glaze on beef, pork, chicken, or salmon.

Cajun Rub

⏱ **TOTAL** 5 MINUTES

2 tablespoons paprika

1 tablespoon coarsely ground black pepper

1 tablespoon ground cumin

1 tablespoon brown sugar

1 tablespoon salt

2 teaspoons ground coriander

1 teaspoon dried thyme

1 teaspoon cayenne pepper

½ teaspoon garlic powder

½ teaspoon ground allspice

IIIIIIIIIIIIIIIIIIIIIIIIIIIIIIIIIIIIII

Use 1 tablespoon **Cajun Rub** per pound of uncooked beef or pork, 2 teaspoons per pound of uncooked fish or chicken.

In small bowl, stir together paprika, pepper, cumin, sugar, salt, coriander, thyme, cayenne, garlic powder and allspice. Store in tightly covered container and use within 6 months. **Makes about ⅓ cup.**

EACH TABLESPOON ABOUT 25 CALORIES, 1G PROTEIN, 5G CARBOHYDRATE, 1G FAT (0G SATURATED), 0G FIBER, 1,400MG SODIUM

The Ultimate Rub

PREP 10 MINUTES
TOTAL 10 MINUTES

¼ cup packed brown sugar
(be sure to break it up)

2 tablespoons kosher salt

2 tablespoons ground
coriander

2 tablespoons ground cumin

2 tablespoons garlic powder

1 tablespoon ground ginger

1 tablespoon smoked paprika

1 tablespoon freshly ground
black pepper

1 teaspoon ground cinnamon

||||||||||||||||||||||||||||||||||||||||

Use 2 tablespoons
for 1½ pounds steak;
1 tablespoon per
pound of vegetables;
¼ cup for 2 pounds
skin-on, bone-in
chicken parts;
3 tablespoons per
pound salmon fillets.

In medium bowl, stir together brown sugar, salt, coriander, cumin, garlic powder, ginger, smoked paprika, pepper, and cinnamon. Store in an airtight container or a resealable plastic bag up to 6 months. **Makes about 1 cup.**

EACH TABLESPOON ABOUT 25 CALORIES, 0G PROTEIN, 6G CARBOHYDRATE, 0G FAT (0G SATURATED), 1G FIBER, 755MG SODIUM

Salt-Free Rubs

You can add tons of flavor with little salt. These salt-free rubs are easy to make, store, and use.

To Store: These zest rubs can be made ahead and stored in airtight containers at room temperature for up to 6 months.

To Use: Pat meat, poultry, or fish dry before sprinkling with the rub. Use just enough to coat the surface lightly—about 1 tablespoon per pound.

Herb Rub

TOTAL 5 MINUTES

- 2 tablespoons crumbled dried rosemary
- 2 tablespoons dried thyme
- 1 tablespoon dried tarragon
- 1 tablespoon coarsely ground black pepper

In small bowl, stir together rosemary, thyme, tarragon, and pepper until blended.

Makes about ⅔ cup.

EACH TABLESPOON ABOUT 5 CALORIES, 0G PROTEIN, 1G CARBOHYDRATE, 0G FAT (0G SATURATED), 0G FIBER, 1MG SODIUM

Use Herb Rub on pork or fish.

Peppercorn Rub

TOTAL 5 MINUTES

- 3 tablespoons coriander seeds
- 3 tablespoons cumin seeds
- 3 tablespoons fennel seeds
- 1 tablespoon black peppercorns

In resealable plastic bag, combine coriander seeds, cumin seeds, fennel seeds, and peppercorns. Place kitchen towel over bag and, with meat mallet or rolling pin, coarsely crush spices.

Makes about ⅔ cup.

EACH TABLESPOON ABOUT 25 CALORIES, 2G PROTEIN, 4G CARBOHYDRATE, 0G FAT, 0MG FIBER, 7MG SODIUM

Use Peppercorn Rub on steak, chicken, or lamb.

Red Chile Rub

TOTAL 5 MINUTES

- 1 tablespoon ground cumin
- 1 tablespoon paprika
- 2 teaspoons chipotle chile powder
- 1 teaspoon dried oregano

In cup, combine cumin, paprika, chipotle powder, and oregano. **Makes about ¼ cup.**

EACH TABLESPOON ABOUT 25 CALORIES, 1G PROTEIN, 3G CARBOHYDRATE, 0G FAT (0G SATURATED) 0G FIBER, 6MG SODIUM

||||||||||||||||||||||||||||||||||||||||||||||||||||

Use Red Chile Rub on pork, chicken, or shrimp.

Lime-Herb Rub

TOTAL 15 MINUTES

- 2 limes
- 2 cups loosely packed fresh cilantro leaves, chopped
- 2 cups loosely packed fresh mint leaves, chopped
- 2 tablespoons brown sugar
- 2 tablespoons minced peeled fresh ginger
- 3 garlic cloves, crushed with press
- 2 green onions, thinly sliced
- 1 teaspoon crushed red pepper

From limes, grate 1 tablespoon peel and squeeze 2 tablespoons juice. In medium bowl, combine lime peel and juice, cilantro, mint, brown sugar, ginger, garlic, green onions, and crushed red pepper. Use rub right away. **Makes about 1 cup.**

EACH TABLESPOON ABOUT 15 CALORIES, 1G PROTEIN, 3G CARBOHYDRATE, 0G FAT (0G SATURATED), 0MG FIBER, 6MG SODIUM

||||||||||||||||||||||||||||||||||||||||||||||||||||

Use Lime-Herb Rub on chicken, pork tenderloin, salmon, or other oily fish.

Recommended Safe Minimum Internal Temperatures

Here are USDA temperature guidelines for meat, poultry, and fish plus grilling times over medium heat. Temperatures should be taken in the thickest part of the food; the thermometer should not touch bone, fat, or gristle (cartilage). Allow all beef, pork, veal, and lamb steaks, chops, and roasts to rest for at least 3 minutes after removing them from the grill. (Note: Cooking temperatures for beef are for medium-rare.)

CUT OF MEAT	INTERNAL TEMPERATURE	APPROXIMATE GRILLING TIME
Ground beef, pork, or lamb burgers (1 inch thick)	160°F	10–12 minutes
Steaks (porterhouse, T-bone, sirloin, rib-eye, top round):		
¾ inch thick	145°F	6–8 minutes
1 inch thick	145°F	11–14 minutes
Steaks (flank or skirt)	145°F	15–20 minutes
Beef tenderloin, whole	145°F	30–40 minutes
Veal chops (1 inch thick)	145°F	10–12 minutes
Lamb chops (¾ inch thick)	145°F	10–12 minutes
Pork chops (rib or loin; 1 inch thick)	145°F	12–14 minutes
Pork tenderloin, whole	145°F	15–25 minutes
Pork tenderloin steaks	145°F	6 minutes
Ham steaks (fully cooked)	Reheat ham steaks packaged in USDA-inspected plants to 140°F and all others to 165°F	5 minutes

CUT OF MEAT	INTERNAL TEMPERATURE	APPROXIMATE GRILLING TIME
Chicken legs, bone-in	165°F	35–40 minutes
Chicken thighs, bone-in	165°F	12–15 minutes
Chicken thighs, boneless	165°F	10–12 minutes
Chicken breasts, bone-in	165°F	30–35 minutes
Chicken breasts, boneless	165°F	10–12 minutes
Whole chicken (3½ pounds)	165°F	1 hour 15 minutes
Ground chicken or turkey burgers (1 inch thick)	165°F	12–14 minutes
Turkey cutlets	165°F	5–7 minutes
Whole turkey (12 pounds)	165°F	2 hours 15 minutes to 3 hours (11–13 minutes per pound)
Salmon fillets (1 inch thick)	145°F	10–12 minutes
Salmon or tuna steaks (¾ inch thick)	145°F	8 minutes
Shrimp (shelled and deveined)	145°F	4–5 minutes
Scallops	145°F	4–5 minutes
Clams and mussels (in shell)	145°F	8–10 minutes

How to Use a Food Thermometer: Use an instant-read meat thermometer to check the internal temperature toward the end of cooking time, but before the food is expected to be "done." Check the temperature in several places to make sure the food is evenly heated. Make sure to clean your thermometer with hot, soapy water before and after each use.

Photography Credits

Index

Note: Page references in *italics* refer to photographs on pages separate from recipes.

Metric Conversion Charts

The recipes that appear in this cookbook use the standard United States method for measuring liquid and dry or solid ingredients (teaspoons, tablespoons, and cups). The information on this chart is provided to help cooks outside the U.S. successfully use these recipes. All equivalents are approximate.

METRIC EQUIVALENTS FOR DIFFERENT TYPES OF INGREDIENTS

STANDARD CUP (e.g., flour)	FINE POWDER (e.g., rice)	GRAIN (e.g., sugar)	GRANULAR (e.g., butter)	LIQUID SOLIDS (e.g., milk)	LIQUID
¾	105 g	113 g	143 g	150 g	180 ml
⅔	93 g	100 g	125 g	133 g	160 ml
½	70 g	75 g	95 g	100 g	120 ml
⅓	47 g	50 g	63 g	67 g	80 ml
¼	35 g	38 g	48 g	50 g	60 ml
⅛	18 g	19 g	24 g	25 g	30 ml

USEFUL EQUIVALENTS FOR LIQUID INGREDIENTS BY VOLUME

¼ tsp	=						1 ml
½ tsp	=						2 ml
1 tsp	=						5 ml
3 tsp	=	1 tbsp	=		½ fl oz	=	15 ml
		2 tbsp	=	⅛ cup	1 fl oz	=	30 ml
		4 tbsp	=	¼ cup	2 fl oz	=	60 ml
		5⅓ tbsp	=	⅓ cup	3 fl oz	=	80 ml
		8 tbsp	=	½ cup	4 fl oz	=	120 ml
		10⅔ tbsp	=	⅔ cup	5 fl oz	=	160 ml
		12 tbsp	=	¾ cup	6 fl oz	=	180 ml
		16 tbsp	=	1 cup	8 fl oz	=	240 ml
		1 pt	=	2 cups	16 fl oz	=	480 ml
		1 qt	=	4 cups	32 fl oz	=	960 ml
					33 fl oz	=	1000 ml = 1 L

USEFUL EQUIVALENTS FOR DRY INGREDIENTS BY WEIGHT

(To convert ounces to grams, multiply the number of ounces by 30.)

1 oz	=	⅟₁₆ lb	=	30 g
2 oz	=	¼ lb	=	120 g
4 oz	=	½ lb	=	240 g
8 oz	=	¾ lb	=	360 g
16 oz	=	1 lb	=	480 g

USEFUL EQUIVALENTS FOR COOKING/OVEN TEMPERATURES

	Fahrenheit	Celsius	Gas Mark
Freeze Water	32°F	0°C	
Room Temperature	68°F	20°C	
Boil Water	212°F	100°C	
Bake	325°F	160°C	3
	350°F	180°C	4
	375°F	190°C	5
	400°F	200°C	6
	425°F	220°C	7
	450°F	230°C	8
Broil			Grill

USEFUL EQUIVALENTS LENGTH

(To convert inches to centimeters, multiply the number of inches by 2.5.)

1 in	=		2.5 cm	
6 in	= ½ ft	=	15 cm	
12 in	= 1 ft	=	30 cm	
36 in	= 3 ft	= 1 yd	= 90 cm	
40 in	=		100 cm	= 1 m